Praise for David Barsamian's interviews

David Barsamian is the Studs Terkel of our generation.
—Howard Zinn

David Barsamian is one of the great journalists of our era,
and a giant of community and public radio.
—Robert McChesney

Louder Than Bombs

Interviews from
The Progressive Magazine

by David Barsamian

South End Press
Cambridge, Massachusetts

Cover design by Nick Jahlen
Cover illustration by Alex Nabaum
Page design and production by the South End Press Collective
This book was designed using Adobe InDesign CS.

Printed by union labor in the US on acid-free, recycled paper
10 09 08 07 06 05 04   1 2 3 4 5

Barsamian, David.
Louder than bombs : interviews from *The Progressive* magazine /
by David Barsamian.
    p. cm.
Includes index.
ISBN 0-89608-725-5 (pbk. : alk. paper)
ISBN 0-89608-726-3 (cloth : alk. paper)
1. Social reformers--Interviews. 2. Political activists--Interviews.
3. Social action. I. *Progressive* magazine. II. Title.
  HN18.B34 2004
  303.48'4'092--dc22   2003027759

South End Press
7 Brookline Street, #1
Cambridge, MA 02139
www.southendpress.org
southend@southendpress.org

Introduction   vii
Matthew Rothschild
Editor of *The Progressive*

Edwidge Danticat   1

Kurt Vonnegut   11

Ahmed Rashid   19

Danny Glover   27

John Pilger   33

Tariq Ali   41

Edward Said   49

Amartya Sen   57

Arundhati Roy   69

Angela Davis   81

Haunani-Kay Trask   91

Juan Gonzalez   101

Ralph Nader   109

Noam Chomsky   119

Eduardo Galeano   135

Edward Said   147

Taylor Branch   163

Eqbal Ahmad   175

Vandana Shiva   189

Howard Zinn   199

Ben Bagdikian   211

Index   221

About David Barsamian   233

About South End Press   234

Acknowledgments

My gratitude and thanks go to all the voices that allowed me to interview them. The theme of the World Social Forum is "Another World is Possible." The participants in *Louder than Bombs* certainly point to that possibility. Alas, two comrades are no longer with us: Eqbal Ahmad and Edward Said. Friends and allies, both were inspired by the Gramscian dictum: Pessimism of the intellect, optimism of the will. Their work and memory endures. The late Erwin Knoll, long time editor of *The Progressive*, always encouraged me in my work. It has been a pleasure working with his successor, Matthew Rothschild. South End Press and Joey Fox have been very supportive of this project. Much appreciation to KGNU in Boulder, one of the best community radio stations anywhere. Thanks to the Lannan Foundation in Santa Fe and to Anthony Arnove for his advice and friendship.

David Barsamian
Boulder, Colorado
March 2004

Matthew Rothschild
Introduction

I'm a sucker for interviews. When I'm in the middle of a magazine or a newspaper, and I've read article after article, essay after essay, on the problems of our society, I'm ready to come up for air. Interviews, if they are done well, provide that oxygen. But they do more than that. They bring a human face into focus, they reveal the intriguing quirks of the person being interviewed, they reflect the crispness and piquancy of spoken English, they come alive with the give and take of two engaged intellectuals, and they offer inspiration. David Barsamian is a master of the form. Since he started conducting interviews for *The Progressive* back in 1997, Barsamian has brought his polyglot and polymath intelligence to bear on a series of subjects. As Eduardo Galeano describes himself in one of these interviews, Barsamian too is *"un curioso"*—a person with a great deal of curiosity: intellectually, culturally, and politically.

Barsamian's interviews, taken together, represent a collage of some of our leading social critics. It's appropriate that the first interview he did for us was with Ben Bagdikian, the great media critic. Appropriate because Barsamian has an enduring interest in corporate control of the media, and he gets Bagdikian to say, colorfully, about newspapers that insist on more cuts even though they're making money: "This is the economics of the fat man at the heavily laden dinner table who doesn't have a choice of three different kinds of roast beef." But appropriate also because, like Barsamian, Bagdikian is an Armenian American. Their Armenian heritage, with both sharing painful family histories of the Armenian genocide in the early twentieth century, makes them acutely aware of the human capacity for mass cruelty. This ability to remember is a prerequisite for being a moral person. It was Hitler who said,

"Who, after all, speaks of the annihilation of the Armenians?" In his first interview, Barsamian and Bagdikian are two who speak of that annihilation.

Asking a good question sometimes means asking a simple one. And that's what Barsamian does when he asks Howard Zinn, "Do you miss teaching?" Zinn answered:

> I miss the classroom and the encounter with students. But I'm not completely divorced from that because I do go around the country and speak to groups of young people, and do a kind of teaching. As a result, I don't miss teaching as much as I might have if I simply retired from teaching and played tennis.

(Somehow, the picture of Zinn at the net makes me laugh.) In that same interview, Zinn offers sage advice about the patience required of political activists, especially in dark days. He tells activists: "Light that match, light that match, light that match, not knowing how often it's going to sputter and go out and at what point it's going to take hold."

Barsamian also squeezes out of Noam Chomsky the confession that he is about to indulge himself. "I have a jock grandson who's finally helping me fulfill a secret dream to have an excuse to go to a professional basketball game. I don't know if I should admit it, but I'm actually going to my first game in around fifty years." And Chomsky admits that Jeff Greenfield, when he was working for *Nightline*, was right when he said there were two reasons Chomsky couldn't come on the show: "First of all, I'm from Neptune. Secondly, I lack concision. I agree with him." Barsamian, always on the quick, asked him why he was from Neptune—you'll have to read that interview to find out.

It is these moments of revelation that, to my mind, are the quintessential Barsamian triumphs, as when the Haitian American writer Edwidge Danticat discusses her fascination with masks:

> Being a shy child, I always longed for a mask. Even in my adult life, I have glasses. They are my mask. When I meet people for the first time, I always put on my glasses because I feel like that's a little something extra between me and them...The story is a mask; the characters you create are masks. That appeals to me.

Or check out Barsamian's interview with Danny Glover, where the actor is in a particularly captious mood: "Did it change the world that Denzel and Halle got Oscars? Did it mean that we're spending what we need to spend on AIDS? Did it mean that there were fewer homeless people?"

Many of Barsamian's subjects look back at how they became rebels in the first place. Vandana Shiva, who campaigns tirelessly against bioengineered food, recalls when she was six years old and wanted a nylon dress like all the other girls she grew up with in India. "I was very keen to get a nylon frock for my birthday. My mother said, 'I can get it for you, but would you rather—through how you live, and what you wear, and what you eat—ensure that food goes into the hands of the weaver or ensure that profits go into the bank of an industrialist?'" Today, Vandana Shiva says she "gets thrills from taking on these big guys and recognizing how, behind all their power, they are so empty."

Arundhati Roy, like Vandana Shiva, also pays a debt to her independent mother. "I thank God that I had none of the conditioning that a normal, middle-class Indian girl would have," she tells Barsamian. "I had no father, no presence of this man telling us that he would look after us and beat us occasionally in exchange. I didn't have a caste, and I didn't have a class, and I had no religion, no traditional blinkers." One tribute to Barsamian is that he does not delete questions and answers even when he is getting scolded. Here is an exchange I love in that same interview with Arundhati Roy:

> Barsamian: You feel a sense of responsibility to these silent voices that are calling out to you.
>
> Roy: No, I don't feel responsibility because that's such a boring word.

You will find amusing lines in here. Eduardo Galeano says, "I know perfectly well that I'm going to hell, and I'm getting trained in warm tropical countries to accept the flames." Kurt Vonnegut says, "Bush is entertaining us with what I call the Republican Super Bowl, which is played by the lower classes using live ammunition." And you will find moments of great self-awareness. Here's Angela Davis, refusing to remain in the pigeonhole of the 1960s. People from that era "tend to use me as a way to think about their own youth," she says:

> That's OK, but it's not really about me, and it can be somewhat straining. I have tried over the years to grow and develop. I am not the same person I was in the early 1970s...I don't want to represent myself, as some people of my generation do, as the veteran with all the answers.

Then there are moments of chilling prescience. The Pakistani American scholar Eqbal Ahmad tells Barsamian in November 1998: "Osama bin Laden is a sign of things to come." Ahmad describes a visit to Afghanistan under Taliban rule, and he sees a boy being sent to his execution for the crime of playing with a tennis ball. Ahmad had no truck with the Taliban, but

Washington did, he points out. And he puts in perspective some of the motives behind the terrorism that erupted on September 11.

> The Arabs are, at the moment, an extremely humiliated, frustrated, beaten, and insulted people...This people has only two choices now, as its young people see it: It's either to become active, fight, die, and recover its lost dignity, lost sovereignties, lost lands, or to become slaves. Terrorism is not without a history.

Edward Said reflects on the horror of September 11 and the "cosmic, demonic quality of mind at work" in those attacks—a mind "which refused to have any interest in dialogue and political organization, and persuasion." Said then gives a warning that Bush has not heeded, to the detriment of us all: "Punish [bin Laden] accordingly, and don't bring down the world around him and ourselves."

It is all here, in these interviews: profound insights into the perilous world we live in, morsels of autobiography, humorous asides, and indispensable advice on how to survive these harrowing times.

A final note or two: Working with David Barsamian is one of the great pleasures I have in my job. He is dogged on the trail of his interview subject, and he does not rest even when he hands in the tape or the transcript. Fastidious to a fault, he is as much his editor as I am, and makes certain that everything is accurate and tight. I also admire his personality and his convictions. A man of incredible energy, an upbeat disposition, and a refreshing, ecumenical approach to progressive politics, Barsamian has no patience for sectarian fights. He once memorably dispatched those on the left who relish such battles, calling them "the tiny savaging the minute in order to become the infinitesimal." You won't find smallness here, but generosity and, above all, curiosity.

Enjoy this collection; I know I have.

Edwidge Danticat
October 2003

Edwidge Danticat won the American Book Award for her 1998 novel, *The Farming of Bones* (Soho Press). Born in Haiti in 1969, she immigrated to Brooklyn in 1981 to join her parents, who had come years earlier. Her father drove a cab, and her mother was a textile worker. After her parents left Haiti, she was raised by her aunt, for whom she has great affection.

Danticat mines the immigrant experience and the history of her native land for material. Her first novel, *Breath, Eyes, Memory* (Soho Press), was published in 1994. The following year, her collection of short stories *Krik? Krak!* (Soho Press) was nominated for a National Book Award. "When you write, it's like braiding your hair," she writes in *Krik? Krak!* "Taking a handful of coarse, unruly strands and attempting to bring them into unity... Some of the braids are long, others are short. Some are thick, others are thin. Some are heavy. Others are light."

Last year, in a departure, she wrote a nonfiction work called *After the Dance: A Walk Through Carnival in Jacmel, Haiti* (Crown Journeys). Rich in reportage, it is a book of both great travel writing and sociological insight. Her forthcoming book is called *The Dew Breaker*. And she's working on a children's book about Anacaona, an Arawak woman who was a chief in pre-independence Haiti.

She does not like to be pigeonholed as some kind of oracle or interpreter of Haitian Americans. "I think I've been assigned that role, but I don't really see myself as the voice of the Haitian American experience," she once said, adding: "There are many; I'm just one."

I first interviewed Danticat when she was in Boulder in the mid-1990s. I was struck then by her acute intellect and her desire to say things precisely, but also by her sense of humor. In that interview, she did not have formulaic answers. That was the case again when I called her in Miami, where she now lives, in early August.

℘   ℞

What's your new book, The Dew Breaker, *about?*

It's a collection of interrelated short stories like *Krik? Krak!* It's centered around a torturer during the thirty-year Duvalier dictatorship. The book is about this person and some of his victims. The main character now lives in Brooklyn and owns a barbershop. I wanted to explore how such a person carries on with his life, and how his victims live with the scars of dictatorship. Often when we migrate, we find ourselves with these types of persons—the torturers and the victims mixed together in the same neighborhood. One of the things that sparked my interest in this is the case of Emmanuel Constant, who started a militia called FRAPH [Front for the Advancement and Progress of Haiti] that was backed by the CIA. FRAPH killed thousands of Haitians in the early 1990s. Now while Constant is living comfortably in Queens, other Haitians are being deported. I wanted to see how those who have been bruised by people like that deal with coming face to face with their torturers.

Faulkner said, "The past is never dead—it's not even past."

Exactly. Especially in the case of people who have migrated from other places. We try so hard to keep some aspects of the past with us and forget others, but often we don't get to choose. We try to keep the beautiful memories, but other things from the past creep up on us. The past is like the hair on our head. I moved to New York when I was twelve, but you always have this feeling that wherever you come from, you physically leave it, but it doesn't leave you.

Constant is wanted in Haiti.

He's been tried in absentia for crimes against the Haitian people, and has been given a life sentence. But he's safely in the United States. And it's not just Haitian torturers who find refuge here. There are examples of people who carried out massacres in the Balkans, Central America, and Indonesia who are now living with impunity in this country. The administration is very selective in whom it considers terrorists.

Your novel The Farming of Bones *traces an important but much overlooked aspect of Haitian history: the 1937 massacre, directed by the Dominican dictator Trujillo. The army, using repatriation as a ruse, rounded up tens of thousands of Haitians who were living in the Dominican Republic. How many people were killed?*

The estimates are from 14,000 to 40,000. I lean more toward the higher number. Afterward, the Dominican Republic offered the Haitian government something like fifty cents in compensation per person killed.

What did you discover in writing that book?

The saddest part of that whole experience was seeing how that event is so linked with what's going on today. We still have our people working in the cane fields in the Dominican Republic. People are still repatriated all the time from the Dominican Republic to Haiti. Some tell of being taken off buses because they looked Haitian, and their families have been in the Dominican Republic for generations. Haitian children born in the Dominican Republic still can't go to school and are forced to work in the sugarcane fields. It really isn't a memory; it's an event that has a continuing relationship. And the massacre is something that people always fear can happen again.

But the whole history between Haiti and the Dominican Republic is complicated. We share the island of Hispaniola, and Haiti occupied the Dominican Republic for twenty-two years after 1804 for fear that the French and Spanish would come back and reinstitute slavery. So we have this unique situation of being two independent nations on the same island, but with each community having their own grievances. Even today people will look at each other and say, "You occupied me," or "Trujillo killed members of my family."

C. L. R. James wrote, Haiti was "the greatest colony in the world, the pride of France, and the envy of every other imperialist nation." Contrast that today with Haiti being one of the most heavily stigmatized countries in the world, almost synonymous with destitution, desperation, violence, boat people, and AIDS.

We were referred to as "the Pearl of the Antilles," the most productive colony—but productive for whom? Not for the slaves working in the plantations. It was a wealthy colony, but once the colonizer left, he left with all the wealth. This is not to make excuses. We made a lot of our own mess, too. But we started out with a lot of negatives that are still against us today.

The Haitian revolution was met by hostility from the United States, which didn't like enslaved blacks leading a revolution and throwing off the French.

This was a "bad" example for US slaves. Haiti was subjected to an embargo from the United States, which, along with many other countries, refused to recognize this new republic.

The leader of that revolt was Toussaint L'Ouverture, someone who is practically unknown in the United States.

He was one of the leaders. There were others: Boukman, a Jamaican who in 1791 organized a Vodou ceremony where people pledged to fight for liberty or to die. There was Mackandal. And then L'Ouverture, who was on a plantation, who started organizing, and had military training. There were also leaders like Jean-Jacques Dessalines, whose motto was, "Cut their heads off, burn their houses." L'Ouverture was taken from Haiti and imprisoned in France, where he died. Wordsworth wrote a poem about him. One of L'Ouverture's most quoted sayings was, when he was about to be taken off by the French, "You can cut the branches of the tree of liberty, but you can't destroy the roots because they are too strong and too many." He was a phenomenal leader, but it's important to acknowledge the others. Because it's a problem we have thinking that one person can make a revolution, whether it's now or in the past.

The United States invaded Haiti in 1915 and remained there until 1934. Decades of dictatorship followed. What kind of legacy has that left on Haiti?

It had a very potent legacy that we're still living with today. For example, the whole military structure in Haiti that existed until the early 1990s was put in place by the American occupation. At the top there were Southern white officers, who led an army that crushed the indigenous resistance—the *cacos*. A high-ranking US officer said when he arrived, "To think these niggers speak French!" Later, Haitian officers attended the notorious School of the Americas at Fort Benning. The threat from the US is something that is always hanging over people's heads: If we don't behave, we'll have occupation again.

You mentioned Boukman. There's a well-known Haitian musical ensemble called Boukman Eksperyans that does roots music. Talk about the relationship between culture and resistance.

Boukman really speaks to the people and the roots of the problem, and their carnivals are often extremely popular. People will sing and dance, but still get a message from it. The group has transformed what was before ceremonial Vodou—notice that it is spelled V-o-d-o-u— and brought it out in a public sphere as beautiful and celebratory but also protest music.

Why do you spell it that way?

Because when people think about this religion, they'll say "voodoo" this and "voodoo" that in the way the Hollywood movies show it: the sticking of pins in dolls. It's very different than Vodou—which is a religion that comes to Haiti from our ancestors in Africa. I want to differentiate it from the stereotypical, sensationalized view that we see of the religion: "voodoo economics," "voodoo this and that." Vodou is one of the religions practiced in Haiti, a rich religion for the people.

In your book After the Dance, *you write about AIDS being "a painfully complicated issue for us Haitians." Why is that?*

In the 1980s, when people were just beginning to talk about AIDS, there were just a few categories of those who were at high risk: homosexuals, hemophiliacs, heroin addicts, and Haitians. We were the only ones identified by nationality. Then it seemed from the media that we were being told that all Haitians had AIDS. At the time, I had just come from Haiti. I was twelve years old, and the building I was living in had primarily Haitians. A lot of people got fired from their jobs. At school, sometimes in gym class, we'd be separated because teachers were worried about what would happen if we bled. So there was really this intense discrimination. The FDA [US Food and Drug Administration] placed us on the list of people who could not give blood. So AIDS was something that was put upon us, and we were immediately identified with it. That is unfair. That is unjust. I always say, "We are all people living with AIDS." It's not like you can avoid it. It's part of our world.

You've looked into the treatment of Haitian immigrants. Attorney General John Ashcroft says Haitian refugees constitute a threat to national security. What's that about?

I recently moved to Florida. I see the sharp inequality between how Haitian and Cuban refugees are treated. Both groups come here because their lives are equally desperate. But on arrival, the Haitians are incarcerated, and some are immediately repatriated, whereas Cubans get to stay and are eligible for citizenship. I'm not saying Cubans don't deserve asylum, but if it is a national security issue, there are people who are coming from Cuba on hijacked airplanes. Why isn't that a national security issue? And recently the attorney general made another astonishing claim, that there were Pakistani terrorists possibly coming on these boats from Haiti. No one has ever seen a Pakistani coming on a boat from Haiti yet. Ashcroft couldn't even name one case.

You've been to these immigration holding centers in Florida. What are they like?

I went with a group of people to Krome, the largest holding center. It's a male facility. We met with a group of people who came to the recreational area. It's sort of out in the middle of nowhere. We met with a lot of people who were depressed, feeling that they were criminalized for having tried to come here. Many men talked about committing suicide. Some had been there for more than a year, and had no idea what their fate was going to be.

What do you think of Bush's attack on Iraq?

That situation could have been resolved in a different way. And the justification—the idea that we have a right to invade another country and determine another people's destiny—is frightening. And I fear really for the future of that occupation. What happens now, and twenty years from now, and forty years from now, given our case? People in the United States may feel like when we don't see it on CNN twenty-four hours a day, it sort of disappears. But it doesn't disappear for the people who have to live under occupation—and their children and their children's children.

What's your assessment of Aristide?

That's a tricky one. My view still is that he was voted in power. I can't really gauge how much change there's been since 1990. I know he has his supporters and detractors. I will quote Brecht: "I'm on the side of the people." Whatever the people decide about him, I will follow. Life's hard in Haiti right now. And the hardest thing is that the future does not lie with one person. A lot of the focus is often put on him. He can't save Haiti. No one individual can. He can't pull the strings and make everything better. It all becomes a personality cult: Can one person save Haiti?

I sense your reticence in talking about Aristide.

I do have trouble talking about him because I just don't know. I can't read the situation very well. I can't say, like some do, that he's all bad, or like some other people, that he's all good.

Tell me about your craft. You've said that at a very early age, writing was a "haven" for you. As a child, you had "secret artistic aspirations." What models did you draw upon?

My models were oral, were storytellers. Like my grandmothers and my aunts. It's true, a lot of people in my life were not literate in a formal sense, but they were storytellers. So I had this experience of just watching somebody spin a tale off the top of her head. I loved that. She would engage an audience, and she would read people's faces to see if what she was saying was captivating them. If it was boring, she would speed up, and if it was too fast, she would slow down. So that whole interaction between the storyteller and the listeners had a very powerful influence on me.

When I started going to school, writing itself was painful. But when I started reading other things—the *Madeline* books about a little girl in France—I thought, well, that's kind of what my grandmother does, except this story never changes. But I don't know where exactly I got it into my mind that I wanted to write, that I could write. It just sort of came about.

I was impressed with After the Dance *as a work of journalism. How did you take it on?*

After the Dance was my first attempt at nonfiction. I'd never really participated in carnival, and I really wanted to go. It sounded like a wonderfully fun thing to do. And I wanted to write something happy about Haiti, something celebratory. And going to carnival gave me a chance to do that, because it is one of the instances in Haiti when people shed their class separation and come together.

Masks are a big part of carnival. You seem drawn to them. Why?

Even when I think of writing fiction, it's being kind of a liar, a storyteller, a weaver, and there's that sense of how much of this is your life. The story is a way you unravel your life from behind a mask. But the idea of just putting on a mask in a big crowd where you can be anybody was always something that was interesting to me because sometimes when we're most shielded is when we are boldest. And, being a shy child, I always longed for a mask. Even in my adult life, I have glasses—they are my mask. When I meet people for the first time,

I always put on my glasses because I feel like that's a little something extra between me and them. It's like the Laurence Dunbar poem "We Wear the Mask." I think we all wear some kind of mask. There are masks that shield us from others, but there are masks that embolden us, and you see that in carnival. The shiest child puts on a mask and can do anything and be anybody. So sometimes we mask ourselves to further reveal ourselves, and it's always been connected to me with being a writer: We tell lies to tell a greater truth. The story is a mask; the characters you create are masks. That appeals to me. Aside from that, too, in the carnival the masks were beautiful and offered a vision of Haitian creativity.

There's a wonderful moment in After the Dance *about the US ambassador, who is attending the carnival.*

On the VIP stand, you had the foreign dignitaries, the carnival queen, the senators, the important people who'd come from afar. And that year, the biggest float was depicting a scene of Haitian refugees with men dressed as Coast Guard officers and people spilling over, and the crowd serving as the sea. Suddenly, the US ambassador heard the crowd sing a popular song about how "we are selling the country in US dollars." It was one of those absurdist moments, where carnival and life merged. Carnival is a celebration of history, and it echoes so much of who we are, from the Arawaks to slavery to colonization to the current day. It's just something that throbs with this living history. People often think of Haiti as a place where you're not supposed to have any joy. I wanted to show that this is a place with joy.

Kurt Vonnegut
June 2003

On February 23, I walked up the steps to Kurt Vonnegut's Midtown Manhattan brownstone and rang the bell. There was a smile and a mass of gray, curly hair to greet me. Then I heard, "Bite him!" At Vonnegut's feet was a meek-looking small white dog. The master's command went unheeded. The dog just looked up at me and seemed terribly bored. Vonnegut lamented that he could not get his dog to obey.

Everything you may have heard about this master storyteller, now eighty, is true. He is irreverent and insouciant. And he is very funny. When I confessed to him that I had not read all his books, he told me, "You can leave now."

He was chain-smoking Pall Malls throughout the afternoon we spent together in his living room. When I pointed the obvious out to him, he said, "I'm trying to die. But it's not working." And then he laughed.

He has recently been writing a column for the magazine *In These Times*, where he fields questions from readers. His disdain for Bush is palpable. "America was certainly hated all around the world long before the Mickey Mouse coup d'état," he wrote recently. "And we weren't hated, as Bush would have it, because of our liberty and justice for all. We are hated because our corporations have been the principal deliverers and imposers of new technologies and economic schemes which have wrecked cultures."

Vonnegut was captured during the Battle of the Bulge in December 1944. He was taken away to a POW camp in Dresden. His experiences there led to his celebrated novel *Slaughterhouse-Five* (Delacorte Press, 1973). It ranks among the great works of antiwar literature. Among his many other books are *Cat's Cradle* (Holt, Rinehart and Winston, 1963), *Breakfast* of *Champions* (Delacorte Press, 1973), *Jailbird* (Delacorte Press, 1979), and *Bluebeard* (Delacorte Press, 1987), as well as what he calls an autobiographical collage, *Fates Worse Than Death* (G.P. Putnam's Sons, 1991).

The same day I saw Vonnegut, he enthralled a standing-room-only crowd honoring Howard Zinn at the 92nd Street Y in New York City. The event celebrated the selling of the millionth copy of *A People's History of the United States*. Vonnegut read from the Zinn classic, as did Alice Walker, James Earl Jones, Danny Glover, Alfre Woodard, and Marisa Tomei, among others.

ॐ ☙

What's your take on George Bush?

We have a president who knows absolutely no history, and he is surrounded by men who pay no attention to history. They imagine that they are great politicians inventing something new. In fact, it's really quite old stuff: tyranny. But they imagine they're being creative.

In 1946, Hermann Goering said at Nuremberg, "Of course, the people don't want war... But, after all, it is the leaders of the country who determine the policy, and it is always a simple matter to drag the people along, whether it is a democracy, or a fascist dictatorship, or a parliament, or a communist dictatorship." Does it work the same way in the United States?

Of course it does. Bush wouldn't know what I'm talking about because he isn't responsive to history, but now we've had our Reichstag Fire. After the First World War, Germany was trying to build a democracy. Then when the Reichstag, the legislature, was burned down in 1933, this was seen as such an emergency that human rights had to be suspended. The attack on the World Trade Center has allowed Bush and his gang to do anything. What are we to do now? I say when there's a code red, we should all run around like chickens with our heads cut off. I don't feel that we are in any great danger.

Today, war is being produced as a made-for-TV event. It's a video game for the army of couch potatoes.

It's incumbent on the president to entertain. Clinton did a better job of it—and was forgiven for the scandals, incidentally. Bush is entertaining us with what I call the Republican Super Bowl, which is played by the lower classes using live ammunition.

You live just a few blocks from the United Nations. On February 15, there was a mass demonstration in New York. You took part in it.

I was simply there, but I didn't speak.

What do you think of the efficacy of people turning out at protests and marching?

I'm an old guy, and I was protesting during the Vietnam War. We killed fifty Asians for every loyal American. Every artist worth a damn in this country was terribly opposed to that war, finally, when it became evident what a fiasco and meaningless butchery it was. We formed sort of a laser beam of protest. Every painter, every writer, every stand-up comedian, every composer, every novelist, every poet aimed in the same direction. Afterwards, the power of this incredible new weapon dissipated. Now it's like a banana cream pie three feet in diameter dropped from a stepladder four feet high. The right of the people to peacefully assemble and petition their government for a redress of grievances is now worth a pitcher of warm spit. That's because TV will not come and treat it respectfully. Television is really something.

The government satirizes itself. All we can wish is that there will be a large number of Americans who will realize how dumb this all is, and how greedy and how vicious. Such an audience is dwindling all the time because of TV. One good thing about TV is, if you die violently, God forbid, on camera, you will not have died in vain because you will be great entertainment.

In Slaughterhouse-Five, *you write about the firebombing of Dresden, and a couple of months later came Hiroshima and Nagasaki.*

The most racist, nastiest act by this country, after human slavery, was the bombing of Nagasaki. Not of Hiroshima, which might have had some military significance. But Nagasaki was purely blowing away yellow men, women, and children. I'm glad I'm not a scientist because I'd feel so guilty now.

At Nuremberg, Supreme Court Justice Robert Jackson, who was the chief US prosecutor, said that to initiate a war of aggression is the supreme international crime.

People are lying all the time as to what a murderous nation we are. So let it be known. We're behaving abominably. It's like having a relative go absolutely nuts. Somebody has to say, "I think Uncle Charlie's off his rocker." We are behaving in a bizarre manner now. George Bush and his gang imagine they are being political geniuses.

You have never seen greatness in a presidency; I have. It was a rich kid who you would think had every reason to be a horse's ass—Franklin Roosevelt. He was humane and wise and resourceful. He was called a traitor to his class. With George Bush, that charge would never stick.

When Bush began to play the Iraq card, it was exactly when there was an enormous amount of attention being paid to the scandals on Wall Street—Global Crossing, Enron, Halliburton. It distracted the public from what was going on in the corporate sector.

One thing I learned, with permission of the school committee of Indianapolis, was that when a tyrant or a government gets in trouble it wonders what to do. Declare war! Then nothing else matters. It's like chess; when in doubt, castle.

The polls demonstrate that 50 percent of Americans who get their news from TV think Saddam Hussein was behind the Twin Towers attack. Man, have they got ways for getting half-truths out right away now, thanks to TV! I think TV is a calamity in a democracy.

What about the importance of reading books?

It's hard to read and write. To expect somebody to read a book is like having someone arrive at a concert hall and be immediately handed a violin and told to go up onstage. It's an astonishing skill that people can read, and read well. Very few people can read well. For instance, I have to be very careful with irony, saying something while meaning the exact opposite. *Slaughterhouse-Five* is read in high schools, and sometimes the teachers tell the students to write the author. Some of them write that the events are not sequential! It's hard enough to read a book with Wednesday followed by Monday.

Your father was an architect. But you said you never saw him read a book. Your uncle Alex, an insurance salesman, was the one who pushed you to read.

Yes, he did. And his recommendations were absolutely first rate.

Like what?

The prefaces to George Bernard Shaw's plays were an enormous influence on me. To hell with the plays. I remember the title to one of his prefaces was "Christianity—Why Not Give It a Try?"

Shaw, who you've described as a hero of yours, was also a socialist.

It's perfectly ordinary to be a socialist. It's perfectly normal to be in favor of fire departments. There was a time when I could vote for economic justice, and I can't anymore. I cast my first vote for a socialist candidate—Norman Thomas, a Christian minister. I had to cast it by absentee ballot. I used to have three socialist parties to choose from—the Socialist Labor Party, Socialist Workers Party, and I forgot what the other one was.

You take pride in being from Indiana, in being a Hoosier.

For being from the state that gave us Eugene Debs.

Eugene Debs of Terre Haute on the Wabash.

Where Timothy McVeigh was executed. Eugene Debs said—and this is merely a paraphrase of the Sermon on the Mount, which is what so much socialist writing is—"As long as there's a lower class, I'm in it; as long as there's a criminal element, I'm of it; as long as there is a soul in prison," which would include Timothy McVeigh, "I am not free." What is wrong with that? Of course, Jesus got crucified for saying the same thing.

With two million souls in prison today in the United States, Debs would be very busy.

Debs would've committed suicide, feeling there was nothing he could do about it.

There is another Hoosier you write about who is unknown, Powers Hapgood of Indianapolis. Who was he?

Powers Hapgood was a rich kid. His family owned a successful cannery in Indianapolis. Powers was radicalized. After he graduated from Harvard, he went to work in a coal mine to find out what that was like. He became a labor organizer. He led the pickets against the execution of Sacco and Vanzetti. I got to know him late in his life when he'd become a local CIO [Congress of Industrial Organizations] official. There was some sort of dustup on a picket line, enough to bring the cops into play. Hapgood was testifying in court about what was to be done about CIO members who had made trouble. The judge stopped the proceedings at one point and said, "Hapgood, why would a man with your advantages, from a wealthy, respected family, Harvard graduate, lead such a life?" Powers Hapgood replied, "Why, the Sermon on the Mount, sir." Not bad, huh?

Incidentally, I am honorary president of the American Humanist Association, having succeeded the great science fiction writer and biochemist Dr. Isaac Asimov. John Updike, who is religious, says I talk more about God than any seminarian. Socialism is, in fact, a form of Christianity, people wishing to imitate Christ.

Christianity pervades your spirit.

Well, of course. It's good writing. I don't care whether it's God or not, but the Sermon on the Mount is a masterpiece, and so is the Lord's Prayer: "Forgive us our trespasses as we forgive those who trespass against us." The two most radical ideas, inserted in the midst of conventional human thought, are $E=mc^2$—matter and energy are the same kind of stuff—and "Forgive us our trespasses as we forgive those who trespass against us." In 1844, Karl Marx said, "Religion is the opiate of the masses." He said this at a time when opium and opium derivatives were the only painkillers. And he said it helped a little. He might as well have said, "Religion is the aspirin of the people." At the time he said this terrible thing, we had human slavery as a perfectly legal enterprise. Now in the eyes of a merciful God, who was more hateful back then? Karl Marx or the United States of America?

You've said that you wouldn't have missed the Great Depression or World War II for anything. Why did you say that?

Well, I actually saw it all. I didn't have to read about it. I was there, so for that reason I wouldn't have missed it for the world. I have really been an infantry private. I didn't read about it; I was it. That's a matter of pride. I was a police reporter for Chicago City News Bureau, which was the outfit that was the inspiration for the play *The Front Page*. I covered Chicago as a street reporter. I really did it. And I've been a teacher and all that. I'm glad for the opportunity to see so much.

When you go to college audiences and give lectures, you're talking to twenty-somethings. What kind of response do you get?

Very warm, very enthusiastic. You think crack cocaine is a high? Try being me facing one of those college audiences. It is marvelous.

Ahmed Rashid
December 2002

A hmed Rashid is a journalist based in Lahore, Pakistan. He has been covering Afghanistan, Pakistan, and Central Asia for more than twenty years for the *Far Eastern Economic Review* and the *Daily Telegraph*. He is the author of *Taliban* (Yale University Press, 2000), a book that has sold a million copies and has been translated into more than twenty languages. His latest book is *Jihad: The Rise of Militant Islam in Central Asia* (Yale University Press, 2002).

Recognized as one of the leading authorities on the Taliban, he has been in high demand since September 11. He has appeared on many radio and TV news shows, has spoken at universities around the world, and has even consulted with the State Department.

Yet Rashid himself became acquainted with the chilly atmosphere in the United States in December 2001. Arriving at Dulles airport to give some talks in Washington, he was stopped by security. "They asked me a few questions and spent about two hours looking through their computers," he recalls. "They finally released me without saying anything. I did not take any umbrage at that. But I thought it quite amusing, having written this book on the Taliban and having been invited by prestigious US institutions to lecture."

A Pakistani citizen, Rashid has not given up on his own country. "There are a lot of people who are struggling consistently for democracy, for human rights, for freedom of the media," he says. "There is a strong and ever growing civil society."

Rashid is helping to build civil society in Afghanistan, as well. He has donated a quarter of the proceeds from his Taliban book to establish the Open Media Fund for Afghanistan. The fund, he says, "is now giving small grants to magazines and newspapers throughout Afghanistan, which had been completely banned by the Taliban. There's a women's magazine, there's one for children. And there's a newspaper in Herat dealing with reconstruction. The idea is to help revive the print media in Afghanistan."

≫ ≪

The standard US media view of the war in Afghanistan is that it was a success. The Taliban were ousted. Al Qaeda has been dispersed. There were a handful of US casualties. Hamid Karzai has been installed in power in Kabul. Maybe a couple of thousand civilians died; sorry about that. The Pentagon can't find Osama bin Laden or Mullah Omar, but all in all America is on its way to winning the war on terrorism. What do you think of that story?

It's true certainly up to a point—to January or February, when the Taliban and Al Qaeda were defeated. But the real problem since then has been a lack of a strategy by the United States as to how to combat terrorism on the ground now that it has taken a different shape and form. The fact that there are no longer large units of Al Qaeda running around means you don't need B-52s. You need intelligence and special forces. And, most importantly, you need to resurrect Afghanistan from what is literally the graveyard of countries and transform it into a normal country, which the Afghans want. The strategy for peace-building is economic aid, reconstruction, international security forces. On those lines, the US has been extremely slow. And it has even blocked expanding security forces from Kabul to other cities. There's a sense of desperation in Afghanistan because of the lack of funding and the fact that the US only has a one-track military strategy. It doesn't have an economic and political game plan.

What do you make of Afghan-born Zalmay Khalilzad, who is Bush's special envoy to Afghanistan?

Khalilzad is being called the governor-general of Afghanistan in the sense that he seems to be taking many of the major decisions in consultation with Hamid Karzai. He can make or break issues. And he reflects the views of the National Security Council and the Defense Department.

There is a kind of love-hate relationship between him and the Afghans. He has done some very sound work in keeping Afghanistan at the top of the Bush administration's agenda and making people notice Afghanistan, which I think is very important. But he's roiled up many groups of Afghans because of what happened during the *loya jirga* in June when he played a very up-front role in trying to block the former king, Zahir Shah, from taking any position. So it's a mixed bag. Overall, Khalilzad is an extremely powerful individual right now.

He also worked for the Rand Corporation and then he was a consultant for Unocal, which has wanted to build a pipeline from Turkmenistan in Central Asia down through Afghanistan and out to Pakistan.

The leaders of all three countries—Turkmenistan, Afghanistan, and Pakistan—are pushing for this, for their own separate reasons. At the moment this is a nonstarter. This would be a pipeline that would cross from Turkmenistan into Afghanistan and end up in markets in Pakistan and India. It is extremely difficult to imagine that any oil company for the next few years is going to want to invest two or three billion dollars in Afghanistan. That confidence is just not there right now. There's a huge security problem. Secondly, the market for that oil and gas is the subcontinent, but Pakistan and India are almost at war with each other. That market is very fragile. It's going to take a lot more than mere intentions to get this pipeline moving.

General Tommy Franks, head of US forces in Afghanistan, says American troops will be in that country "for years." What are the implications of that?

Very serious. You have a lot of suspicion from the neighbors of Afghanistan about US intentions. Iran is already, to some extent, trying to undermine the US in Afghanistan. Russia is now becoming increasingly nervous about a more permanent US presence in Central Asia. And China is not keen that the US should be so close to its borders over a long period of time. Certainly, if the US is going to be there for a long time, it's going to exacerbate regional tensions.

The idea of a permanent US military presence, as opposed to an economic presence, is going to create a new wave of hostility toward the United States. In the south amongst the Pashtuns, that sentiment is already strong. And I don't equate this with the Pashtuns becoming pro-Taliban or pro-Al Qaeda. Pashtun nationalism is reasserting itself. Its political history spans several hundred years. The Pashtuns are angry at the Americans because, one, they're still being bombed, and two, they perceive that the Americans are backing the Tajik faction, which controls the army and security forces in Kabul.

The problem right now, which I've been pointing out very bluntly to American officials in Washington, is that the US has no economic presence in Afghanistan. The Afghans can't point and say, "Oh, the Americans built that road. They built that telecommunications facility. They built that electricity powerhouse," because nothing has been built so far.

Karzai recently survived an assassination attempt. How secure is he?

The situation is extremely fragile, with widespread anger in the Pashtun belt at the Karzai government and the Americans. The Pashtuns feel discriminated against by the Americans because they supported the Taliban and the war is still going on in their region with continued US bombing. They are also disgruntled at the overwhelming power of their ethnic rivals the Tajiks, who dominate the security forces in Kabul and control the key levers of political power. Although Karzai is a Pashtun, many Pashtuns consider him a hostage to the Tajiks and Americans.

We should remember that the Pashtuns are the largest ethnic group in Afghanistan. Of course, many of them did support the Taliban. But you cannot equate all Pashtuns with the Taliban. There has to be a better ethnic representation in all areas of government. This is the biggest issue that Karzai is facing.

There is also the issue of the continuing threats posed by the warlords. The fact is, they are defying Kabul. They're not accepting its authority, they're trying to keep their fiefdoms. They're raising their own revenues and maintaining their own armies.

The US, by failing until now to allow for the expansion of the ISAF [International Security Assistance Force] to other cities and by failing to take the lead in helping reconstruct the country and urging other Western nations to provide fast-moving funding, has created a precarious situation. There is an impasse. The warlords are stronger than they were some months ago. The Tajiks are more in control, more decisive and more unwilling to compromise; the central government authority has actually shriveled and not expanded outside Kabul.

The situation can only be changed if the US is willing to play a leadership role amongst the Western donors, essentially by expanding ISAF by whatever means and getting money and reconstruction projects into the country fast, and, in particular, into the Pashtun belt.

Speaking of those pre-Taliban warlords, they are people like Abdul Rashid Dostum, the Uzbek leader in the north, Ismail Khan in Herat, and Gul Agha Shirzai in Kandahar.

Karzai's strategy, which is questionable, has been to try to bring the warlords into Kabul and to persuade them to leave their fiefdoms. He's given a lot of senior posts to them, but many have refused his offers. Ismail Khan, for example, has been offered the vice presidency but he prefers to stay in his fiefdom in Herat. Dostum has been named special representative of the government to the north, but he stays in the north.

The real problem for Karzai is extending the writ of the central government. It is a political issue, but more than that, it's an economic issue. Unless Karzai can say, "Either you behave or I have money and I can build a road in your area. Either you behave and join the central government and cooperate with me, or I won't build this road, I'll build it somewhere else," he won't have any clout. The fact is, he has no money. As long as this continues, the warlords know Karzai is extremely weak.

Let me ask you a bit more about Dostum. He's one of the most powerful of the warlords, and he's the deputy defense minister. Newsweek *recently revealed new information about Dostum and his forces being involved in war crimes, the murdering of hundreds of captured prisoners in the Mazar-e-Sharif area. Do you have any information on that?*

This is not a new story. Immediately after the fall of Mazar-e-Sharif and Kunduz to the Northern Alliance, it was well documented that large numbers of Taliban prisoners suffocated to death as they were being transported in sealed containers from Kunduz and Mazar to Sheberghan. Amnesty International, the American-based Human

Rights Watch, documented all this. Because the war was on, and defeating the Taliban was the main priority, this was ignored. *Newsweek* has presented considerable new evidence. And Physicians for Human Rights has unearthed mass graves. Clearly, something has to be done. The Afghan government actually condemned the mass killing and said that they would help any kind of investigation. But this is a very difficult issue. All the main perpetrators are part of the government.

What is the situation of women in Afghanistan today? Have you seen any improvement?

There has been an enormous improvement. Something like three million children have gone back to school. In the program, something like 50,000 women have gone back to work as teachers. That has been a huge accomplishment. The key to breaking the Taliban taboo against women and the cultural brainwashing that the Taliban imposed upon many Afghans is to get women back into the workforce. And that is happening at a pace that is quite remarkable. There's been a lot more progress in Kabul than in other cities, however, because they have not received reconstruction support.

There are several women in his government, though not in the top posts. That is one of the criticisms that came out of the *loya jirga*.

Before the Taliban took power in 1996, Afghanistan was the major source of the world's supply of heroin. During the Taliban rule, poppy cultivation was significantly curtailed. So much so that in May 2001 Secretary of State Colin Powell sent $43 million to the Taliban as thanks for the fine job they were doing in the war on drugs. What's the situation today?

The West has had a distorted understanding of how to cope with drugs. Right after the government was formed in Kabul, it was the season for harvesting poppy crops. The Americans and the British raised $50 million and threw it at the farmers to try to get them to cut down their crops. This program was not successful. There was corruption.

Afghan farmers have no access to other seeds, other crops, irrigation, tools, and all the other incentives that are needed to wean themselves from a black-market economy. That again is part of the reconstruction effort. If there had been a speedier input of money and incentives for farmers in this key area where poppies are grown on a large scale, you might not have stopped this year's crop but you would have stopped last year's crop. But now it's time to get ready for planting next year's crop, and there's still very little activity going on in the agricultural sector. So this could have been tackled on an emergency basis if there had been a serious investment in agriculture. Even if it couldn't be done across the country it could have been done in the key poppy areas.

Before October 7, 2001, and the beginning of the US bombing campaign, I remember seeing signs in Urdu: "Afghanistan: Amreekon ka Qabirstan"— "Afghanistan: Graveyard for the Americans." I recall you predicting there would be fierce resistance to the US onslaught. That simply didn't happen. Why not?

What everyone underestimated was the acute unpopularity of the Taliban, even in the Pashtun areas. People like myself were saying the Taliban would be driven out very swiftly from the north of the country, but given that their main support base was in the Pashtun belt, there would be greater resistance there. That didn't happen. The Taliban had become deeply unpopular and were actually discarded by the Pashtun population almost as quickly as they were in the north. I don't see the Taliban coming back in any way.

What's happening in the tribal areas of Pakistan bordering Afghanistan? There's been numerous reports that many Taliban and Al Qaeda fighters have taken refuge there.

There's no doubt that Al Qaeda has taken refuge not just in the tribal areas but also in Pakistan. We should remember that Al Qaeda had developed very close links to Pakistan over the last ten years, especially over the six years when the Taliban controlled Kabul. Some Pakistanis fought for the Taliban. Pakistani extremist groups provided infrastructural support to Al Qaeda. There was a coming and going of Al Qaeda militants and leaders between Afghanistan and Pakistan for several years. All that has really happened is that Al Qaeda has escaped from Afghanistan, come into Pakistan, got in touch with their contacts and friends in these extremist groups, which then provided them with safe houses, cars, and not just in the border areas but also in the cities. Rooting out Al Qaeda in Pakistan now is where the main battle is being fought. And it's a very difficult one.

Is Musharraf saying and doing one thing while his Inter-Services Intelligence is saying and doing something completely different?

I don't think it's a problem of division within the Pakistani military. I think the real problem is that there has been some disingenuity by Musharraf himself. He is, for example, cracking down on Al Qaeda. Pakistan has delivered to the Americans over 300 of the 900-plus people incarcerated in Guantanamo Bay. He's catching Al Qaeda. He's catching some of the extremist, sectarian groups, who have carried out the horrendous assassinations of Pakistani Christians and Westerners in recent months.

At the same time, he's backsliding on the pledges he's made to Pakistanis and to the West about containing the larger Islamic parties, which are equally important. The reason he's been backsliding on that is because they are involved in fighting in Kashmir, and the army needs these groups' support for the war in Kashmir and for confronting India. It's a mixed bag. Musharraf is walking a very fine line.

The Bush administration is focused on Iraq. The mantra is "regime change." The show is basically over in their view in Afghanistan. There will be a few mop-up operations but now we're off to new battlegrounds.

It would be hugely detrimental for the Afghan people, because Afghanistan will then disappear from the radar screen and will not get noticed. It will become even less likely that Afghanistan will get the kind of funding and aid to revive society than it would otherwise. But the other really big strategic issue here is that the war on terrorism will take a back seat. There is no way the Americans are going to be able to carry out a full-scale war against Iraq and at the same time maintain the same kind of pressure on the Al Qaeda network in countries as diverse as Indonesia, the Philippines, and Pakistan, as well as in Europe. With the victory in Afghanistan, the Bush administration is imagining that they can fight many wars, in many places, and win everywhere.

Danny Glover
December 2002

Danny Glover is board chair of the TransAfrica Forum, founded by Randall Robinson, that deals with issues relating to Africa and the Caribbean. He has traveled widely, promoting reparations and debt relief for African nations. In response to the AIDS crisis in Africa, he has extended his tenure as goodwill ambassador for the United Nations Development Program. He is an active board member of the Algebra Project, a math empowerment program developed by civil rights veteran Bob Moses.

Glover attended San Francisco State University and trained at the Black Actors' Workshop of the American Conservatory Theater. He appeared in numerous stage productions, but it was his performance in New York in *Master Harold and the Boys*, by the South African playwright Athol Fugard, that first brought Glover national recognition.

"The only reason I'm an actor," Glover told one interviewer, "is because of Fugard." Beyond the hijinks of the *Lethal Weapon* series, Glover gave solid performances in such films as *Places in the Heart*, *The Color Purple*, and *Beloved*. And his role as a homeless man in the independent movie *The Saint of Fort Washington* was memorable.

Glover is a hybrid of progressive politics and artistic sensibility in an industry that commodifies everything and reduces social commitment to late-night TV jokes. He knows what the *Lethal* movies are about: big paydays. But he takes the money and does things with it that are meaningful.

I called Glover in late August in Toronto, where he was working on a film. His marvelous grainy voice and infectious vitality made me want more time with him, but the set was beckoning.

ॐ   ॐ

At an event in New York City late last year called "Imagining Peace," you read from Martin Luther King's historic 1967 Riverside Church speech, "Beyond Vietnam." You quoted this passage: "Even when pressed by the demands of inner truth, men do not easily assume the task of opposing their government's policy, especially in time of war." Why did you pick that King speech?

At the time I spoke, it was just a matter of three months after September 11. We were in the midst of an undeclared war of indefinite length. A war that most people, even today, have difficulty understanding. I wanted to draw out the connections of that war to past events. Today, as the drums of war again beat louder and louder, the voices of those who oppose the war are drowned out by those voices that support the expedient way.

As King noted, it's always dangerous to speak out. His speech marked his transformation from civil rights leader to human rights leader. It made him vulnerable, perhaps even more vulnerable than during the darkest days of the civil rights movement. And his assassination occurred a year to the date of that speech. In the speech, he talked about creating a new way for African Americans and people of color to look at Vietnam, to see how that war had eviscerated the social programs that were supposed to help the poor. Yet the war not only drained valuable resources but took the lives of thousands of Americans already scarred by poverty.

King's speech reverberates today. It should be as clear to us as it was to him that beyond the rhetoric of war and terrorism lies a different reality. Look at the world around us and see what is happening. Wealth has increased. The disparity between poor and rich nations has widened. Two billion people in the world live on less than a dollar a day. The gap inside of countries has also widened. People go hungry here in the United States.

Your opposition to the death penalty and the war on terrorism embroiled you in some controversy. There was a call to boycott your film The Royal Tenenbaums. *What was that all about?*

I gave a speech at Princeton about the death penalty at the invitation of the local Amnesty International chapter. I reminded the audience that the United States is one of the few countries that still imposes the death penalty while it considers itself civilized. The European Union does not allow the death penalty and supports its abolition around the world. I was asked if my views on the death penalty applied to Osama bin Laden. I said they did. And I added that I was opposed to military tribunals, and to detentions that are still happening. After that I was tagged by elements of the right as unpatriotic.

Earl Hilliard, an African American congressman from Alabama, was defeated in June. In August, Cynthia McKinney, five-term progressive congresswoman from Georgia, was also defeated. Both were critical of Israeli policies vis-à-vis the Palestinians. In McKinney's case, her opponent outspent her two-to-one. What do you make of that?

Congresswoman McKinney represented a very important voice not only in the Black Caucus but in the Progressive Caucus. We're at a dangerous moment in terms of our ability to speak out on certain issues. And we have to find ways in which we can offset the role of money in the electoral process.

There was a rally in mid-August in Washington, DC, in favor of reparations for descendants of African American slaves. What's your position on that?

It's important that we continue to knock at the door of reparations. But if we're talking about giving someone forty acres and a mule and sending him off, that demeans the whole idea of reparations. It should be about a much larger thing: a way to enhance people's lives and provide them with resources to build community-based institutions. I was at the World Conference on Racism in Johannesburg. The issue of reparations came up, not only for African Americans but for Senegalese, Afro-Brazilians, Afro-Colombians, Angolans. Angola was engaged in a civil war for almost three decades. The US government supported the notorious Jonas Savimbi and his faction.

As the board chair of TransAfrica, I favor a Marshall Plan for the continent: a comprehensive effort to develop Africa's infrastructure and harness its resources. So, that's what I'm talking about in terms of reparations.

You spoke at Paine College in Augusta, Georgia, this past spring. Even though you were born in San Francisco, you said you felt really "at home." What did you mean by that?

Paine College is my mother's alma mater. My mother, Carrie M. Glover, graduated from there sixty years ago this year. She was the first to graduate from college in her family. My grandparents had a farm about forty miles from Augusta in Jefferson County. My mother was born and raised in that county. I spent a good deal of time in Georgia as a child. We visited the farm all through my childhood. That's a tradition that is still strong within the African American community. You can talk to a lot of people, and they will tell you about going to visit their grandparents on a farm after the Great Migration.

At Paine College, you recited from memory Langston Hughes's great poem "The Negro Speaks of Rivers," with that refrain, "My soul has grown deep like the rivers." What's your connection with Hughes?

For the last fifteen years I've traveled around the country, and often at campuses and at community events I've recited Langston, or read from his work. He's an incredible figure to understand, and his work reflects his profound love for people of African descent.

He came from a very interesting family. His maternal grandmother's first husband was part of John Brown's group that raided Harper's Ferry in 1859. He was killed there. In fact, one of Langston's most prized possessions was the bullet-riddled shawl that he wore. Members of his family held prominent positions during Reconstruction. He was half Native American, so he had strong indigenous roots. He wrote at a strategic moment in the modernity of African Americans.

He went to Columbia University in 1921 and soon became a prominent voice in this enormous black mecca called the Harlem Renaissance. Then came the Depression, which had an incredible impact on people and the way in which they saw themselves in relationship to government. Langston wrote about that. His politics reflected that. If you look at one of my favorite poems, "Let America Be America Again," he talks about all those issues.

It was also a very dark period for him. In his poem "Drum," he talks about his views on life and existentialism, as well. He supported the Spanish Republic against Franco's fascism. Then he came through the war period, and the brutal McCarthy era, where he was targeted, as many artists were. And then he threw himself into African liberation movements in Africa. He wrote a powerful poem about Patrice Lumumba called "Lumumba's Grave."

You see this continuity as an artist, and as a voice, against oppression. Take his poem "Bitter River," written in 1942 after the lynching of two fourteen-year-old kids in Mississippi. It was at the beginning of the war against fascism, and here's two kids swinging from trees in Mississippi. The contradiction and the irony of that!

There was a big to-do at the Academy Awards this year with Denzel Washington and Halle Berry both winning Oscars. How are African Americans faring in Hollywood, not just on the screen but in the executive suites?

We have to change the way we look at what is happening. This is a business that is primed on sequels, a business that caters to kids in the nine-to-fourteen age bracket. And here we are, grown adults, running around saying this is important, that is important.

If we matter, we matter tangentially to what the real situation is. So why do we talk about it? How important is it that African Americans won Oscars this year? I don't know. You can talk about stuff long enough so that you say, "Oh, this means something." But, really, what does it mean? And to respond to it, is what? Did it change the world that Denzel and Halle got Oscars? Did it mean that we're spending what we need to spend on AIDS? Did it mean that there are fewer homeless people?

Are you getting the kind of roles you're looking for?

I don't think you ever do that. I'm looking for stories. Am I seeing the kinds of stories I want to see? Not necessarily.

I see them in foreign films. I saw a wonderful Inuit film called *The Fast Runner* and an excellent Indian film called *Monsoon Wedding*. Look, I'm trying to find work that I find meaning in. What's a role? Does he look like a judge? Is that a good role? Sitting on the bench where he isn't a big part of the plot? I don't know, man.

You told the Washington Post *that careers come and go, and that your career could be on the downside, but you're not going to sit around playing golf.*

I don't play golf. I'm not going to sit around. All I know is that I can go and speak my truth. That's all I have control over. My truth doesn't come from how many meetings I have with Hollywood execs. My truth comes from trying to be in the world and trying to talk about issues and trying to understand—and underline the word "understand"— what is happening around us and around me. And maybe if I get a chance to put that on screen in some way or realize that on screen, that's great. But there are positive things happening with such groups as the Boggs Center in Detroit, which works on environmental justice and community building, or Barrios Unidos in Santa Cruz, which works to prevent gang violence. There's an organization called Street Soldiers in Oakland, which gives out an Urban Peace Award to gang members who preserve the peace in the neighborhood.

Those are the kinds of things I pay attention to. Those are the kind of things I support, when I can. I don't do the work, but I support those who are doing the work.

John Pilger
November 2002

Corporate journalism in the United States preaches "objectivity" and scorns those who take the side of the dispossessed and disenfranchised. But the mainstream media in Britain makes a few allowances. John Pilger, the Australian-born, London-based journalist and filmmaker, is one.

"I grew up in Sydney in a very political household," Pilger told me, "where we were all for the underdog." His father was a Wobbly, a member of the Industrial Workers of the World. Like Orwell, whom he admires, Pilger has a direct style. For example, he uses the term "imperialism" and does not hesitate to attach it to the adjective "American."

He was a featured speaker at the mass peace rally in London on September 28. He told the crowd, estimated at between 150,000 and 350,000, "Today a taboo has been broken. We are the moderates. Bush and Blair are the extremists. The danger for all of us is not in Baghdad but in Washington." And he applauded the protesters. "Democracy," he told them, "is not one obsessed man using the power of kings to attack another country in our name. Democracy is not siding with Ariel Sharon, a war criminal, in order to crush Palestinians. Democracy is this great event today representing the majority of the people of Great Britain."

For his reporting, Pilger has twice won the highest award in British journalism. His latest book is *The New Rulers of the World* (Verso, 2002). His political films include *Paying the Price: Killing the Children of Iraq, Death of a Nation: East Timor, The New Rulers of the World,* and *Palestine Is Still the Issue.* These documentaries are shown all over Britain, Canada, Australia, and much of the rest of the world but are rarely seen in the United States. PBS, the Public Broadcasting Service, which has seemingly unlimited space to air specials on animals, cannot seem to find a spot for Pilger's work.

"The censorship is such on television in the US that films like mine don't stand a chance," Pilger told me, and he illustrated this point with the following anecdote. Some years ago, PBS expressed interest in one of his films on Cambodia, but it was concerned about the content. In something out of Orwell's Ministry of Truth, the network appointed what it called a "journalistic adjudicator" to decide whether the film was worthy of airing. The adjudicator adjudicated. The film did not air. PBS also rejected another film on Cambodia that Pilger did. But WNET in New York picked it up—the only station in the country to do so. On the basis of that one showing, Pilger was awarded an Emmy.

I called him at his home in London the day before he spoke at the huge peace rally.

℘   ℭ

Is the war on terrorism a new version of the white man's burden?

Classic nineteenth-century European imperialists believed they were literally on a mission. I don't believe that the imperialists these days have that same sense of public service. They are simply pirates. Yes, there are fundamentalists, Christian fundamentalists, who appear to be in charge of the White House at the moment, but they are very different from the Christian gentlemen who ran the British Empire and believed they were doing good works around the world. These days it's about naked power.

Why do you say that?

The attack on Iraq has been long planned. There just hasn't been an excuse for it. Since George H. W. Bush didn't unseat Saddam in 1991, there's been a longing among the extreme right in the United States to finish the job. The war on terrorism has given them that opportunity. Even though the logic is convoluted and fraudulent, it appears they are going to go ahead and finish the job.

Why is Tony Blair such an enthusiastic supporter of US policy?

We have an extreme right-wing government in this country, although it's called the Labour government. That's confused a lot of people, but it's confusing them less and less. The British Labour Party has always had a very strong Atlanticist component, with an obsequiousness to American policies, and Blair represents this wing. He's clearly obsessed with Iraq. He has to be because the overwhelming majority of the people of Britain oppose a military action. I've never known a situation like it. To give you one example, the *Daily Mirror* polled its readers and 90 percent were opposed to an attack on Iraq. Overall, opinion polls in this country are running at about 70 percent against the war. Blair is at odds with the country.

In your new book, you talk about the group around Bush that is essentially forming war policy, people like Vice President Dick Cheney, Defense Secretary Donald Rumsfeld, and Deputy Secretary of Defense Paul Wolfowitz. You single out Richard Perle, who was assistant secretary of defense in Reagan's Pentagon. You highlighted his comment "This is total war."

I interviewed Perle when he was buzzing around the Reagan administration in the 1980s, and I was struck by how truly fanatical this man was. He was then voicing the views of total war. All of Bush's extremism comes from the Reagan years. That's why people like Perle, Wolfowitz, and other refugees from that period have found favor again. I singled out Perle in the book because I thought he rather eloquently described the policies of the Bush regime. September 11 has given this clique an opportunity from heaven. They never really believed they would have the legitimacy to do what they are doing. They don't, of course, have legitimacy because most of the world is opposed to what they are doing. But they believe it has given them if not a legitimacy then a constituency in the United States.

They are also part of an administration that came to power under shady circumstances.

I don't regard them as an elected group. It's quite clear that Gore won most of the votes. I think the accurate description for them is a military plutocracy. Having lived and worked in the United States, I must add that I don't want to make too much of the distinction between the Bush regime and its predecessors. I don't see a great deal of difference. Clinton kept funding Star Wars. He took the biggest military budget to Congress in history. He routinely bombed Iraq, and he kept the barbaric sanctions in place. He's really played his part. The Bush gang has taken it just a little further.

At least on the level of rhetoric, it seems that the top officials of the Bush administration are much more bellicose. They've taken their gloves off. They speak in extreme language: "You're either with us or you're with the terrorists."

We're grateful to them because they've made it very clear to other people just how dangerous they are. Before, Clinton persuaded some people that he was really a civilized character and his administration had the best interests of humanity at heart. These days we don't have to put up with that nonsense. It's very clear that the Bush administration is out of control. It contains some truly dangerous people.

How do you assess US policy toward Israel?

Israel is the American watchdog in the Middle East, and that's why the Palestinians remain victims of one of the longest military occupations. They don't have oil. If they were the Saudis, they wouldn't be in the position they are now. But they have the power of being able to upset the imperial order in the Middle East. Certainly, until there is justice for the Palestinians, there will never be any kind of stability in the Middle East. I'm absolutely convinced of that. Israel is the representative of the United States in that part of the world. Its policies are so integrated with American policies that they use the same language. If you read Sharon's statements and Bush's statements, they're virtually identical.

You write for the Mirror, *the British tabloid with a circulation of two million plus. How did you get that job?*

I wrote for the *Mirror* for twenty years. I joined it back in the 1960s when I arrived from Australia. You don't really have anything like the *Mirror*—as it was, and as it is trying to be again—in the United States. The *Mirror* is a left-leaning tabloid. It's really a traditional supporter of the Labour Party in this country. I suppose its politics are center-left. During the time I was there, it was very adventurous politically. It reported many parts of the world from the point of view of victims of wars. I reported Vietnam for many years for the *Mirror*. In those days, it played a central role in the political life of this country. It then fell into a long, rather terrible period, trying to copy its Murdoch rival, the *Sun*, and just became a trashy tabloid.

Since September 11, the *Mirror* has reached back to its roots, and decided, it seems, to be something of its old self again. I received a call asking if I would write for it again, which I've done. It's a pleasure to be able to do that. It's become an important antidote to a media that is, most of it, supportive of the establishment, some of it quite rabidly right wing. The *Mirror* is breaking ranks, and that's good news.

In one of your articles, you called the United States "the world's leading rogue state." This incurred the wrath of the Washington Times, *which is owned by the Moonies. They called your paper "a shrill tabloid read by soccer hooligans." Your fellow Australian Rupert Murdoch, head of News Corporation, called the* Mirror *a "terrorist-loving London tabloid."*

There's one correction I want to make there. Murdoch is not a fellow Australian. He's an American.

But he was born in Australia.

No, he's an American. He gave up his Australian citizenship in order to buy television stations in the United States, which is symptomatic of the way Murdoch operates. Everything is for sale, including his birthright. The *Mirror* is not read by soccer hooligans. It's read by ordinary people of this country. That comment is simply patronizing. But to be criticized by the Moonies and Murdoch in one breath is really just a fine moment for me.

George Orwell in his essay "Politics and the English Language" describes the centrality of language in framing and informing debate. He was particularly critical of the use of euphemisms and the passive voice. Today we have "collateral damage," "free trade," and "level playing fields," and such constructions as "villages were bombed," and "Afghan civilians were killed." You compare the rhetoric surrounding the war on terrorism to the kind of language Orwell criticized.

Orwell is almost our litmus test. Some of his satirical writing looks like reality these days. When you have someone like Cheney who talks about "endless war" or war that might last fifty years, he could be Big

Brother. You have Bush incessantly going on about the evil ones. Who are these evil ones? In *1984*, the evil one was called Goldstein. Orwell was writing a grim parody. But these people running the United States mean what they say. If I were a teacher, I would recommend that all my students very hurriedly read most of Orwell's books, especially *1984* and *Animal Farm*, because then they'd begin to understand the world we live in.

And the use of passive voice?

Using the passive voice is always very helpful. Mind you, a lot of that propaganda English emanates from here. The British establishment has always used the passive voice. It's been a weapon of discourse so those who committed terrible acts in the old empire could not be identified. Or, today, the British establishment uses "the royal we," as in, "We think this." You hear a lot of that these days. It erroneously suggests that those who are making the decisions to bomb countries, to devastate economies, to take part in acts of international piracy involve all of us.

What's wrong with journalism today?

Many journalists now are no more than channelers and echoers of what Orwell called the official truth. They simply cipher and transmit lies. It really grieves me that so many of my fellow journalists can be so manipulated that they become really what the French describe as *functionaires*, not journalists.

Many journalists become very defensive when you suggest to them that they are anything but impartial and objective. The problem with those words "impartiality" and "objectivity" is that they have lost their dictionary meaning. They've been taken over. "Impartiality" and "objectivity" now mean the establishment point of view. Whenever a journalist says to me, "Oh, you don't understand, I'm impartial, I'm objective," I know what he's saying. I can decode it immediately. It means he channels the official truth. Almost always. That protestation means he speaks for a consensual view of the establishment. This is internalized. Journalists don't sit down and think, "I'm now going to speak for the establishment." Of course not. But they internalize a whole set of assumptions, and one of the most potent assumptions is that the world should be seen in terms of its usefulness to the West, not humanity. This leads journalists to make a distinction between people who matter and people who don't matter. The people who died in the Twin Towers in that terrible crime mattered. The people who were bombed to death in dusty villages in Afghanistan didn't matter, even though it now seems that their numbers were greater. The people who will die in Iraq don't matter. Iraq has been successfully demonized as if everybody who lives there is Saddam Hussein. In the buildup to this attack on Iraq, journalists have almost universally excluded the prospect of civilian deaths, the numbers of people who would die, because those people don't matter.

It's only when journalists understand the role they play in this propaganda, it's only when they realize they can't be both independent, honest journalists and agents of power, that things will begin to change.

Tariq Ali
January 2002

Tariq Ali was born in 1943 in Lahore, in what was then British-controlled India. He was educated in Pakistan and then at Oxford. His opposition to the military dictatorship in Pakistan during the 1960s led to permanent exile in Britain. He was active in the antiwar movement in Europe during the late 1960s.

Ali is a long-standing editor of *New Left Review* and has written more than a dozen books on history and politics. His forthcoming book is *The Clash of Fundamentalism: Crusades, Jihad, and Modernity* (Verso, 2002). He also has been working on two sets of novels. Three novels of the *Islamic Quintet* have been published by Verso: *Shadows of the Pomegranate Tree*, *The Book of Saladin*, and *The Stone Woman*. They portray Islamic civilization in a way that he says "runs counter to the standard views." His *Fall of Communism* trilogy has seen the publication of *Redemption* and *Fear of Mirrors*. Ali's creative output extends to scripts for stage and screen. A short play of his on Iraq was recently performed at Cooper Union in New York. A veritable "all 'rounder," as they say in South Asia, he is currently working on an opera on Ayatollah Khomeini.

In late October, he was detained at the Munich airport. "The inspector's eyes fell on a slim volume in German that had been given to me by a local publisher," he said. "It was still wrapped in cellophane. In a state of some excitement, the inspector rushed it over to an armed policeman. The offending book was an essay by Karl Marx, *On Suicide*." Ali said he was rudely instructed to repack his bag, minus the book, and was then taken to police headquarters at the airport. The arresting officer, Ali added, "gave me a triumphant smile and said, 'After September 11, you can't travel with books like this.' At this point, my patience evaporated."

Ali demanded to call the mayor of Munich, who had earlier interviewed him on the current crisis at a public event in the city. The threat of the call was sufficient, and Ali was allowed to continue on his journey.

Ali lives in London, and I spoke with him in late November by phone.

80   08

A Pakistani general once told you, "Pakistan was the condom that the Americans needed to enter Afghanistan. We've served our purpose and they think we can be just flushed down the toilet." That was in the 1980s, when the United States and Pakistan funded and armed the mujahideen to defeat the godless Soviet Union. Is the US again using Pakistan as a condom?

I think the Americans fished out the same condom but found it had too many holes in it. So they supplied a new one, and they've gone in again. But this time they couldn't go in with the Pakistani army, since the Pakistani army created the Taliban and propelled it to victory. It could hardly be expected to kill its own offspring. The US forced the Pakistani army to withdraw its support, which it did, reluctantly. But it had to. Once Pakistani support was withdrawn from the Taliban, they collapsed like a house of cards, though one hardline faction will probably carry on in the mountains for a bit.

Most Americans may not know the history of Pakistani-US support for the Taliban. In a talk you gave in late September, you said, "People are taught to forget history." What did you have in mind there?

In the West, since the collapse of communism and the fall of the Soviet Union, the one discipline both the official and unofficial cultures have united in casting aside has been history. It's somehow as if history has become too subversive. The past has too much knowledge embedded in it, and therefore it's best to forget it and start anew. But as everyone is discovering, you can't do this to history; it refuses to go away. If you try to suppress it, it reemerges in horrific fashion. That's essentially what's been going on.

It's a total failure of the Western imagination that the only enemy they can see is Adolf Hitler. This is something that actually started during the Suez War of 1956, what I call the first oil war. Gamal Abdel

Nasser, the nationalist leader of Egypt, was described by British prime minister Anthony Eden as an Egyptian Hitler. Then it carried on like that. Saddam Hussein became Hitler when he was no longer a friend of the West. Then Milosevic became Hitler. Now Al Qaeda and the Taliban are portrayed as fascists. The implication strongly is that Osama bin Laden is a Hitler, even though he has no state power at all. It's just grotesque if you seriously think about it. In reality, the only player in this game who was soft on the Nazis was King Zahir Shah, who then sat on the Afghan throne. He hoped the Nazis would defeat the British in India, and he, having collaborated with them, might share part of the spoils!

But the reason they can get away with it is that history has been totally downplayed. We have populations now in the West with a very short memory span. One reason for this short memory span is that television over the last fifteen years has seen a big decline in the coverage of the rest of the world. History, when they do it, is ancient history, and they sensationalize even that. Contemporary history is virtually ignored on television. If you see what passes as the news on the networks in the United States, there's virtually no coverage of the rest of the world, not even of neighboring countries like Mexico or neighboring continents like Latin America. It's essentially a very provincial culture, and that breeds ignorance. This ignorance is very useful in times of war because you can whip up a rapid rage in ill-informed populations and go to war against almost any country. That is a very frightening process.

Contrast the last wars of the twentieth century with the first war of the twenty-first century.

One difference is that the previous wars were genuinely fought by coalition. The United States was the dominant power in these coalitions, but it had to get other people on its side. In both the Gulf War and in Kosovo, the US had to get the agreement of other people in these alliances before it moved forward. The war in Afghanistan, the first war of the twenty-first century, shows the United States doing what it wants to do, not caring about who it antagonizes, not caring about the effects on neighboring regions. I don't think it's too bothered with what happens afterwards, otherwise it would be more worried about the Northern Alliance. The US is telling the Northern Alliance to kill Taliban prisoners. It's totally a breach of all the known conventions of war. Western television networks aren't showing this, but Arab networks are showing how prisoners are being killed and what's being done to them. Instead, we're shown scenes that are deliberately created for the Western media: a few women without the veil, a woman reading the newspaper on Kabul television, and 150 people cheering.

All these wars are similar in the way ideology is being used. It's the ideology of so-called humanitarian intervention. We don't want to do this, but we're doing this for the sake of the people who live there. This is, of course, a terrible sleight of hand because all sorts of people live there. By and large, they do it to help one faction and not the other. In the case of Afghanistan, they didn't even make that pretense. It was essentially a crude war of revenge designed largely to appease the US public. In Canada in mid-November, I was debating Charles Krauthammer, and I said it was a war of revenge and he said, "Yeah, it was, so what?" The more hardline people, who are also more realistic, just accept this.

And the United States has perfected the manipulation. The media plays a very big, big role.

In what way?

During the Gulf War, journalists used to challenge government news managers and insisted they wouldn't just accept the official version of events. It seems that with the war in the Balkans and now this, journalists have accepted the official version. Journalists go to press briefings at the Ministry of Defense in London or the Pentagon in Washington, and no critical questions are posed at all. It's just a news-gathering operation, and the fact that the news is being given by governments who are waging war doesn't seem to worry many journalists too much.

The task does really devolve to alternative networks of information and education. The Internet has been an invaluable acquisition. I wonder how we would do without it. Information can be sent from one country to the other within the space of minutes, crossing channels, crossing oceans, crossing continents. But still, we can't compete with the might and power and wealth of those who dominate, control, and own the means of the production of information today. These are the five or six large companies that control and own the media, publishing houses, and the cinema.

Tony Blair has occupied center stage in the war on terrorism. In many ways he is even more visible than Bush. What accounts for Blair's enthusiasm for the war?

Blair does it to get attention. He does it to posture and prance around on the world stage, pretending that he is the leader of a big imperial power when, in fact, he's the leader of a medium-sized country in Northern Europe.

I think Clinton certainly liked using him. But the Bush administration doesn't take him that seriously.

Noam Chomsky points out that Britain did not bomb Boston and New York, where major IRA [Irish Republican Army] supporters and financial networks are located.

I think Noam's right. But to just even raise the point goes to show that Britain isn't an imperial power and the United States is. The United States is now The Empire. There isn't an empire; there's The Empire, and that empire is the United States. It's very interesting that this war is not being fought by the NATO high command. NATO has been totally marginalized. The "coalition against terrorism" means the United States. It does not wish anyone else to interfere with its strategy. When the Germans offered 2,000 soldiers, Rumsfeld said we never asked for them. Quite amazing to say this in public.

In a recent article, you cited a poem by the tenth-century secular Arab poet al-Maarri: "And where the Prince commanded, now the shriek / Of wind is flying through the court of state: / 'Here,' it proclaims, 'there dwelt a potentate / Who would not hear the sobbing of the weak.'" Talk about "the sobbing of the weak."

The sobbing of the weak today is the sobbing of the victims of neoliberal policies. They consist of billions of people all over the world. These are the people who leave their countries. These are the people who cling onto the belly of a plane leaving Africa for Europe, not caring if they are killed in the process, and many of them are.

This desperation is the result of globalization. The question is, will the weak be able to organize themselves to bring about changes or not? Will the weak develop an internal strength and a political strength to ever challenge the rulers that be? These are the questions posed by the world in which we live. People are increasingly beginning to feel that democracy itself is being destroyed by this latest phase of globalization and that politics doesn't matter because it changes nothing. This is a very dangerous situation on the global level, because when this happens, then you also see acts of terrorism. Terrorism emanates from weakness, not strength. It is the sign of despair.

Dear old al-Maarri was a great skeptic poet. He wrote a parody of the Koran, and his friends would tease him and say, "al-Maarri, but no one says your Koran." And he said, "Yes, but give me time. Give me time. If people recite it for twenty years it will become as popular as the other one." It was a good moment in Islam when people were actually challenging authority at every level. Very different from the world we live in now, incidentally.

And in this world, the United States is projecting a long war on terrorism. They're talking about it lasting for ten or fifteen years, and involving up to sixty countries. The Bush administration reminds us almost on a daily basis that the war on terrorism is still in its earliest stages. What are the implications of that?

The main implication is a remapping of the world in line with American policy and American interests. Natural resources are limited, and the United States wants to make sure that its own population is kept supplied. The principal effect of this will be for the US to control large parts of the oil which the world possesses. There are some people who say this war is about oil. I honestly don't believe it. But that doesn't mean once they have sorted out the first phase of it, the war won't be used to assert or reassert US economic hegemony in the region.

They want to do it in the Middle East, as well. A big problem in the Middle East is that the Iraqi state and Syrian state are potential threats to Israel just by the very fact they exist. Iraq also sits on a great deal of oil, and as that cutthroat Kissinger once said, "Why should we let the Arabs have the oil?" Since Israel is the central ally of the United States in the region, the US would like to weaken the potential opposition. Attacking Iraq, and possibly even Syria, is one way to do that. This is a policy fraught with danger for those who carry it out because it totally excludes the reaction of ordinary people. Could there be mass explosions? And if there are, then you will see countries like Saudi Arabia going under. No one would weep if the royal family were overthrown; but if that were to happen, they would probably be replaced by a US protectorate or a US colonial-type administration, or the US disguised as the UN. Other corrupt sheikdoms, like the United Arab Emirates, would crumble, as well. Then what will the US do? Have the Israelis acting as guardians of oil in the whole region? That will mean permanent guerrilla warfare. Or will they have American and European troops guarding these regions? That, too, would mean limited guerrilla warfare. The only way they'll be able to rule is by killing large numbers of people who live there.

What about Iraq?

If they attack Iraq in the next phase, it could create big problems for them. I'm sure that in Europe the antiwar movement would just mushroom. The Arab world could really explode. That is what their close allies in Saudi Arabia and Egypt are telling them: Do not attack Iraq. The coalition will break up, and even Turkey is saying that it will not be party to an attack on Iraq. Probably the plan is to create an independent state in a corner of Iraq, and then use that as a base to destroy Saddam Hussein. If they go down that route, the world then becomes a very unpredictable and very dangerous place. The one thing that it will not do is curb terrorism. It will increase terrorism, because the more governments you destroy, the more the people will seek revenge.

After flirting with neo-isolationism, the US is now deciding it wants to run the world. The US should come out openly and say to the world, "We are the only imperial power, and we're going to rule you, and if you don't like it, you can lump it." American imperialism has always been the imperialism that has been frightened of speaking its name. Now it's beginning to do so. In a way, it's better. We now know where to kneel.

Edward Said
November 2001

Urbane and sophisticated, Edward W. Said is in many ways the quintessential New Yorker. His love for the city is palpable. "New York," he says, "plays an important role in the kind of criticism and interpretation which I have done." He mirrors the city's restless energy and diversity. In addition to his great love for literature and his unflagging interest in politics, he is an inveterate devotee of opera and classical music. An accomplished pianist, he opens his home on New York's Upper West Side to artists, writers, and musicians from all over the globe.

He has been a New Yorker since 1963 when he accepted a position at Columbia, where he now holds the position of University Professor. Born in Jerusalem and educated at schools there and in Cairo, Said came to the US in the early 1950s and attended Princeton and Harvard. There is lots of talk these days about public intellectuals. Much of it is hot air. Said is the real thing. His creative intellectual talents and abilities are infused with passion and a sense of outrage at the hypocrisies, contradictions, and indignities of what passes for political commentary, particularly when it comes to the Middle East. He is no doubt the most prominent spokesperson for the Palestinian cause in the United States.

His productivity and range of interests are impressive. A relentless and indefatigable worker, he maintains a rigorous schedule while struggling against leukemia. A prolific author, he most recently published *Reflections on Exile* (Harvard University Press, 2000) and *Power, Politics, and Culture* (Pantheon Books, 2001). Much of his political writing is not only excavating buried memories and affirming the Palestinian presence but also pointing toward a future where peace is possible.

We have done many interviews over the years, and what always strikes me is his tremendous intellectual energy and, yes, enthusiasm to talk. He remains doggedly hopeful. His oppositional role, he says, is "to sift, to judge, to criticize, to choose so that choice and agency return to the individual." He envisions a community that does not exalt "commodified interests and profitable commercial goals" but values instead "survivability and sustainability in a human and decent way. Those are difficult goals to achieve. But I think they are achievable." I talked with him by phone in late September.

The events of September 11 have bewildered and confused many Americans. What was your reaction?

Speaking as a New Yorker, I found it a shocking and terrifying event, particularly the scale of it. At bottom, it was an implacable desire to do harm to innocent people. It was aimed at symbols: the World Trade Center, the heart of American capitalism, and the Pentagon, the headquarters of the American military establishment. But it was not meant to be argued with. It wasn't part of any negotiation. No message was intended with it. It spoke for itself, which is unusual. It transcended the political and moved into the metaphysical. There was a kind of cosmic, demonic quality of mind at work here, which refused to have any interest in dialogue and political organization and persuasion. This was bloody-minded destruction for no other reason than to do it. Note that there was no claim for these attacks. There were no demands. There were no statements. It was a silent piece of terror. This was part of nothing. It was a leap into another realm—the realm of crazy abstractions and mythological generalities, involving people who have hijacked Islam for their own purposes. It's important not to fall into that trap and to try to respond with a metaphysical retaliation of some sort.

What should the US do?

The just response to this terrible event should be to go immediately to the world community, the United Nations. The rule of international law should be marshaled, but it's probably too late because the United States has never done that; it's always gone it alone. To say that we're going to end countries or eradicate terrorism, and that it's a long war over many years, with many different instruments, suggests a much more complex and drawn-out conflict for which, I think, most Americans aren't prepared. There isn't a clear goal in sight. Osama bin Laden's organization has spun out from him and is now probably independent of him. There will be others who will appear and reappear. This is why we need a much more precise, a much more defined, a much more patiently constructed campaign, as well as one that surveys not just the terrorists' presence but the root causes of terrorism, which are ascertainable.

What are those root causes?

They come out of a long dialectic of US involvement in the affairs of the Islamic world, the oil-producing world, the Arab world, the Middle East—those areas that are considered to be essential to US interests and security. And in this relentlessly unfolding series of interactions, the US has played a very distinctive role, which most Americans have been either shielded from or simply unaware of.

In the Islamic world, the US is seen in two quite different ways. One view recognizes what an extraordinary country the US is. Every Arab or Muslim that I know is tremendously interested in the United States. Many of them send their children here for education. Many of them come here for vacations. They do business here or get their training here. The other view is of the official United States, the United States of armies and interventions. The United States that in 1953 overthrew the nationalist government of Mossadegh in Iran and brought back the shah. The United States that has been involved first in the Gulf War and then in the tremendously damaging sanctions against Iraqi civilians. The United States that is the supporter of Israel against the Palestinians.

If you live in the area, you see these things as part of a continuing drive for dominance, and with it a kind of obduracy, a stubborn opposition to the wishes and desires and aspirations of the people there. Most Arabs and Muslims feel that the United States hasn't really been paying much attention to their desires. They think it has been pursuing its policies for its own sake and not according to many of the principles that it claims are its own—democracy, self-determination, freedom of speech, freedom of assembly, international law. It's very hard, for example, to justify the thirty-four-year occupation of the West Bank and Gaza. It's very hard to justify 140 Israeli settlements and roughly 400,000 settlers. These actions were taken with the support and financing of the United States. How can you say this is part of US adherence to international law and UN resolutions? The result is a kind of schizophrenic picture of the United States.

Now we come to the really sad part. The Arab rulers are basically unpopular. They are supported by the United States against the wishes of their people. In all of this rather heady mixture of violence and policies that are remarkably unpopular right down to the last iota, it's not hard for demagogues, especially people who claim to speak in the name of religion, in this case Islam, to raise a crusade against the United States and say that we must somehow bring America down.

Ironically, many of these people, including Osama bin Laden and the mujahideen, were, in fact, nourished by the United States in the early 1980s in its efforts to drive the Soviets out of Afghanistan. It was thought that to rally Islam against godless communism would be doing the Soviet Union a very bad turn indeed, and that, in fact, transpired. In 1985, a group of mujahideen came to Washington and was greeted by President Reagan, who called them "freedom fighters." These people, by the way, don't represent Islam in any formal sense. They're not imams or sheiks. They are self-appointed warriors for Islam. Osama bin Laden, who is a Saudi, feels himself to be a patriot because the US has forces in Saudi Arabia, which is sacred because it is the land of the prophet Muhammad. There is also this great sense of triumphalism, that just as we defeated the Soviet Union, we can do this. And out of this sense of desperation and pathological religion, there develops an all-encompassing drive to harm and hurt, without regard for the innocent and the uninvolved, which was the case in New York. Now to understand this is, of course, not at all to condone it. And what terrifies me is that we're entering a phase where if you start to speak about this as something that can be understood historically—without any sympathy—you are going to be thought of as unpatriotic, and you are going to be forbidden. It's very dangerous. It is precisely incumbent on every citizen to quite understand the world we're living in and the history we are a part of and we are forming as a superpower.

Some pundits and politicians seem to be echoing Kurtz in Heart of Darkness *when he said, "Exterminate all the brutes."*

In the first few days, I found it depressingly monochromatic. There's been essentially the same analysis over and over again and very little allowance made for different views and interpretations and reflections. What is quite worrisome is the absence of analysis and reflection. Take the word "terrorism." It has become synonymous now with anti-Americanism, which, in turn, has become synonymous with being critical of the United States, which, in turn, has become synonymous with being unpatriotic. That's an unacceptable series of equations. The definition of terrorism has to be more precise, so that we are able to discriminate between, for example, what it is that the Palestinians are doing to fight the Israeli military occupation and terrorism of the sort that resulted in the World Trade Center bombing.

What's the distinction you're drawing?

Take a young man from Gaza living in the most horrendous conditions—most of it imposed by Israel—who straps dynamite around himself and then throws himself into a crowd of Israelis. I've never condoned or agreed with it, but at least it is understandable as the desperate wish of a human being who feels himself being crowded out of life and all of his surroundings, who sees his fellow citizens, other Palestinians, his parents, sisters, and brothers, suffering, being injured, or being killed. He wants to do something, to strike back. That can be understood as the act of a truly desperate person trying to free himself from unjustly imposed conditions. It's not something I agree with, but at least you could understand it. The people who perpetrated the terror of the World Trade Center and Pentagon bombings are something different because these people were obviously not desperate and poor refugee dwellers. They were middle class, educated enough to speak English, to be able to go to flight school, to come to America, to live in Florida.

In your introduction to the updated version of Covering Islam: How the Media and the Experts Determine How We See the Rest of the World, *you say: "Malicious generalizations about Islam have become the last acceptable form of denigration of foreign culture in the West." Why is that?*

The sense of Islam as a threatening Other—with Muslims depicted as fanatical, violent, lustful, irrational—develops during the colonial period in what I called Orientalism. The study of the Other has a lot to do with the control and dominance of Europe and the West generally in the Islamic world. And it has persisted because it's based very, very deeply in religious roots, where Islam is seen as a kind of competitor of Christianity. If you look at the curricula of most universities and schools in this country, considering our long encounter with the Islamic world, there is very little there that you can get hold of that is really informative about Islam. If you look at the popular media, you'll see that the stereotype that begins with Rudolph Valentino in *The Sheik* has really remained and developed into the transnational villain of television and film and culture in general. It is very easy to make wild generalizations about Islam. All you have to do is read almost any issue of the *New Republic* and you'll see there the radical evil that's associated with Islam, the Arabs as having a depraved culture, and so forth. These are impossible generalizations to make in the United States about any other religious or ethnic group.

In a recent article in the London Observer, *you say the US drive for war uncannily resembles Captain Ahab in pursuit of Moby Dick. Tell me what you have in mind there.*

Captain Ahab was a man possessed with an obsessional drive to pursue the white whale which had harmed him—which had torn his leg out—to the ends of the Earth, no matter what happened. In the final scene of the novel, Captain Ahab is being borne out to sea, wrapped around the white whale with the rope of his own harpoon and going obviously to his death. It was a scene of almost suicidal finality. Now, all the words that George Bush used in public during the early stages of the crisis—"wanted, dead or alive," "a crusade," etc.—suggest not so much an orderly and considered progress towards bringing the man to justice according to international norms, but rather something apocalyptic, something of the order of the criminal atrocity itself. That will make matters a lot, lot worse, because there are always consequences. And it would seem to me that to give Osama bin Laden—who has been turned into Moby Dick, he's been made a symbol of all that's evil in the world—a kind of mythological proportion is really playing his game. I think we need to secularize the man. We need to bring him down to the realm of reality. Treat him as a criminal, as a man who is a demagogue, who has unlawfully unleashed violence against innocent people. Punish him accordingly, and don't bring down the world around him and ourselves.

Amartya Sen
August 2001

A martya Sen of India won the Nobel Prize in economics in 1998 for his pioneering work on development issues. He has focused attention on the social sources of famine, poverty, and inequality, and he has highlighted the need for women's empowerment.

Sen was born in Santiniketan, north of Calcutta, in 1933. His family lived there and in Dhaka, which was then part of India but is now the capital of Bangladesh. Sen studied at Presidency College, Calcutta and at Trinity College, Cambridge. He is Master of Trinity College, Lamont University Professor Emeritus at Harvard, and honorary president of the Oxford Committee for Famine Relief (OXFAM). He has also taught at the London School of Economics, Oxford University, and Delhi University. And he helped establish the United Nations' Human Development Index, which compares the social welfare of people across countries.

One of his better known works is *Poverty and Famines: An Essay on Entitlement and Deprivation* (Oxford University, 1981), which challenges the view that a shortage of food is the main cause of famine. Sen proved, instead, that famines have a class basis and occur only in undemocratic countries. His most recent book is *Development as Freedom* (Knopf, 1999), a collection of lectures he gave at the World Bank.

I talked with Sen in his office at Harvard in mid-April. Sen told me he was "always a little worried" about doing interviews for fear that his views would be misrepresented.

But when he found out I had spent some years in India, it seemed to set him at ease a bit. Sen told me of his admiration for the Indian poet and fellow Nobel Prize–winner Rabindranath Tagore (1861–1941), who was, it turns out, a friend of the family.

Tagore actually gave him his first name, Amartya, which means immortal. "I had met him a number of times as a child," he said. "I remember him as a benign, friendly presence." Sen's mother was a dancer and "played the lead role in several of Tagore's dance dramas in Calcutta," he told me. Today, at ninety, she edits a literary magazine in Bengali. Tagore's emphasis on the power of "reasoned scrutiny" and his appreciation for the "seamless whole of world civilization" were imprinted on him, Sen said. "I grew up in that culture."

Other influences he cited were John Stuart Mill, Adam Smith, Karl Marx, and Mahatma Gandhi. He also expressed admiration for Akbar, the great sixteenth-century Mughal emperor, who viewed India as a place where a multiplicity of peoples and cultures could live together.

A cosmopolitan man, Sen got choked up when recounting the opening story of this interview.

৳০   ৎ৪

Tell me about the childhood experience you had in Dhaka that made a big impression on you.

It happened when I was about ten. I was playing alone in the garden of our home when I was suddenly made aware of the presence of somebody. I looked up and there was a person profusely bleeding from his stomach. He had clearly been knifed. He came through the door wanting help and some water. I shouted for help while trying to make him lie down on the ground. He was a Muslim daily laborer named Kader Mia, who had come for work in this largely Hindu area called Wari. He had come despite knowing that these were troubled times, where in Hindu areas Muslims were getting butchered and in Muslim areas Hindus were getting butchered. He came with great reluctance, but he was poor. His family had very little to eat. He was offered a job. He was on his way there when he was knifed. He kept on telling me that his wife had said not to go to such a dangerous area. But he felt economically compelled to do so in order to have an income. The penalty of that economic unfreedom proved to be death.

This incident had a tremendous impact on me. It was incredible to me that members of one community could kill members of another not for anything personal that they did but simply based on their identity. That's still a hard thought for a human mind to comprehend:

Why should you take the life of someone who has done you no harm, whom you don't even know, just because he belongs to some group? I found that terrifying and utterly perplexing, both from an ethical point of view and intellectually. What kind of thought process was it?

It also made me deeply skeptical of community-based identities. Even to this day, I remain instinctively hostile to communitarian philosophy and communitarian politics. Part of that hostility is based on some analyses, which I've tried to present in my writings. But I think the instinctive revulsion is connected with having seen some of the ugly sides of community identity. That was a very strong thing. I knew that there were riots going on, but until I held somebody in my own arms who was bleeding to death—and he did finally die in the hospital—it wasn't as real to me. Kader Mia's moving explanation of why he could not listen to the wise counsel of his wife has held a strong presence in my thinking. Because of the lack of freedom in his life, he had to take every opportunity that came his way, even at great personal risk, if he was to be a good father and feed his children. He took the risk and lost his life. That made me realize that lack of economic freedom could be a very major reason for loss of liberty, in this case, liberty of life. The fact that different kinds of freedom interrelate has become a central notion for me. The beginning of that idea was in those moments.

Another important experience was the Bengal famine of 1943. I read that as a child you handed out a tin of rice to starving refugees as they passed your grandfather's house in Santiniketan.

First, a comment on the tin of rice. Somehow, in one of the interviews that was done of me, I did mention that my grandfather allowed me to take a cigarette tin of rice from the large jar we had and give it to any family that came for help. But it's not a big thing, and it's not my strong memory. The main memory that I have of that period is not of my trying to help in a tiny little way, but the bewilderment as to why suddenly people were dying in such numbers. Where did they come from? I didn't know any of them. They didn't come to the school that I went to, not a rich person's school, but a middle-class school with a very nominal fee.

Like all famines, this was a rigidly class-based one. Depending on which occupational group you belonged to, which class you came from, you either got decimated or you had no problem whatsoever. Ninety to 95 percent of Bengalis' lives went on absolutely normally, while 3 million died. They all came from a small community, a small class. The people who died were primarily rural wage earners, but also wage workers in river transport or other trades and services, like barbers and craftsmen. Once the famine hit, there was no market for them. This small group of people were economically most vulnerable. They got drowned by the flood of the famine.

So the class basis of the famine was a very strong memory. Later I would find that hardly any famine affects more than 5 percent, almost never more than 10 percent, of the population. The largest proportion of a population affected was the Irish famine of the 1840s, which came close to 10 percent over a number of years.

There was also considerable evidence, which I gathered from my parents and others, that the harvest hadn't been bad in any sense, so it was surprising that there would be a famine. The Bengal famine happened during World War II. The Japanese were in Burma, and the British army was in Bengal. There was war-based high demand and inflation. Prices shot up. In normal circumstances, sharecroppers and cash-wage laborers are almost equally poor. But when prices shot up, the wage earners, with fixed-money wages, started going down right away, whereas sharecroppers, since they got part of their income in the form of food, were not distressed at all in the way that cash-wage laborers were.

At the age of ten, when I watched the famine and its class-based nature, its suddenness and its contrariness, I had the beginning of the recognition that the complexity of the entire economic system must be brought into the story.

In Development as Freedom, *you write: "No famine has ever taken place in the history of the world in a functioning democracy." Why is that?*

It became increasingly clear to me by the 1970s that, empirically, famines have actually not occurred in functioning democracies and that this didn't seem like a fluke but there was a good reason for it. My first book on the subject, *Poverty and Famines,* came out in 1981, and by then I understood something about how famines operate and how easy it is to prevent them. You can't prevent undernourishment so easily, but famines you can stop with half an effort. Then the question was, "Why don't the governments stop them?"

The first answer is that the government servants and the leaders are upper class. They never starve. They never suffer from famine, and therefore they don't have a personal incentive to stop it. Second, if the government is vulnerable to public opinion, then famines are a dreadfully bad thing to have. You can't win many elections after a famine, and you don't like being criticized by newspapers, opposition parties in parliament, and so on. Democracy gives the government an immediate political incentive to act.

Famines occur under a colonial administration, like the British Raj in India or for that matter in Ireland, or under military dictators in one country after another, like Somalia and Ethiopia, or in one-party states like the Soviet Union and China.

The Chinese had the failure of the Great Leap Forward, which led to a famine between 1958 and 1961 in which nearly 30 million people died. While tens of millions were dying, the disastrous policies of the government were not revised. This would be unthinkable in a democracy. Similarly, while the famine was going on, there was also a starving of information. This is an additional factor, the informational connection as opposed to the political incentive connection. People in each collective obviously saw that they were not doing very well themselves but they read in the papers that everything was fine in the rest of the country. That's what censorship does. They all came to the conclusion respectively that they alone were failing. So rather than admitting failure, they cooked the numbers. When Beijing added these up at the height of the famine, they thought they had 100 million more metric tons of rice than they actually had. So the censorship of the press, which often goes with the lack of a democratic system, had the effect of hoodwinking not only the public but ultimately hoodwinking the state.

Something similar happened in the Soviet Union. They were partly deluded and partly theoretically arrogant. Of course, in the case of the famine in the Ukraine, there was also a dislike of one group, the Kulaks. But on top of that, the lack of political incentives that goes with the absence of democracy and the lack of information added to the story.

India is often hailed in the Western press as the world's largest democracy. Yet paradoxically, it's being led by a nationalist, Hindu party, the BJP [Bharatiya Janata Party], which has some very fanatical elements. What has led to the "jihadization" of politics in India?

I don't think that India is much celebrated for its democracy. Democracy has been a very neglected commodity at home and abroad. In India, it did not get much praise from others whom I would see to be roughly on the left because there is a tendency to dismiss democracy as bourgeois and a sham. Such a view was very strong in my student days, when I was active in left-wing politics. Nearly everybody else who was active in politics thought it was an amiable eccentricity on my part to regard democracy as such a big thing. Similarly, in the West, people have taken relatively little interest in Indian democracy. The governments and the hardheaded military establishment and the general conservative part of America have never taken much interest in democracy, anyway. But also on the left there is a deep skepticism about what democracy means if you are hungry and poor. The celebration, in that context, of China—which had many reasons to be celebrated but not for its lack of democracy—acted as a kind of barrier to see that India was doing something major. So I want to correct that impression.

I regret, of course, the fact that the BJP is in power. I've never voted for it and never will. However, it has to be said that the BJP has not been opposed to democracy as such. There has never been a proposal to suspend the constitution, to change voting rights, or to dispense with elections. So, in that respect, you couldn't say that a nondemocratic party had been elected to run the government. That's not the case. But their interest, of course, is much more in favor of one community in a multicommunity country. India, I believe, is quintessentially multicommunity, multireligious, multicultural, with Hindus and Muslims and Sikhs and Christians and Jains and others making up the population. The political underpinning of the BJP lies very much in Hindu sectarianism. But the BJP has always tried to argue that it has Muslim members. I don't take that terribly seriously. They're not very powerful. But it's interesting that even with that sectarian base, given the nature of Indian polity, they have to claim that they are somehow multicultural themselves, which to me is a kind of backhanded tribute to the constitutional democratic secularism that we are lucky enough to have in India.

The BJP gets about a quarter of the vote. Its share of the vote has not grown for many years now. It is in a coalition government, and it has made good electoral alliances, more skillfully than the Congress Party or the left coalition has managed to do.

As a good democrat, I think it's only right that they should run the government. You have to take the rough with the smooth, and the BJP is part of the rough edge of Indian politics.

In May 1998, India conducted nuclear tests. A month later Pakistan followed. What was your reaction?

I thought this was a disastrous development. But it was part of the BJP's agenda during the election campaign to carry forward the nuclear program, and this they did.

A lot of the writing in the West has underestimated the extent to which there was opposition to it. It's very easy to capture pictures of jubilant people in the street after the nuclear bomb. But there were no pictures of morose people sitting in their kitchens and living rooms. After the initial euphoria, which was mainly in urban areas, was over, the government got nothing in terms of popular support for nuclearization.

The nuclear tests made the entire subcontinent less safe. It was predictable that Pakistan would retaliate. Everybody knew that Pakistan had the capability to produce the bomb. It doesn't matter that its capability is much less than that of India because if they share in a nuclear holocaust you get hundreds of millions dying anyway.

On top of that, from an economic point of view, India diverted a lot of resources that could have been much more productively used for economic and social development.

You are a strong advocate for women's rights, and you've written about the connection between the lack of women's empowerment and increased fertility rates.

There's a clear and strong connection between fertility reduction and women's literacy and empowerment, including women's gainful employment. If you look at the more than 300 districts of India, the strongest influences in explaining fertility variations are women's literacy and gainful economic employment. No matter what the effect of the rapid rise of the population may be in the long run for the environment, the immediate impact of constant bearing and rearing of children is on the lives, liberty, and freedom of young women. Anything that increases the voice of young women tends therefore to reduce the fertility rate.

It seems to me to be kind of inescapable that one has to be interested in the issue of gender and gender equality. I don't really expect any credit for going in that direction. It's the only natural direction to go in. Why is it that some people don't see that as so patently obvious as it should be?

What are your views on globalization?

Globalization is a complex issue, partly because economic globalization is only one part of it. Globalization is greater global closeness, and that is cultural, social, political, as well as economic. I think the whole progress over the last two or three millennia has been entirely dependent on ideas and techniques and commodities and people moving from one part of the world to another. It seems difficult to take an anti-globalization view if one takes globalization properly in its full sense. I'm beginning on this high ground because it's hard to be opposed just to economic globalization while you want globalization in everything else. The anti-globalization movement is one of the biggest globalized events of the contemporary world, people coming from everywhere—Australia, Indonesia, Britain, India, Poland, Germany, South Africa—to demonstrate in Seattle or Quebec. What could be more global than that?

We live in a world community, and economic contact has partly contributed to that. It's also the case that economic opportunity opened up by economic contact has helped to a great extent to reduce poverty in many parts of the world. East Asia's success is in that direction. Going further back, the escape from poverty in Western Europe and North America is also connected with the use of economic opportunity that international trade helped foster.

But the United States was built on genocide and expropriation of an entire continent, and Europe's wealth was directly connected to its colonial empires.

I think one has to separate out the different factors in it. To say that certainly America was very lucky to get a large amount of land, and the native Indians were extremely unlucky to have white men coming over here, is one thing. But to say that the whole of the American prosperity was based on exploiting the indigenous population would be a great mistake. To a great extent, it was based on the productivity of modern industries, which Karl Marx overall saw very clearly. When he asks, in volume one of *Capital*, what is the one great event of the contemporary world, he singles out the American Civil War. What is the Civil War about? Replacing a non-trade-based relationship, namely slavery, with a wage-based relationship. He doesn't talk about 1848 and the Paris Commune as a great event because Marx, as a realist, saw that industrial capitalism was bringing about a big change that was never achievable earlier and that could be the basis of a prosperous society. He may have got somewhat mixed up as to how you might have a more egalitarian basis of that, thinking about a socialist future. But certainly he was a great follower of Adam Smith and David Ricardo in seeing that a market economy had enormous opportunity for expanding wealth and enabling people to escape poverty.

What about Europe and colonialism? Bengal itself was stripped of its wealth, pauperized.

Bengal got a very raw deal. Its development was put back. There's no question that Bengal suffered enormously from colonialism. But to say that Europe would not have had any industrial revolution but for the colonies is a mistake. I don't think that's the analysis you get. Ultimately, imperialism made even the British working classes suffer. This is a point which the British working classes found quite difficult to swallow, but they did, actually. To say that the whole of the industrial experience of Europe and America just shows the rewards of exploiting the third world is a gross simplification.

Look at some other country, like Japan. It became an imperialist country in many ways, but that was much later, after it had already made big progress. I don't think Japan's wealth was based on exploiting China. Japan's wealth was based on its expansion in international trade.

One has to be realistic. One's concern for equity and justice in the world must not carry one into the alien territory of unreasoned belief. That's very important.

What about the downside of economic globalization?

I'm generally in favor of economic globalization. Having said that, it doesn't always work and does not immediately work in the interest of all. There are sufferers. What we have to look at is not a kind of wholesale denunciation of globalization, which gets us nowhere. This is like King Kanute trying to discipline the sea. Quite aside from the importance of globalization, it's inescapable. It's a question of how to make it more humane and just. That requires paying attention to the underdog.

I believe that virtually all the problems in the world come from inequality of one kind or another. And what we're looking at is inequality. We have to see how we can make it more equitable. That requires that we pay a great deal of attention particularly to labor conditions. It requires much more activism by the labor movement. It requires a revival of cooperative efforts. It requires revision of the financial architecture of the world, because as it emerged in the 1940s it reflected a reality that is no longer true.

Even though I'm pro-globalization, I have to say thank God for the anti-globalization movement. They're putting important issues on the agenda. The themes that the anti-globalization protesters bring to the discussion are of extraordinary importance. However, the theses that they often bring to it, sometimes in the form of slogans, are often oversimple. But just because the theses may be easy to reject—and a skillful economist or even a skillful financial journalist will be able to shoot them down—does not mean that the process itself is valueless. The process is basically putting certain items on the agenda.

Globalization can be very unjust and unfair and unequal, but these are matters under our control. It's not that we don't need the market economy. We need it. But the market economy should not have priority or dominance over other institutions. We need democracy. We need political activism. We need social movements of various kinds. We need the NGOs [nongovernmental organizations]. We live in a world where there is a need for pluralistic institutions and for recognizing different types of freedom, economic, social, cultural, and political, which are interrelated. It's that complexity that cannot be captured by either being anti-globalization or being pro-globalization without qualification.

What drives you?

I am not sure that I am very "driven." But let me try to say why we might have reason to be driven! We live for a short stretch of time in a world we share with others. Virtually everything we do is dependent on others, from the arts and culture to farmers who grow the food we eat. Quite a lot of the differences that make us rich and poor are matters just of luck. To somehow revel in one's privilege would be a mistake. An even bigger mistake would be trying to convert that into a theory that the rich are so much more productive than many of us. It's scandalous when one thinks about the people who live in a world in which they need not be hungry, in which they need not die without medical care, in which they need not be illiterate, they need not feel hopeless and miserable so much of the time, and yet they are.

But this is not just a matter of poverty. There are some people who say that they're concerned only with poverty but not inequality. But I don't think that is a sustainable thought. A lot of poverty is, in fact, inequality because of the connection between income and capability—having adequate resources to take part in the life of the community. So you have to be interested in inequality. The issue of inequality and that of poverty are not separable.

We need to ask the moral questions: Do I have a right to be rich? And do I have a right to be content living in a world with so much poverty and inequality? These questions motivate us to view the issue of inequality as central to human living. Ultimately, the whole

Socratic question—"How should I live?"—has to include a very strong component of awareness and response to inequality.

Arundhati Roy
April 2001

There is a high-stakes drama playing out in India these days, and the novelist Arundhati Roy is one of its most visible actors. Multinational companies, in collusion with much of India's upper class, are lining up to turn the country into one big franchise. Roy puts it this way: "Is globalization about 'the eradication of world poverty,' or is it a mutant variety of colonialism, remote controlled and digitally operated?"

Roy, forty-one, is the author of *The God of Small Things* (Random House, 1997), which won the Booker Prize, sold six million copies, and has been translated into forty languages. Set in a village in the southwestern state of Kerala, the novel is filled with autobiographical elements. Roy grew up in Kerala's Syrian Christian community, which makes up 20 percent of the population. She laughs when she says, "Kerala is home to four of the world's great religions: Hinduism, Islam, Christianity, and Marxism." For many years, Kerala has had a Marxist-led government, but she hastens to add that party leaders are Brahmins and that caste still plays a strong role.

The success of Roy's novel has brought lucrative offers from Hollywood, which she takes impish delight in spurning. "I wrote a stubbornly visual but unfilmable book," she says, adding that she told her agent to make the studios grovel and then tell them no. In Kerala, the book has become a sensation. "People don't know how to deal with it," she says. "They want to embrace me and say that this is 'our girl,' and yet they don't want to address what the book is about, which is caste. They have to find ways of filtering it out. They have to say it's a book about children."

Roy lives in New Delhi, where she first went to become an architect. But she is not working as an architect or even a novelist these days. She has thrown herself into political activism. In the central and western states of Madhya Pradesh, Maharashtra, and Gujarat, a series of dams threaten the homes and livelihoods of tens of millions. A huge, grassroots organization, the Narmada Bachao Andolan (NBA), has arisen to resist these dams, and Roy has joined it. Not only did she give her Booker Prize money (about $30,000) to the group, she has also protested many times with it, even getting arrested.

Roy skillfully uses her celebrity status and her considerable writing gifts for this effort, as well as in the cause of nuclear disarmament. Her devastating essay on dams, "The Greater Common Good," and her searing denunciation of India's nuclear testing, "The End of Imagination," have literally kindled bonfires. The upper class did not appreciate her critique of development, and the nationalists abhorred her for questioning India's nuclear arsenal. (These two essays comprise her latest book, *The Cost of Living*, Modern Library, 1999.)

By now, Roy is used to criticism. "Each time I step out, I hear the snicker-snack of knives being sharpened," she told one Indian magazine. "But that's good. It keeps me sharp."

Her most recent essay is called "Power Politics." In it, she takes on Enron, the Houston-based energy corporation that is a large financial backer of George W. Bush. In India, Enron is trying to take over Maharashtra's energy sector. The scale of what is happening, she says, makes California's power woes look like child's play.

On a cold, mid-February afternoon, Roy gave the annual Eqbal Ahmad lecture at Hampshire College in Amherst, Massachusetts, before a huge crowd. It was a powerful, political talk, and afterward she was besieged by a long line of mostly young South Asian women, many of whom are studying at one of the five colleges in the Amherst area. She donated her lecture fee to earthquake relief in Gujarat.

The next morning, I interviewed her in the backseat of a car taking her from Amherst to Logan Airport in Boston. The two-hour drive went by in a flash.

ဢ   ஜ

You grew up in Kerala. What's the status of women there?

Women from Kerala work throughout India and the world earning money to send back home. And yet they'll pay a dowry to get married, and they'll have the most bizarrely subservient relationships with their husbands. I grew up in a little village in Kerala. It was a nightmare for me. All I wanted to do was to escape, to get out, to never have to marry somebody there. Of course, they were not dying to marry me [laughs]. I was the worst thing a girl could be: thin, black, and clever.

Your mother was an unconventional woman.

She married a Bengali Hindu and, what's worse, then divorced him, which meant that everyone was confirmed in their opinion that it was such a terrible thing to do in the first place. In Kerala, everyone has what is called a *tharawaad* [lineage]. If you don't have a father, you don't have a *tharawaad*. You're a person without an address. That's what they call you. I grew up in Ayemenem, the village in which *The God of Small Things* is set. Given the way things have turned out, it's easy for me to say that I thank God that I had none of the conditioning that a normal, middle-class Indian girl would have. I had no father, no presence of this man telling us that he would look after us and beat us occasionally in exchange. I didn't have a caste, and I didn't have a class, and I had no religion, no traditional blinkers, no traditional lenses on my spectacles, which are very hard to shrug off. I sometimes think I was perhaps the only girl in India whose mother said, "Whatever you do, don't get married" [laughs]. For me, when I see a bride, it gives me a rash. I find them ghoulish, almost. I find it so frightening to see this totally decorated, bejeweled creature who, as I wrote in *The God of Small Things*, is "polishing firewood."

Tell me a little more about your mother.

She is like someone who strayed off the set of a Fellini film. She's completely nuts. But to have seen a woman who never needed a man, it's such a wonderful thing, to know that that's a possibility, not to suffer. We used to get all this hate mail. Though my mother runs a school and it's phenomenally successful—people book their children in it before they are born—they don't know what to do with her, or with me. The problem is that we are both women who are unconventional in their terms. The least we could have done was to be unhappy. But we aren't, and that's what bothers people.

By the way, my mother is very well known in Kerala because in 1986 she won a public interest litigation case challenging the Syrian Christian inheritance law that said a woman can inherit one-fourth of her father's property or 5,000 rupees, whichever is less. The Supreme Court actually handed down a verdict that gave women equal inheritance retroactive to 1956. But few women take advantage of this right. And the churches have gone so far as to teach fathers to write wills that disinherit their daughters. It's a very strange kind of oppression that happens there.

Since you wrote your novel, you've produced some remarkable political essays. What was that transition like?

It's only to people in the outside world, who got to know me after *The God of Small Things*, that it seems like a transition. In fact, I'd written political essays before I wrote the novel. I wrote a series of essays called "The Great Indian Rape Trick" about a woman named Phoolan Devi, and the way the film *Bandit Queen* exploited her, and whether or not somebody should have the right to restage the rape of a living woman without her consent. There are issues I've been involved with for a while.

I don't see a great difference between *The God of Small Things* and my works of nonfiction. As I keep saying, fiction is truth. I think fiction is the truest thing there ever was. My whole effort now is to remove that distinction. The writer is the midwife of understanding. It's very important for me to tell politics like a story, to make it real, to draw a link between a man with his child and what fruit he had in the village he lived in before he was kicked out, and how that relates to Mr. Wolfensohn at the World Bank. That's what I want to do. *The God of Small Things* is a book where you connect the very smallest things to the very biggest: whether it's the dent that a baby spider makes on the surface of water or the quality of the moonlight on a river or how history and politics intrude into your life, your house, your bedroom.

Estha, one of the main characters in your novel, is walking "along the banks of the river that smelled of shit and pesticides bought by World Bank loans." The World Bank scheme for the Narmada River Valley envisioned the construction of more than 3,000 dams. The bank has since withdrawn from the project, and the government of India has taken it over. Tell me about the Narmada Bachao Andolan, the NBA.

When I first met people from the NBA, they told me, "We knew that you would be against the dams and the World Bank when we read *The God of Small Things.*" The remarkable thing about the NBA is that it is a cross-section of India. It is a coalition of Adivasis [India's indigenous people], upper-caste big farmers, the Dalits [formerly known as untouchables], and the middle class. It's a forging of links between the urban and the rural, between the farmers and the fishermen and the writers and the painters. That's what gives it its phenomenal strength, and it's what a lot of people criticize it for in India, saying, you know, these middle-class protesters! That makes me furious. The middle-class urban engineers are the people who came up with this project! You can't expect the critique to be just Adivasi. You isolate them like that, and it's so easy to crush them. In many ways, people try to delegitimize the involvement of the middle class, saying, how can you speak on behalf of these people? No one is speaking on behalf of anyone. The point is that the NBA is a fantastic example of people linking hands across caste and class. It is the biggest, finest, most magnificent resistance movement since the independence struggle.

One protest you were involved in last year took place at a village on the banks of the Narmada at the site of one of the proposed dams. You were among many who were arrested there. What was that like?

It was absolutely fantastic. I was in a village called Sulgaon. All night, all over the valley, people started arriving, by tractor, by motorcar, by foot. By three in the morning there were about 5,000 of us. We started walking in the dark to the dam site. The police already knew that the dam site would be captured, but they didn't know from where the people would come. There's a huge area of devastation there. So we walked in the dark. It was amazing. Five thousand people, mostly villagers, but also people from the cities—lawyers, architects, journalists—walking through these byways and crossing streams in absolute silence. There was not a person that lit a *bidi* or coughed or cleared their throats. Occasionally, a whole group of women would sit down and pee and then keep walking. Finally, at dawn, we arrived and took over the dam site. For hours, the police surrounded us. Then there was a baton charge. They arrested thousands of people, including me. The jails were full.

You say that the government of India is "hell-bent on completing the project." What's driving it?

There are many things. First of all, you have to understand that the myth of big dams is something that's sold to us from the time we're three years old in every school textbook. Nehru said, "Dams are the temples of modern India." So they're like some kind of huge, wet national flags. Before the NBA, it was like, the dam will serve you breakfast in bed, it will get your daughter married and cure your jaundice. People have to understand that they're just monuments to political corruption, and they derive from very undemocratic political institutions. You just centralize natural resources, snatch them away from people, and then you decide who you're going to give them to.

The first dam that was built in the Narmada was the Bargi, completed in 1990. They said it would displace 70,000 people and submerge 101 villages. One day, without warning, the government filled the reservoir, and 114,000 people were displaced and 162 villages were submerged. People were driven from their homes when the waters rose. All they could do was run up the hill with their cattle and children. Ten years later, that dam irrigates 5 percent of the land that they said it would. It irrigates less land than it submerged. They haven't built canals. Because for contractors and politicians, just building the dam in itself is a lot of money.

What happens to those who are displaced?

Nobody knows. When I was writing "The Greater Common Good," what shocked me more than the figures that do exist are the figures that don't exist. The Indian government does not have any estimate of how many people have been displaced by big dams. I think that's not just a failure of the state, but a failure of the intellectual community. The reason that there aren't these figures is because most of the people that are displaced are again the non-people, the Adivasis and the Dalits. I did a sanity check based on a study of fifty-four dams done by the Indian Institute of Public Administration. According to that study, just reservoir-displaced, which is only one kind of displacement, came to an average of something like 44,000 people per dam. Let's assume that these fifty-four dams are the bigger of the big dams. Let's quarter this average. We know that India has had 3,600 big dams built in the last fifty years. So just a sanity check says that it's 33 million people displaced. They all just migrate to the cities. And there, again, they are non-citizens, living in slums. They are subject to being kicked out at any minute, anytime the housewives of New Delhi's upscale areas decide that all these slum people are dangerous.

You've compared this uprooting to a kind of garbage disposal.

It's exactly like that. The Indian government has managed to turn the concept of nonviolence on its head. Nonviolent resistance and nonviolent governance. Unlike, say, China or Turkey or Indonesia, India doesn't mow down its people. It doesn't kill people who are refusing to move. It just waits it out. It continues to do what it has to do and ignores the consequences. Because of the caste system, because of the fact that there is no social link between those who make the decisions and those who suffer the decisions, it just goes ahead and does what it wants. The people also assume that this is their lot, their karma, what was written. It's quite an efficient way of doing things. Therefore, India has a very good reputation in the world as a democracy, as a government that cares, that has just got too much on its hands, whereas, in fact, it's actually creating the problems.

But you say about your own politics that you're "not an anti-development junkie or a proselytizer for the eternal upholding of custom and tradition."

How can I be? As a woman who grew up in a village in India, I've spent my whole life fighting tradition. There's no way that I want to be a traditional Indian housewife. So I'm not talking about being anti-development. I'm talking about the politics of development, of how do you break down this completely centralized, undemocratic process of decision making? How do you make sure that it's decentralized and that people have power over their lives and their natural resources? Today, the Indian government is trying to present privatization as the alternative to the state, to public enterprise. But privatization is only a further evolution of the centralized state, where the state says that they have the right to give the entire power production in Maharashtra to Enron. They don't have the right. The infrastructure of the public sector in India has been built up over the last fifty years with public money. They don't have the right to sell it to Enron. They cannot do that. Three-quarters of our country lives on the edge of the market economy. You can't tell them that only those who can afford water can have it.

Still, I sense some optimism on your part about what you call the "inherent anarchy" of India to resist the tide of globalization.

The only thing worth globalizing is dissent, but I don't know whether to be optimistic or not. When I'm outside the cities I do feel optimistic. There is such grandeur in India and so much beauty. I don't know whether they can kill it. I want to think they can't. I don't think that there is anything as beautiful as a sari. Can you kill it? Can you corporatize a sari? Why should multinationals be allowed to come in and try to patent basmati rice? People prefer to eat *roti* and *idlis* and *dosas* rather than McDonald's burgers. Just before I came to the US, I went to a market in Delhi. There was a whole plate of different kinds of dal, lentils. Tears came to my eyes. Today, that's all it takes to make you cry, to look at all the kinds of dal and rice that there are, and to think that they don't want this to exist.

Talk about the material you covered in "The End of Imagination" concerning nuclear testing on the subcontinent.

It's so frightening, the nationalism in the air. I'm terrified by it. It can be used to do anything. I know that a world in which countries are stockpiling nuclear weapons and using them in the ways that India and Pakistan and America do to oppress others and to deceive their own people is a dangerous world. The nuclear tests were a way to shore up our flagging self-esteem. India is still flinching from a cultural insult, still looking for its identity. It's about all that.

You said that the jeering young Hindu men celebrating the nuclear test were the same as the ones who were thrilled with the destruction of the Babri mosque.

Indian intellectuals today feel radical when they condemn fundamentalism, but not many people are talking about the links between privatization, globalization, and fundamentalism. Globalization suits the Indian elite to a T. Fundamentalism doesn't.

It's also a class problem. When people stop some film from being shot or burn a book, it's not just that they are saying, this is against Indian culture. They are also saying, you Westernized, elite, English-speaking people are having too much of a good time. It's a very interesting phenomenon. I think it has to be addressed together, not separately. The religious right-wingism is directly linked to globalization and to privatization. When India is talking about selling its entire power sector to foreign multinationals, when the political climate gets too hot and uncomfortable, the government will immediately start saying, should we build a Hindu temple on the site of the Babri mosque? Everyone will go baying off in that direction. It's a game. That's something we have to understand. With one hand, you're selling the country out to Western multinationals. And with the other, you want to defend your borders with nuclear bombs. It's such an irony! You're saying that the world is a global village, but then you want to spend scores of rupees on building nuclear weapons.

You use a metaphor of two truck convoys. One is very large, with many people going off into the darkness. The other is much smaller and is going into the light of the promised land. Explain what you mean.

India lives in several centuries at the same time. Every night outside my house I pass a road gang of emaciated laborers digging a trench to lay fiber-optic cables to speed up our digital revolution. They work by the light of a few candles. That is what is happening in India today. The convoy that melts into the darkness and disappears doesn't have a voice. It doesn't exist on TV. It doesn't have a place in the national newspapers. And so it doesn't exist. Those who are in the small convoy on their way to this glittering destination at the top of the world have completely lost the ability to see the other one. So in Delhi the cars are getting bigger and sleeker, the hotels are getting posher, the gates are getting higher, and the guards are no longer the old *chowkidars*—the watchmen—but they are fellows with guns. And yet the poor are packed into every crevice like lice in the city. People don't see that anymore. It's as if you shine a light very brightly in one place, the darkness deepens around. They don't want to know what's happening. The people who are getting rich can't imagine that the world is not a better place.

You made a decision, or the decision was made for you, to identify with, or to be part of, that large convoy.

I can't be a part of the large convoy because it's not a choice that you can make. The fact that I'm an educated person means that I can't be on that convoy. I don't want to be on it. I don't want to be a victim. I don't want to disappear into the darkness. I am an artist and a writer, and I do think that one always places oneself in the picture to see where one fits. I left home when I was sixteen and lived in places where it was very easy for me to have fallen the other way. I could have been on the large convoy because I was a woman and I was alone. In India, that's not a joke. I could have ended up very, very badly. I'm lucky that I didn't.

I think my eyes were knocked open and they don't close. I sometimes wish I could close them and look away. I don't always want to be doing this kind of work. I don't want to be haunted by it. Because of who I am and what place I have now in India, I'm petitioned all the time to get involved. It's exhausting and very difficult to have to say, "Look, I'm only one person. I can't do everything." I know that I don't want to be worn to the bone where I lose my sense of humor. But once you've seen certain things, you can't un-see them, and seeing nothing is as political an act as seeing something.

Are you thinking about writing any new fiction?

I need fiction like you need to eat or exercise, but right now it's so difficult. At the moment, I don't know how to manage my life. I don't know how I'll ever be able to make the space to say, "I'm writing a book now, and I'm not going to be able to do x or y." I would love to.

You feel a sense of responsibility to these silent voices that are calling out to you.

No, I don't feel responsibility because that's such a boring word.

You're in a privileged position. You are a celebrity within India and also outside.

But I never do anything because I'm a celebrity, as a rule. I do what I do as a citizen. I stand by what I write and follow through on what I write. It's very easy for me to begin to believe the publicity about myself, whether for or against. It can give you an absurd idea of yourself. I know that there's a fine balance between accepting your own power with grace and misusing it. And I don't ever want to portray myself as a representative of the voiceless. I'm scared of that.

But one of the reasons some people get so angry with me is because I have the space now that a lot of others who think like me don't. It was a mistake maybe for so many people to have opened their hearts to *The God of Small Things*. Because a lot of dams and bombs slipped in along with it.

Angela Davis
February 2001

If you are of a certain age, the name Angela Davis is etched in memory. Close your eyes, and you can see her signature Afro and clenched fist raised high. But the Angela Davis of yore and the educator, scholar, and activist of today are quite different. Unlike some of her peers from the 1960s who traffic in nostalgia, Davis has kept up with the times. Her pathbreaking work on the prison-industrial complex has helped push this issue to center stage.

Davis was born and raised in Birmingham, Alabama. "Even though Birmingham was entirely segregated, I learned not to assume that that was the way things were supposed to be," she recalled. "I can remember my parents saying, 'This may be the situation now, but it will not be this way forever.' From a very early age, I managed not to feel imprisoned."

She graduated magna cum laude from Brandeis University in 1965 and pursued graduate studies at the Goethe Institute in Frankfurt and the University of California at San Diego, where she received her master's in 1968. A year later, she was fired from her teaching position as an assistant philosophy professor at UCLA by Governor Ronald Reagan for her political activities in the Communist Party and the Black Panther Party. After a 1970 shootout in a courthouse in Marin County, California, Davis, who was not even in the area at the time, made the FBI's Ten Most Wanted list. After going on the lam, she was apprehended and jailed on charges of conspiracy, kidnapping, and murder. The trial, which was an international cause célèbre, resulted in her acquittal in 1972.

A tenured professor at the University of California at Santa Cruz, she's the author of *Women, Race, and Class* (Random House, 1981) and *Women, Culture, and Politics* (Random

House, 1989). Her latest book is *Blues Legacies and Black Feminism* (Pantheon, 1998). She is just finishing up a collection of essays on the prison-industrial complex called *Dispossessions and Punishment*.

It's one thing to read Davis's work and quite another to hear her speak. Her voice is a musical instrument. I know of few speakers who use pauses and silences so effectively. She measures her words like a composer crafting a melody. She fills halls all over the world and is in such demand as a speaker she could probably lecture every night of the year. Still, she has a shyness and humility about her. She doesn't flaunt her celebrity or talk down to her audiences. She is like the classic Thelonious Monk tune "Straight, No Chaser."

ℭ   ℜ

I think it's fair to say that you have almost iconic status, linked as you are to a legendary era when it seemed revolutionary change was possible. What's it like being Angela Davis?

I don't think about that very much. I do recognize that people associate me with another time. It seems to me that when people approach me and say, for example, "I'm from the sixties," they tend to use me as a way to think about their own youth. That's OK, but it's not really about me, and it can be somewhat straining. I have tried over the years to grow and develop. I am not the same person I was in the early 1970s, when many people became familiar with my name. The impetus for radical social movements has always come from young people. I don't want to represent myself, as some people of my generation do, as the veteran with all of the answers.

You ran for vice president twice on the Communist Party ticket in the 1980s. Did I hear you right recently when you said you're now a Green Party member?

I'm registered as a Green Party member. I've never been registered as a member of one of the major parties. I've been registered as a Communist, and I am now a registered member of the Green Party, and I do believe that independent politics basically are absolutely necessary. Independent politics provide us with the only vote for accomplishing anything significant within the electoral arena.

W. E. B. DuBois in his classic work The Souls of Black Folk *wrote, "The problem of the twentieth century is the problem of the color line." Where is that color line today?*

The color line about which DuBois spoke is not nearly as clear as it was at that time. Racialization processes are now far more complicated. Class is an important category to consider as it intersects with race and gender. The prominence of black middle classes today combined with the putative eradication of racism within the legal sphere means that we have to think in a much more complicated way about the structures of racism and how they continue to inform US society. We need to develop an analysis that incorporates gender and class and sexuality, as well.

A lot of academics write about the criminal justice system, but you actually spent time in jail, sixteen months, most of it in solitary confinement. How did that affect your work?

Certainly the fact that I was once incarcerated has inspired me to do activist as well as scholarly work around prison issues. But no matter what particular work progressive people are doing today, it is incumbent upon them to discover some way to relate their scholarship, their activism, to the campaign against the prison-industrial complex. This is not, however, to underestimate the importance of involving people who have direct experience of the prison system. As a matter of fact, when one looks at the campaign against the death penalty, it certainly can be argued that Mumia Abu-Jamal is one of the most eloquent and most powerful opponents of it. When we organized three years ago the conference "Critical Resistance: Beyond the Prison-Industrial Complex," we attempted to involve former prisoners and people who were at that time in prison.

My approach to the study of prisons and also to prison activism is informed by prison abolitionism. In other words, I, along with many other people, believe that we should seek ways of minimizing the use of imprisonment. Therefore, when I talk about a prison that seems to be more attentive to the humanity of those it imprisons, it is against the backdrop of an abolitionist strategy.

The current prison population is eight times what it was in 1970. More than 2 million people are behind bars—70 percent people of color, 50 percent African Americans, 17 percent Latinos. And Native Americans have the highest per capita rate of incarceration.

The role of race in creating the raw material for the prison industry is undeniable. While you've mentioned the statistics that relate to US prisons, one can also point to prisons in Europe or Australia. It's generally the case that you find a disproportionate number of people of color or immigrants. I recently visited a prison in Stockholm and discovered that large numbers of people there are refugees from Turkey and Yugoslavia, as well as people from Africa and Latin America. In the Netherlands, you see a vast number of people of African descent, from the Caribbean, and from Indonesia, the former colony of the Netherlands. In Australia, while aboriginal people constitute 1 to 2 percent of the population, in the prisons they constitute 20 to 30 percent. So the racialization of prison populations is not simply a characteristic of the US system.

Unfortunately, in this era of globalization, the US prison model is being exported around the world. When I visited Australia a year and a half ago, I found that the largest women's prison there, which is outside of Melbourne, is owned and operated by Corrections Corporation of America, which is headquartered in Nashville, Tennessee. It is not only the tendency to incarcerate ever greater numbers of people that one can see in European countries and Australia, but also the supermaximum prisons have been exported. There are supermaximum prisons in the Netherlands, South Africa, and even Sweden. The security housing unit, which is a particularly repressive formation originating in the US, has invaded their prisons, as well. We're talking about countries such as the Netherlands, which for a very long time attempted to use strategies of decarceration. Now, under the impact of the drug war and the peculiarly North American ways of addressing the drug issue, one sees ever larger numbers of people going to prison and therefore the historical strategy of decarceration has been basically dismissed.

You've also looked at the prisons in Cuba. What's it like there?

In Cuba, at least in the women's prisons I visited, the women—unlike women in the US or in other countries—did not feel disconnected from the larger society. The effort to pay close attention to the UN standard minimum rules for the treatment of prisoners was very obvious. Perhaps the most impressive aspect of the system itself was the fact that prisoners were allowed to continue to work in their fields if their offense was not related to their particular profession. I talked to a woman who was a veterinarian, for example, and she continued to be a veterinarian in the prison. I talked to a woman who was a doctor, and she continued to be a physician in the particular prison where she was incarcerated. That in itself was interesting because it inverts the hierarchies of prisoners and guards. As the doctor, she was in charge of civilian nurses, for example, and was treated not as a prisoner, not as an inferior person, but rather as a doctor. Furthermore, people who work, and virtually everyone works who is in prison, receive the same wages and salaries as they would receive if they were working in the same job on the outside. It was a striking difference with respect to the US, where prisoners can receive as little as ten cents an hour. It seems to me that the trade union movement in this country could learn a great deal by looking at the integration of Cuban prisoners into unions and not separating them as inferior workers.

When you use the term "prison abolition," how do people react?

Many more people are willing to think seriously about the importance of decreasing the role of punishment in society. The vast expansion of the prison system, which happened largely without any major protest, has reached critical proportions. But, at the same time, over the last five years, the interventions of activists have been important in encouraging people to think differently about the prison system, particularly the use of the term "prison-industrial complex" as an example of a new vocabulary that allows people to think critically rather than to respond based on their own emotional reactions.

Would you favor incremental strategies of prison reform?

Reform is a difficult question. Certainly it is important to think about the kinds of reform that will, in fact, assist the people who are so unfortunate as to live behind prison walls. But at the same time, if one looks at the history, it is clear that reforms have played pivotal roles in actually bolstering the prison system.

Michel Foucault in his work *Discipline and Punish* points out that from the very origin of the prison, reform played that central role. As a matter of fact, imprisonment as punishment was a reform designed to replace capital punishment and corporal punishment. During the 1970s, the very dramatic prison movement that emerged around the rebellion in Attica and the many other uprisings in prisons throughout the country gave rise to what many of us felt was significant reform, such as the abolition of the indeterminate prison sentence. However, we need to consider the fact that prison sentences have become far longer and that developments such as truth in sentencing and three strikes have relied precisely on this reform in sentencing practices. All of which is to say we need to be very cautious about supporting those reforms that have the potential of creating a more powerful prison system. I would suggest that we measure the reforms we propose against the potential for rendering the prison system less powerful.

Let me give you another example of the potential dangers of certain kinds of reforms. At the moment, there is a very impressive movement against the death penalty. Many people now say it should be abolished pending the possibility of guaranteeing that there's not a single innocent person on death row. With the new DNA technology, innocence is something that is demonstrated scientifically. I find that extremely problematic because precisely in proving innocence through DNA, there's also the concomitant demonstration of guilt, so that what appears to be a progressive movement may well, in fact, make it even more difficult to abolish the death penalty as a form of punishment.

One other problem in the death penalty movement as it stands today is that there is a tendency to argue that life imprisonment should be offered as an alternative to capital punishment. The danger of seeing life imprisonment as the alternative is precisely that life imprisonment will be legitimized not only for people who would otherwise have been sentenced to death but for a whole class of people far beyond those who might have been subject to capital punishment.

According to a report by Human Rights Watch and the Sentencing Project, 2 percent of all Americans have lost the right to vote because of felony convictions.

It's important to point out that we're talking about not only currently incarcerated prisoners who have lost the right to vote. In many states, former felons are divested of their political rights, as well. In the state of Alabama, one-third of all black men, according to that report by Human Rights Watch and the Sentencing Project, have permanently lost the right to vote and will be unable to exercise it unless they receive a pardon by the governor.

A lot of your work has focused on women prisoners.

A number of activists and scholars, myself included, suggest that we think about other ways of punishing women in conjunction with the state apparatus of punishment. And we see that historically women have been punished in mental institutions, within the patriarchal structure of the family, or within intimate relations. There is a connection between violence against women in the domestic sphere and the punishment of women by the state. The recent reports by human rights organizations such as Human Rights Watch and a report by the United Nations Special Rapporteur on Violence Against Women have demonstrated that sexual violence is quite pervasive in US prisons. Some women prisoners point out that being imprisoned is structurally similar to being in a violent relationship. I make this point because the current movement against violence against women, which has become highly professionalized over the recent period, could benefit from an effort to engage with the politics of imprisonment. And, at the same time, the movement against the prison-industrial complex needs to integrate an analysis of gender.

In October, there was a state hearing in Chowchilla, home of California's two largest women's prisons. One person testified that the health care there was "something the Three Stooges would do on Saturday Night Live. Breast lumps and vaginal tumors are left untreated for months. Treatable illnesses become terminal." What about the issue of health care and women in prison?

The issue of health care reveals how systematically US prisons violate the human rights of women. The prison in Chowchilla is the largest women's prison in the world, and numerous health violations have been revealed there by organizations such as the San Francisco group Legal Services for Prisoners with Children. I know of one particular case of a woman at the prison right across the street, the Central California Women's Facility, who was diagnosed with a brain tumor shortly after she was incarcerated last February. But because there was no neurosurgeon on staff of the local hospital, the Madera Community Hospital, she had to be taken to a hospital in another city, Fresno. However, on the two occasions when she was transferred to that hospital, the prison failed to transfer the chart, and therefore her appointments were canceled and she was returned to the prison undiagnosed. After many months of delayed treatment, the tumor had grown so large and had become entangled with her brain stem that they were not able to remove it. This is a horror story, just one of many.

You've taught in the University of California system for years. Starting in the mid-1990s, California began spending more money on prisons than on its university system. What kind of impact has that had?

There is a vastly deteriorated educational system. The impact of Proposition 209 has meant that affirmative action can no longer be used in admission processes in the state of California. On the other hand, affirmative action, it appears, is quite alive in the recruitment of prison personnel. As a matter of fact, people of color increasingly play major roles in the California correctional system. Certainly there is an invisible affirmative action program at work with respect to the population of the prisons. As the Justice Policy Institute reported a couple of years ago, a black man in the state of California is five times more likely to be found in a prison cell than in one of the state colleges or universities.

What's your sense of student activism today as you travel around the country?

I'm extremely impressed by the student activists. I don't envy them. The difficulties are far greater than they were during the 1960s. The stakes are far greater today. The issues are far more complex. But I think that the younger generation will be able to go much further.

I've seen the impact that you have, particularly on young women of color, at your public appearances. At the end of your speech, there's a rush to talk to you, to touch and even embrace you.

That often happens, that's true. I try to trouble their attitude toward celebrity, and, at the same time, I try to encourage them to find their own way. I try not to provide answers and solutions but to raise questions and to encourage people to think differently about their own lives.

Haunani-Kay Trask
December 2000

Haunani-Kay Trask is an eloquent voice affirming indigenous Hawaiian rights. Hawaii (also spelled Hawai'i) is an "exotic colony" of the United States, she says. She fights against the sexploitation of native women, the misappropriation of the culture (the theme parks featuring Polynesian revues with hula girls adorned with leis and prancing around luaus), and the devastation that tourism and the US military presence have wrought, economically, culturally, and environmentally.

Trask projects *mana* (power). She is a commanding speaker and a formidable organizer. She and her sister Mililani have largely been responsible for publicizing the issue of native sovereignty. An agitator par excellence, she gets under the skin of most *haoles* (white people) in Hawaii. And she doesn't mind a bit.

Trask is a professor at the Center for Hawaiian Studies at the University of Hawaii. She is cofounder of, and longtime activist with, Ka Lahui Hawai'i, the major organization advocating Hawaiian sovereignty.

Her classic book, *From a Native Daughter* (Common Courage Press, 1993), has just been revised and reissued by the University of Hawaii Press. Alice Walker calls it "a masterpiece" and a work "so powerful it will change the way you think about Hawaii, and all lands seized by force."

She is also the author of *Light in the Crevice Never Seen* (Calyx Books, 1999), the first poetry collection by an indigenous Hawaiian to be published in North America. And she coproduced the 1993 award-winning film *Act of War: The Overthrow of the Hawai'ian Nation*.

I first met Trask in 1993 when she was at the University of Colorado on a Rockefeller Fellowship. I caught up with her again earlier this year when she returned to Boulder as a keynote speaker for International Women's Week.

ॐ   ॐ

In the introduction to your poetry collection, you recount the following incident: You were stopped one day at an airport by a breathless American woman. She said, "Oh, you look just like the postcard." You responded, "No, the postcard looks like me." What does that reveal?

It reveals how distant we Hawaiians are as human beings from the image that tourists have of us. People literally think that I'm an artifact of what I really am. It skews any kind of human interaction. People look at you, tourists in particular, as an object of their desire instead of as another fully endowed human being. When you do that on a mass basis, what you have is a people whose entire image is as servants, dancers, waiters, and entertainers. This image creates an almost impossible gap. I am constantly enraged when I'm in Hawaii. I'm known there as a very angry person. But normally I'm not an angry person. I just find it very difficult to live in a situation where my people are constantly exploited and commercialized.

You write, "No matter what, we are not happy natives." What might make you happy?

Fewer tourists. We have more than thirty tourists for every native. We don't need any more tourists. We don't want them. We don't need any more tourist resorts. The idea that there is some pristine place—whether in the Pacific or the Caribbean or some other place in the third world—where tourists can come and spend their money and have a fantasy fourteen-day rest from the maniacal life of the first world is false. My advice is, if you're thinking about Hawaii, don't come. Stay right where you are. If you do come, remember that you're contributing to the oppression of a native people in their home country.

Hawaii has nearly 7 million tourists a year. We have only maybe a million residents, of whom only about 200,000 are natives.

We are inundated with golf courses, which use all kinds of pesticides, insecticides, and herbicides. These courses are built on lands where native people have been evicted. They are usually part of massive resort complexes where people can enjoy a "complete" tourist experience. That's a form of environmental racism and environmental pollution.

One of your sisters worked in the tourism industry.

When my youngest sister, Damien, tried to get a job, the Sheraton told her to sit in a canoe all day and take pictures with tourists. That lasted exactly three days before she quit. Later, she was selling suntan lotion. Later still, she was a model. At a certain point, she quit the whole thing altogether. But that trajectory is not unfamiliar to our young women. Then there is local prostitution in the brothels of Waikiki and parts of Maui and Kona. There is prostitution of our culture, our women, and our land.

Four million tourists a year come from the state of California alone. But increasingly now we have tourists from Japan, Taiwan, Hong Kong, and Australia. Tourism is destructive to the fragility and beauty of our environment. Tourists are always complaining that Waikiki is heavily congested with cars and people. It's a mile and a quarter in area. Its traffic is horrific. So tourists spread out to other islands. Of course, they just reproduce the same conditions within short order.

Tourism is the single greatest cause of homelessness. Our people cannot afford the prices of living and renting. Many Californians come as tourists and then buy land, build second homes, and live in fabulous gated communities because they don't want to have anything to do with natives. They want to live on our land, but they don't want to see us. Real estate speculation has resulted in a tremendous increase in housing costs. Homelessness among our people is a serious problem. There are beach shanties springing up all over the different islands. The state evicts people because the image is bad for tourism.

You write of jam-packed freeways, in contrast to the conventional postcard of beautiful, deserted beaches.

There aren't any postcards of the freeways at seven o'clock in the morning and at four thirty to six thirty at night. That would be bad for tourism.

What about the US military presence?

The Pacific command is planned and deployed from Pearl Harbor, which was essentially stolen from us in the 1880s, even before the formal US takeover. The Seventh Fleet, the largest of the US Navy, patrols the entire Pacific and the Atlantic, to the coast of Africa. It is stationed in Pearl Harbor. Nuclear submarines are stationed there. Bombing exercises by the Pacific Rim countries, Japan, Canada, the US, are planned and deployed from the base. So it is critical to US military dominance of both Asia and the Pacific, north and south.

Define your cause.

We would like the return of a portion of our land base, which in US law has already been identified as ours. We seek a status very like the nation-within-a-nation status that recognized American Indian nations have. We want to control both the economy and the physical space of that land base. We created our own government in exile in 1987, Ka Lahui Hawai'i. My sister Mililani was the first elected *Kia'ina* [governor] of our nation. We spent a great deal of time mapping out the claims we have on identifiable geographic areas, and we've conveyed these claims to the state and the federal government. We work with other native nations to push our cause on the continent, in the Congress.

In 1993, our favorite apologist, Bill Clinton, issued an apology to the Hawaiian people for the overthrow of our government by US Marines. Part of the apology says that Hawaiians and the US need a process of reconciliation. We are now working on that process.

My people have lived in the Hawaiian Islands since the time of *Papa*—Earth Mother—and *Wkea*—Sky Father. Like many other native people, we believed that the cosmos was a unity of familial relations. Our culture depended on a careful relationship with the land, our ancestor, who nurtured us in body and in spirit.

For over a hundred generations, we tended the earth. Then, in 1778, white people arrived on our shores. They brought disease, iron, and capitalism. And they also brought violence, the violence of first contact, the violence of plague and death, the violence of dispossession.

By the arrival of the first missionaries in Hawaii in 1820, more than half the estimated one million Hawaiians present in 1778 were dead from foreign epidemic diseases. Within another twenty years, the population had been halved again. Conversion to Christianity occurred in the chaos of physical and spiritual dismemberment.

In 1893, the American military invaded Hawaii, overthrew our government, and put an all-white puppet government in its place. We were forcibly annexed to the United States in 1898. Hawaii has been an occupied country ever since.

Colonial occupation? Most Americans view Hawaii as a state and a tourist mecca.

Most tourists who visit Hawaii have no sense of our history. The perception is a very romanticized and false one that we were willing natives who wanted our archipelago taken over by the US. The truth, of course, is that the US not only invaded and took our country but went on out into the Pacific at the end of the nineteenth century to take Wake and Guam and then the Philippines and later, in the Caribbean, Puerto Rico. The taking of Hawaii is the first great push of US overseas imperialism.

One of your poems is in fact entitled "Pax Americana: Hawai'i 1848"

I am always falling
toward that dark, swollen
river filled with tongues
drunk and baptized

new priests waving foreign
flags and parchment
calling in the conquered
to hungry bankers

sacred places gone for coin
and rotting ships
diseased through
by poisoned seas

in greenish light
hooks and stripes
the lash across my face
and pale white stars

nailed to coffins
filled with dying
flesh cast off
from a dying land

only my scream in the homeless wind
and murdered voices

This poem is really about the division of our lands in 1848 by US missionaries right when diseases were collapsing our population. There's no term other than collapse for what happened to us. The missionaries actually rejoiced in it. They enjoyed the fact that the Hawaiians were dying off and said it was because we were sinful and primitive. They started preaching about things that are foreign to natives, like sin and covering up our bodies, because the body itself is the source of sin. They propagated the idea that native culture is inferior, whether it's because of our ways of planting or fishing or because of our nakedness and customs. They implanted in the native people a self-doubt that makes them feel inferior to a system that is not only foreign to them but that is dangerous—genocidal, in fact.

What does "Haunani" mean?

It's the diminutive of Haunaniokawekiu O Haleakala, which means "the beautiful snows of the highest summits of Haleakala Mountain," a volcano on the island of Maui. Haunani by itself, which is not an uncommon name in Hawaii, means "beautiful ice" or "beautiful cold heights," or "beautiful snow," since we have only one word for all three.

Taro figures significantly in Hawaiian cosmology. What is it?

Taro is a tuber that is common, indigenous all over the Pacific. It has beautiful green leaves. The tuber is underground. From that we make poi, probably the most famous thing about Hawaiian food. You can steam taro, which the Samoans and the people in Papua New Guinea and the Tahitians do, in an earth oven, which we call *imu*. It's kind of like a sweet potato. In our creation story, taro is the parent of the Hawaiian people. It is planted in the ground by Earth Mother, and Sky Father created the Hawaiian people. This story is not unlike American Indian stories of the sweet potato or corn or squash, where the land actually is our elder brother, elder sibling, and protects us and takes care of us. We are people of the land.

Another Hawaiian word that has seeped into the lexicon is mana.

It means power in both a spiritual and a kind of electrical sense. You can actually feel people's mana. In the current Hawaiian sovereignty movement we say that many of our leaders, for example, my sister Mililani, who founded our nation and wrote our constitution, have great mana. It is something you can actually feel when you're next to great people. It's not dissimilar to what people felt in the presence of a Martin Luther King or a Malcolm X, people with tremendous personal electricity. Our chiefs were thought to possess mana. Today we say our great leaders still possess mana.

Explain what you mean when you describe the native Hawaiian experience as "exile at home."

We're exiled at home because even though we are born in Hawaii and we are connected for centuries to this place, we are not secure. We don't have land. In our case, our lands are almost entirely owned by foreigners, including the American government and military. There is no respect for our language, culture, way of life, and customs. There is tremendous racial discrimination against Hawaiians. We are one of the few people still classified by blood quantum, which is considered racist on its face by the UN. We have the same status in many ways as American Indians do, where we are the original inhabitants of the land but we are treated with the utmost disregard. That is the experience of being an exile at home.

In your writings, you mention three people who inspired you: Malcolm X, Ngugi Wa Thiongo, and Frantz Fanon.

All three were very central to the evolution of my thinking. I first read Malcolm X when I went to the University of Chicago for a year. Frantz Fanon first came to my attention when I was at the University of Wisconsin at Madison, where I spent ten years during some of the greatest student uprisings against the war in Vietnam.

Ngugi Wa Thiongo I came to later. *Decolonizing the Mind* [Heinemann, 1986] is probably his most famous work. In it, he says that before there is any political decolonization there must be a decolonization of the mind, by which he means the ideological and conceptual oppression of our capacity to think through our own subjugation. Fanon did talk about that, but Ngugi has turned it into a quest for the recovery of native languages.

One way to decolonize is to recover your own metaphors, your own pronunciations, the language that is the language of the place from whence you come. That has resonated throughout the colonized world.

Our language was banned in 1898. I grew up speaking and reading English, but I never had an opportunity to speak and read my own language. The Hawaiian language was unbanned for tourist purposes in 1978. So we, the Hawaiian people, are very close to other native peoples who are trying to recover and teach their native languages.

Your three intellectual progenitors are all men. Have any women inspired you?

I'm very inspired by poets like Adrienne Rich and by theorists like Rosa Luxemburg and by political leaders like Rigoberta Menchú and Maori women from whom I derive great strength. But theoretically, the people that have moved me the most have been, interestingly, black people, whether black Caribbean, black American, or black African. I've also been influenced by American Indians as well, mostly through working with them more than theoretically.

Are you connected with women activists elsewhere?

Although my major focus is native rights, the fact that I am a woman leader for many women, regardless of their color or class, is something that they take sustenance from. Leadership by women is incredibly important. I belong to the Indigenous Women's Network, founded by Winona LaDuke, an Anishanaabe, who ran as the vice presidential candidate of the Green Party. I also have lots of friends, mentors, and colleagues in struggle in the South Pacific, especially among the Maori people.

What are the areas of common ground that you have with other native people of the South Pacific?

We have the Nuclear-Free and Independent Pacific Movement that's over twenty years old now. The first meeting I went to was in 1980 in Hawaii. We have been somewhat successful in raising the question of nuclear testing. The French testing in Tahiti has stopped. Of course, the effects of radiation will continue. There has been a lot of work done regarding the Marshall Islands; we've been explaining to the world why we need to get rid of nuclear weapons, nuclear testing, nuclear fuel. We've worked with people in Japan. There's a very large movement there because of the bombings of Hiroshima and Nagasaki. I was in Saskatchewan doing some work with native people. I didn't realize until I was there that Canada's biggest uranium mining is in that province. So all native peoples that I've been able to work with have some kind of story to tell about nuclear testing, nuclear radiation effects, and uranium mining. It's critical that people try to figure out where all of this mining is done. In the North American continent, it's usually connected to native land.

How are things looking for your cause?

We're moving right along in the sovereignty struggle. I really think we can do it. It's a question of will and not a question of how.

Juan Gonzalez
July 2000

Juan Gonzalez is an award-winning columnist with the *New York Daily News*. Born in Ponce, Puerto Rico, he grew up in a New York City housing project and studied at Columbia University, where he got involved in the 1968 student strike.

"When I was studying at Columbia," he told me, "one of the great halls was named after one of the big sugar barons who owned South Puerto Rico Sugar Company."

A founding member of the Young Lords, a Puerto Rican activist group, Gonzalez later served as president of the National Congress for Puerto Rican Rights. Along with his *Daily News* column, he writes regularly for the magazine *In These Times*. And for the past four years, he has been a twice-weekly cohost with Amy Goodman on Pacifica Radio's *Democracy Now*.

"Juan sees the world through the lens of an insider and outsider," says Goodman. "He brings a depth of national and international experience to the program."

Gonzalez is the author of *Roll Down Your Window: Stories from a Forgotten America* (Verso, 1995) and *Harvest of Empire: A History of Latinos in America* (Viking, 2000).

In *Harvest of Empire*, I was particularly struck by a passage about his public school experience in New York. "Most of us became products of a sink-or-swim public school philosophy," he wrote,

> immersed in English-language instruction from our first day in class and actively discouraged from retaining our native tongue. 'Your name isn't Juan,' the young teacher told me in first grade at PS 87 in East Harlem. 'In this country it's John. Shall I call you John?' Confused and afraid, but sensing this as some fateful decision, I timidly said no. But most children could not summon the courage, so school officials routinely anglicized their names.

Though I had spoken only Spanish before I entered kindergarten, the teachers were amazed at how quickly I mastered English. From then on, each time a new child from Puerto Rico was placed in any of my classes, the teachers would sit him beside me so I could interpret the lessons. Bewildered, terrified, and ashamed, the new kids grappled with my clumsy attempts to decipher the teacher's strange words. Inevitably, when the school year ended, they were forced to repeat the grade, sometimes more than once, all because they hadn't mastered English. Even now, forty years later, the faces of those children are still fresh in my mind. They make today's debates on bilingual education so much more poignant, and the current push toward total English immersion so much more frightening.

Gonzalez was named one of the nation's one hundred most influential Hispanics by *Hispanic Business* and has received a lifetime achievement award from the Hispanic Academy of Media Arts and Sciences.

I caught up with him in Boulder on a sunny Friday morning during his national book tour for *Harvest of Empire*. He had been at the Tattered Cover bookstore in Denver the previous night, and as soon as we finished, he was off to Breckenridge in the high Rockies for yet another event.

ℰ ℛ

Tell me more about the faces of those schoolchildren that are still fresh in your mind.

I never forget the fear that these children had being in a country where they didn't understand anything that was going on in school, and yet somehow they were grappling to learn subject matter. I believe that the whole question of the learning of a new language depends to a great degree on how young you are when you begin the process. Since I was a Spanish speaker when I entered kindergarten, I really began to learn English from the very beginning and was able to dominate the language fairly rapidly. You take children who come in when they've already spent four years in school in the Dominican Republic or Venezuela—or worse, when they come in as teenagers—at that point the mastery of another language becomes a far more difficult and psychologically taxing process. You're not only learning to speak another language; you're learning to think one, too.

I grew up on East 87th Street in New York, not too many blocks from your old neighborhood. My parents were immigrants from Armenia. When my mother used to speak to me in Armenian in the street in front of my friends, the American kids, I wanted to crawl into the nearest sewer, feeling this enormous shame.

That is the classic immigrant experience that is repeated over and over in the US. My wife, who comes from the Dominican Republic, is a Spanish-language teacher in a New York high school. She finds the kids who most resist learning Spanish are the Latinos. To them, Spanish is a negative—second-class. It pains her. She says she has to do much more counseling of the Latino children just to get them interested in being able to study Spanish as a foreign language. But Spanish is not a foreign language in the US. The annexation of the Mexicans to the Southwest and the Puerto Ricans meant that those groups did not come to the US. The US came to them and made them citizens, speaking their own language in their original territories.

What do you think of bilingual education?

I think bilingual transitional education is a good idea. I don't think it's the responsibility of the public schools to maintain another language or culture, but I do think it is their responsibility to provide enough transitional education so that people don't fall back in other subjects. The important thing is that in those parts of the US like South Texas or California or New York where you have huge Latino populations, everybody should learn Spanish—the English population as well as the Spanish-speaking population—and break out of monolingual ghettos. Then you will have more cultural understanding.

There are thirty million Latinos in the US, a very fast-growing population. What are the political implications of that?

In another fifty years, one out of every four people in the country will be Latino. By 2100, it could be half the population. If something is not done to raise the economic level of Latin America, everyone is going to keep coming. The implication is that the entire social and cultural fabric of the US is going to go through a transformation.

So you have a choice. Either you raise the economic level of Latin America so that more people will want to stay in their own country, or you accept the fact that the US itself, like the old Roman Empire, will be changed from within by the very people it conquered.

What are you trying to do in Harvest of Empire?

I talk about the whole process of Americanization or lack of Americanization by Latinos, and what has happened psychologically as well as socially on this assimilation road.

You write, "In this country, meanwhile, few children in the public schools, including Puerto Rican children, are taught anything about Puerto Rico except for its geographical location and the fact that it 'belongs' to the US."

I am perpetually amazed at the lack of basic knowledge that most Americans have about Puerto Rico. Even to the point of whether Puerto Ricans are foreigners or Americans. I was just asked recently by someone when I was doing a reading in Texas whether Puerto Ricans had to have passports to enter the US. Puerto Ricans, without asking for it, were all made American citizens by a declaration of Congress in 1917, the Jones Act. In fact, the House of Delegates of Puerto Rico, the only elected Puerto Rican representatives at the time, unanimously rejected the citizenship and told Congress they didn't want it. Yet Congress imposed it anyway. Since that time, Puerto Ricans travel back and forth without a passport, as if moving from one state of the Union to another.

You say Puerto Ricans "are in a different position from Italians or Swedes or Poles. Our homeland is invaded and permanently occupied, its patriots persecuted and jailed by the very country to which we migrated."

There was a recent congressional hearing over Puerto Rico. Louis Freeh, the head of the FBI, apologized to Congressman [José] Serrano, Democrat of New York, for the role the bureau played in its notorious COINTELPRO [counter intelligence program] activities, which repressed the independence movement by creating divisions and disruptions.

Technically speaking, the island is a commonwealth. What does that mean?

A commonwealth is a fancy word that doesn't have anything like the implications of the British Commonwealth. The various countries that were formerly colonies of Britain and are part of the British Commonwealth have their own separate national sovereignty, their own representation in international bodies, and their own independent existence. Puerto Rico's commonwealth is different. Puerto Ricans are able to vote for local officials to run their local government, but the local government is subservient to, and must abide by, the laws that are passed by Congress. Whenever Congress wants to change a Puerto Rican law, it has the right to do so. Whenever Congress wants to ignore a Puerto Rican law, it has the right to do so. There's currently a big battle because the Puerto Rican constitution abolished the death penalty. Federal law has reinstituted the death penalty. That directly conflicts with the Puerto Rico constitution. In all of those conflict areas, federal law supersedes Puerto Rican law. That's one way that Puerto Rico remains under the control of Congress.

The citizenship of Puerto Ricans is not a citizenship of birth; it is a citizenship of law. Congress has granted citizenship to Puerto Ricans, and if Congress decides in the future that everyone born in Puerto Rico from 2001 on is not a US citizen, they can do that. I was born in Ponce, Puerto Rico. I'm a US citizen but I could never be elected president, and neither could anyone else born in Puerto Rico, because the Constitution requires that you must have been born in the US to be president. On the one hand, there is a citizenship. On the other hand, it is a second-class citizenship. Puerto Ricans do not vote for president. They don't elect any voting members to the Senate or the House.

I'm interested that you cite Frantz Fanon's Wretched of the Earth, *which talks about the internalizing of colonial ideas.*

I think the Puerto Rican experience is the one which is closest to what Fanon was talking about. This extends not only to language, but to all the things that language is a transmission belt for: the historical memories of a people, and their sense of themselves. Fanon wrote:

Colonialism is not satisfied merely with holding a people in its grip and emptying the native's brain of all form and content. By a kind of perverted logic, it turns to the past of the oppressed people, and distorts, disfigures, and destroys it ... The effect consciously sought by colonialism [is] to drive into the natives' heads the idea that if the settlers were to leave, they would at once fall back into barbarism, degradation, and bestiality.

This sense of the psychological effect of colonialism—what many years ago when I was in the Young Lords we used to call the "colonial mentality"—exists among Puerto Ricans. Many Puerto Ricans, for instance, throughout the 1950s and 1960s would say, if Puerto Rico were to be an independent country, it would starve. It would not be able to survive without the US. Where did this concept come from? It came from the US, from those who administered the Puerto Rican colony throughout the early 1900s. For the first fifty years of the century Puerto Ricans did not even have their own governors. There were American governors appointed by the president that administered the colony. All the major figures of the Puerto Rican cabinet were Americans. It was not until 1948 that Puerto Ricans elected their own governor, even though he was still limited in power. But there was always this sense that Puerto Rico was powerless to function as a sovereign or independent country. It didn't have the resources or the capacity to be able to function.

Surprisingly, there must be at least a dozen countries in the Caribbean that are far smaller than Puerto Rico and with less population and fewer resources that have managed quite well to survive as independent countries. But the Puerto Rican doesn't believe, for the most part, that the island could function as an independent nation.

A lot of the resistance in Puerto Rico since the 1898 US takeover has manifested itself in music and literature. Why is that?

Puerto Rico was a colony of Spain for 400 years. Ever since 1898 it has been a colony of the US. So for 500 years Puerto Rican society has been ruled or administered by a foreign nation. That doesn't mean that a Puerto Rican nation doesn't exist. It just has never gotten its own political sovereignty. As a result, what has happened is that culture and language have become the vehicles by which Puerto Ricans express their nationality. The ability of Puerto Ricans to maintain a

separate cultural identity—whether in music, poetry, theater, or art—
has been an important part of national consciousness. It's almost as
if people compensated in the cultural arena for what they lacked in
the political arena. Today, more than one-third of all Puerto Ricans
live outside of Puerto Rico, within the US. Those Puerto Ricans who
moved to the US or who were raised here have a dual identity as both
part of the American experience as well as part of the Puerto Rican
experience. So you have a whole host of writers, poets, musicians who
have developed their art within the US but still see Puerto Rico as the
fountainhead of their identity.

*What is your sense of the independence movement on the island today?
And won't Congress be reluctant to integrate a large Spanish-speaking
community into the US if Puerto Rico becomes a state?*

I happen to be of the belief that Puerto Rico will never become a
state of the US.

Why not?

Because it is a separate nation. Puerto Ricans and Americans
know that. Virtually every state that was admitted into the Union
had at that time either a majority white settler population or a large
plurality white settler population. Puerto Rico has been a territory of
the US for one hundred years. After one hundred years, the number
of white Americans living in Puerto Rico doesn't even pass 3 or 4
percent. Because it is an island, because it is not a contiguous territory,
and because unlike Hawaii it has a huge population, the island has
basically stayed as a Spanish-speaking Latin American population.

The admission of Puerto Rico into the US would change the
character of the American nation more dramatically than has ever
happened in the past. All the Republicans in Congress understand
that, and even many of the Democrats. That's why they're saying,
before you become a state you've got to agree that the official language
will be English. Puerto Ricans are saying, no, we don't want to give up
our language. We would like to have coequal official languages.

Another reason I don't think Puerto Rico will become a state is it's
so big. Its admission into the Union would instantly raise to a higher
point of importance the question of the District of Columbia. African

Americans will say, if you're going to admit Puerto Rico as a state, why leave the District of Columbia out? The last things the Republicans want are two states coming in that would have such huge, poor, non-white, and probably Democratic populations. Puerto Rico right now has a greater population than twenty-four states in the Union.

Still, as a longtime supporter of independence, I have to recognize certain realities. The bulk of the people in Puerto Rico have been voting in these beauty contest referenda either for statehood or for commonwealth. Independence continues to remain a choice of 4 to 5 percent of the voting public.

What's the answer then?

Acquiring a colony is a lot easier than divesting yourself of it, just as getting married is a lot easier than getting divorced. In the divorce process that must occur between the US and Puerto Rico, both sides must get something. I think that the real solution to the dilemma of the Puerto Rico–US relationship is something that's called free association, which is recognized by the UN as a form of decolonization. The UN recognizes three forms of decolonization: annexation into the colonial territories, which is statehood; independence; and free association. Free association is a status where the colonial nation is recognized as a sovereign state and is able to exercise international relations, negotiate its own trade treaties, have a seat in the UN, and be recognized as a separate nation. However, it chooses to be in a voluntary association with its former colonial master, sometimes having dual citizenship, but maintaining an ongoing relationship.

So I think that eventually this will be the solution that will meet the needs of all sides. Puerto Rico will be able to keep its language and its culture, have a relationship with the US, continue to have the travel back and forth, but not have the animosity that has existed because of its second-class citizenship.

In Congress, they argue that's not in the Constitution. That's what amendments are for. There are twenty-seven amendments to the Constitution. And if it requires an amendment to the Constitution to finally give Puerto Rico a status both Americans and Puerto Ricans can live with, why not do it?

Ralph Nader
April 2000

"Get something on this guy… Get him out of our hair… Shut him up." These were the directions General Motors gave to a private detective hired to snoop on Ralph Nader. In 1965, Nader incurred GM's wrath with his best-selling book *Unsafe at Any Speed* (Grossman, 1965), which exposed the company's poor auto safety record and its notorious Corvair car. But GM did not "get him." Instead, it had to pay Nader a large sum in an invasion of privacy suit. Nader used that money to seed his first public interest organization. Since bursting onto the national scene in the mid-1960s, he has maintained his crusade to correct the misdeeds and abuses of the corporate sector and the political system.

Nader is a catalytic converter who has sparked such organizations as Public Citizen, Public Interest Research Group, the Center for Auto Safety, the Center for Science in the Public Interest, and the Center for the Study of Responsive Law, as well as magazines such as *Multinational Monitor*. He was influential in the passage of the National Traffic and Motor Vehicle Safety Act in 1966. He helped create the Environmental Protection Agency in 1970 and four years later the Freedom of Information Act. His health and safety efforts have saved hundreds of thousands of lives. In recent years, he has been in the forefront of the struggles around NAFTA (North American Free Trade Agreement) and the WTO (World Trade Organization). That the term "corporate welfare" is in the public discourse may be attributed to Nader's insistent references to it.

His Spartan-like habits are legendary. And he expects everyone around him to be as hardworking as he. It is sometimes tough to match the efforts of the tall Arab American from the small town of Winsted, Connecticut, but working for Nader has been a training ground for two generations of activists, progressive lawyers, and muckraking journalists.

In 1996, he was the Green Party's presidential candidate. He did little campaigning and managed to get on the ballot in only twenty-two states. He received only 0.7 percent of the vote. This year, he is again a candidate. According to one staffer, Nader's goal is to help build the Green Party. If Nader gets at least 5 percent of the national vote, the Green Party would qualify for millions of dollars in federal election funding in the 2004 Presidential election.

A favorite Nader metaphor is the acorn and the oak: Mighty accomplishments have modest beginnings.

I've been interviewing Nader throughout the 1990s, and he is a regular on my *Alternative Radio* series. I talked with him by phone in late February just a few days after he announced his candidacy and a few days before his sixty-sixth birthday.

℘   ℘

The last time you ran, you didn't seem to give it your all. Are you more into it this time?

In 1996, I started getting letters from environmental groups and others in various states asking, would I put my name on the ballot of the Green Party? I said, I'm willing to do that, but I don't want to indicate in any way that I'm going to run, raise money, or campaign. I said, I will do media interviews, etc., and I fulfilled that promise. They knew right from the beginning that I was just standing in for the Green Party.

Now it's different. Now I'm running. It's a serious campaign to build the Green Party to significant status and to increase the likelihood that we'll have a national discussion on corporate power abuses and winner-take-all political rules. We're going to raise $5 million. We're going to go for matching funds. We have a very good web site at VoteNader.com. We're going to have some very good people in place, very energetic, very committed. We hope to have a staff of thirty in Washington and around the country. The first order of business is to get on the ballot in these difficult states like Michigan, Illinois, Oklahoma, Texas, Georgia, North Carolina, Pennsylvania, and West Virginia.

So in 1996, I stood. In the year 2000, I'm running.

The question of this campaign is, to every citizen, do you want to be more powerful? Are you tired of being pushed around? Are you tired of being entertained into trivial pursuits? Are you tired of having your children exploited by corporate hucksters? Are you tired of having the promise of America being held back by the greed and power of a few dominating the many? It's not going to be, support me and I will do this and that. It's, do you really want to be more powerful in your role as taxpayers against corporate welfare, as workers to organize trade unions, as consumers to advance the health, safety, and economic rights of ordinary people, and as voter citizens to be able to build the most important instrument for justice ever devised, a strong democracy? Do you want to be stronger? That's the question. If you do, you'll join this campaign.

In your 1996 campaign, you insisted on focusing on the abuses of corporate power. You made a comment to William Safire of the New York Times *that stung a lot of people. You said you weren't interested in "gonadal politics." Is this year going to be any different?*

First of all, the concentration of the campaign will be on building democracy and opposing the concentration of corporate power and wealth over our government, marketplace, workplace, environment, childhood, and educational institutions. Secondly, I didn't mean that comment in any pejorative way. If you look it up in any Oxford dictionary, the word "gonadal" means that which begets. I could have used the phrase "sexual politics." I guess it would have been more understandable. But no one goes back longer in terms of fighting for civil rights and civil liberties. My first article, for example, was on American Indians and their plight on the reservations. I fought against the restrictions on women being prohibited from civil juries way back before some of the more prominent issues of homosexual rights and abortion came onto the political scene.

The Green Party has an excellent position on all these issues. They have people who are far more experienced in these areas than I am, and they will be speaking out on these issues as well. I feel most comfortable speaking out specifically on issues I've worked on.

I understand that, but you're going to face questions on other issues like Roe v. Wade. *If Bush is elected because of votes going toward the Greens, he'll appoint Supreme Court justices who will overturn* Roe v. Wade.

There are massive numbers of important issues that the two parties are blocking, such as significant arms control, control of devastating environmental contamination, heading off a rampaging genetic engineering industry, not to mention poverty, avoidable disease, illiteracy, collapsing infrastructure, corporate welfare, distortions of public budgets, etc. So while we all have our major issue or two, we have to keep in mind that there's a lot else at stake in trying to replace the present corrupt political system.

Having said that, I don't think that *Roe v. Wade* will ever be overturned. I think the Republicans will destroy their party if they push this to the limit. They're already very, very cautious about not taking a hard stand the way Pat Buchanan has, for example. The reason why they're doing that is because they know they're going to lose a lot of votes if they do.

People will also want to know your views on sanctions against Iraq, on the Comprehensive Test Ban Treaty, on Chechnya, on Kosovo. You've got to be prepared to answer those questions.

They'll be answered in terms of frameworks. Once you get into more and more detail, the focus is completely diffused. The press will focus on the questions that are in the news. If Chechnya is in the news, they'll want to focus on that. We should ask ourselves, what kind of popular participation is there in foreign and military policy in this country? Very little indeed. We want to develop the frameworks. For example, do we want to pursue a vigorous policy of waging peace and put the resources into it from our national budget in the same way that we pursue the policy of building up ever-new weapons systems? Corporations are very much involved in a lot of these foreign policy and military policy issues.

I know you want to focus on that which you know and do best, and that is corporate power. Nevertheless, it wouldn't take more than a couple of minutes to state your views, for example, on the Comprehensive Test Ban Treaty. I don't know what your position is on it.

Of course I'm for it. Arms control is extremely important, yes.

These are the kinds of things your campaign will need to flesh out.

That is not off my experience screen. I'm quite aware of how the arms race is driven by corporate demands for contracts, whether it's General Dynamics or Lockheed Martin. They drive it through Congress. They drive it by lobbying and hiring ex-Pentagon officials in the Washington military-industrial complex, as Eisenhower phrased it.

This is not a completely black-and-white issue. For example, US corporations are dying to get into Cuba and Iran. Ideology is keeping them out. What are your views on that—on Cuba?

How are they dying to get in? They were dying to get in Iraq and sell Saddam Hussein military weapons before 1990. They want to get into other countries to sell arms. I don't think that's a good way to get in. What do they want to sell Cuba?

Casinos and hotels.

Of course. Casinos, hotels, and junk products, and junk food. They'll try to undermine Cuba's organic agriculture expansion and its more self-reliant health system and get people into dependency through all kinds of pharmaceuticals. They're trying to export their model of economic expansion that is destructive of the environment and of self-reliant communities.

I'd like you to address the fear that the Greens will act as spoilers and help elect a worse alternative.

The political system is dominated by the two parties, two subsidiaries of business money, which carve up districts where each one of them is dominant and not competitive with the other. These two parties have generated such a spoiled system, it's impossible to spoil them in any third-party manner. You can only purge them, displace them, or at the least discipline them to remind them that they're supposed to represent people, not big corporations.

So the spoilers are the two-party duopoly, really one corporate party with two heads wearing different makeup. If you want to have politics regenerated, you have to give small seeds a chance to sprout.

We have a winner-take-all political system that discourages small parties and independent candidates from trying to start a new direction or a new movement. That's why we need a debate on proportional representation, which I think can be quite practically applied relatively soon at some municipal jurisdictions and then we can work up from there.

You've got about seventy-five House districts in 1998 that did not have an opposing major party candidate, even on the ballot, against the incumbent, whether Republican or Democrat. I think the Greens can begin picking those vacuums, not only at the congressional level, but also at the state and local levels. I don't think enough has been known and publicized about how many one-party districts there are in the US, where the other opposing party has forfeited the trust of the public in participating in at least a two-party competition process, never mind that the two parties are Tweedledum and Tweedledee. I think those are real openings for Greens.

For years, the lesser-of-two-evils argument has been advanced as a reason to vote for either the Democrat or the Republican. Peace activist Dave Dellinger calls that the "evil of two lessers."

Most people are not interested in being told, you've got two choices: Go vote for the least worst, or stay home. They want more choices. If they want to buy a car, they don't want to have to choose from just two cars. If they want to buy a house, they don't want to be told, You've got to buy one of these two houses in this city. They want choices.

They also, judging by the reactions in my audiences, are overwhelmingly supportive of a binding None-of-the-Above law. So if you don't like who's on the ballot, you can go down and vote for None of the Above in your voting precinct. If None of the Above wins more votes than any of the other candidates, it cancels that particular election, sends the candidates packing, and orders a new election and new candidates within thirty or forty-five days.

What else are your audiences responding to?

The whole issue of corporate globalization, the corporate model of economic development, the autocratic systems of governance embedded in the WTO, which subvert our legitimate local, state, and national sovereignties and imperil our existing health and safety laws. The mandate of the WTO is trade über alles. Trade subordinates all our consumer, environmental, health, safety, and workplace standards.

Today, it isn't just that a majority of workers are making less, inflation adjusted, than they made in 1979, despite record macro-prosperity whose gains are being siphoned off by the top few percent of the wealthiest people. It's not just that. It's that they're having to put more and more time in, 163 hours more a year compared to twenty years ago. And they're having to spend money on things that they didn't have to spend money on thirty or forty years ago because of more commutes, more cars per family, more auto insurance policies, more fast food restaurants instead of eating at home, more time away from the kids. When you have to buy $70 Nintendo games and bring the commercial entertainment into the home, that's a form of a pay cut. One reason people think they're so hard-pressed is they're having to spend more on things that they didn't have to spend money on years ago, before this corporate, mall-dominated, suburban sprawl–dominated political economy got established.

All these issues are going to be part of this campaign.

The Green Party national convention is going to be held in Denver on the weekend of June 23. In 1996, Winona LaDuke ran as your vice presidential running mate. Have you talked to her about possibly running again?

I have, and she's committed to running again. I'm absolutely delighted. I urge that everyone read her new book called *All Our Relations*, which describes the ravages of corporations and government activity on the reservations of our first natives. This is a beautifully written book published by South End Press.

Few people know of your Arab heritage. Your parents were born in Lebanon. You rarely mention this. I was wondering how that background, growing up with that heritage, influenced you.

It was a very civically responsible upbringing. My parents said to the children, "The other side of freedom is civic responsibility." So we were always encouraged to participate and try to improve our community and not be passive onlookers or bystanders. Our parents would take us to town meetings in my hometown, which were often pretty robust displays of discussion between the citizenry and the selectmen and mayor. I think it was also a time when children had some solitude. They weren't glued to video games and television thirty or forty hours a week. We played in the backyard instead of sitting on a couch gaining weight, getting out of shape, munching potato chips, and watching some violent cartoon show.

What about the heritage of Arab culture?

We grew up learning the language—the proverbs were always a part of encouragement, admonition in the household. It was a very nurturing type of cultural upbringing.

I have a sense that you're sometimes shy of using your prestige and position to advance a progressive agenda.

You're probably right. I really don't like to brag about our past achievements, although they are, over thirty-five or forty years, quite significant, and I think they improved the health and safety of the country and showed what individual citizens can do and exposed a lot of corporate and government abuses. But I always look forward. I never achieve anywhere near what I'd like to achieve.

It is important to remind people, though, especially young people who are demoralized and disengaged, that we've had some great victories, whether it was getting the coal mine health and safety laws through in the late 1960s or the environmental and consumer protection laws.

All these started with a very small number of people who built up a public constituency and developed what Judge Learned Hand called the "essential public sentiments" in behalf of needed changes. Now it's becoming more and more difficult to do that, as corporations have taken over the government and turned it almost actively against its own people, either by blocking access to participation or by impeding the consumer, environmental, labor, small taxpayer, and clean-money reform efforts.

I always like Cicero's definition of freedom—to show you how little has changed in terms of wise insights in this world. This was a little over 2,000 years ago. He said, "Freedom is participation in power."

I also recall Supreme Court Justice Louis Brandeis's statement. He said, back a little over sixty years ago, "We can have democracy, or we can have the concentration of wealth in the hands of a few. We cannot have both." That's really the touchstone of this campaign.

Noam Chomsky
September 1999

Noam Chomsky, longtime political activist, writer, and professor of linguistics at the Massachusetts Institute of Technology, is the author of numerous books and articles on US foreign policy, international affairs, human rights, and the media. His works include *Manufacturing Consent*, with Ed Herman (Pantheon, 1988), *Deterring Democracy* (Verso, 1991), *World Orders Old and New* (Columbia University, 1994), *Profit Over People* (Seven Stories, 1999), and *Fateful Triangle* (South End Press, revised edition, 1999). His latest book is *The New Military Humanism* (Common Courage, 1999).

I first wrote to Chomsky around 1980. Much to my surprise, he responded. We did our first interview four years later. We have done scores since then, resulting in a series of books as well as radio programs. The interview collections have sold in the hundreds of thousands, which is remarkable since they have had virtually no promotion and have not been reviewed even in Left journals.

In working with Chomsky over the years, I have been struck with his consistency, patience, and equanimity. There are no power plays or superior airs. In terms of his intellectual chops, he is awesome in his ability to take a wide and disparate amount of information and cobble it into a coherent analysis.

Chomsky, now seventy, is indefatigable. In addition to producing a steady stream of articles and books on politics and linguistics, he maintains a heavy speaking schedule: He is in enormous demand and is often booked years in advance. He draws huge audiences wherever he goes, though not because of a flashy speaking style. As he once told me, "I'm not a charismatic speaker, and if I had the capacity to do so, I wouldn't do it. I'm really not interested in persuading people.

What I like to do is help people persuade themselves." And this he has done probably with more diligence over a longer period of time than any other intellectual.

The *New Statesman* calls him "the conscience of the American people." To cite just one example of his solidarity, last year I asked him to come to Boulder to speak at KGNU community radio's twentieth anniversary. Notwithstanding being fatigued from recent surgery, he not only came but waived his fee.

Often Chomsky is introduced as someone who exemplifies the Quaker adage of speaking truth to power. He takes exception to that. He says the powerful already know what's going on. It is the people who need to hear the truth.

As a kid growing up in Philadelphia, when he was not writing articles in the school newspaper on the Spanish Civil War, he was a long-suffering Athletics baseball fan. In those days, he recalls, the A's were always getting creamed by the Yankees. "For children of first-generation Jewish immigrants, it was considered part of your Americanization to know more about baseball than anybody else," he says. Today, after years of not paying attention to sports, Chomsky takes his grandchildren to games. Nevertheless, his trenchant critique remains. "Sports," he says, "plays a societal role in engendering jingoist and chauvinist attitudes. They're designed to organize a community to be committed to their gladiators." If you are playing on a team, according to Chomsky, it's not much better. "They build up irrational attitudes of submission to authority."

I can see it now. Chomsky at the plate. Barsamian on the mound. The count is three and two, bottom of the ninth. His team is, of course, losing. Here's the pitch. And Chomsky swings, there's a long drive to deep left, and that ball is...

This interview is culled from four hours
     in early February in Lexington and Cambridge, Massachusetts.

ᔆᴏ   ᴄ℟

Our interviews are a kind of roulette. You really don't know where the questions are coming from or what kind of detail you'll need. How do you feel about that?

You've got the upper hand. I'm just your servant. So I have the easy job. I just follow where you lead.

You've said many times that you're not Amnesty International. What determines your involvement in an issue?

If you can't do anything about some problem, it doesn't help a lot to make big statements about it. We could all get together and say, "Condemn Genghis Khan," but there's no moral value. So the first question is, to what extent can we influence things? To the extent that US power is directly involved, we can influence it more than if it's not directly involved, for example.

If it's a very popular issue, I don't feel that there's much advantage in my talking about it. Take South Africa. I said very little about apartheid, although I think overcoming it was an extremely important thing. It didn't seem like a useful contribution of my time to say "I agree," which I often did. I'd rather take issues that are being kept out of the public sphere and on which we can really do a lot and that are intrinsically important.

There are other things that are just personal. Ever since childhood, I happen to have been concerned with Israel, or what was Palestine. I grew up in that environment. I've lived there, read the Hebrew newspapers, have a lot of friends there—so naturally I'm involved in that.

The last time you were on National Public Radio's All Things Considered *was during the Gulf War in February 1991. You did a commentary on countries violating Security Council resolutions. You were imagining a US bombing attack on Tel Aviv, Ankara, and Jakarta.*

If you look at the list of leading recipients of US aid, virtually every one of them is a major human rights violator. In the Western Hemisphere, the leading recipient of military aid through the 1990s has been mostly Colombia, which also has the worst human rights record. That was the point of that comment. Of course, you don't have to bomb these countries. If you want to stop the terror and atrocities that they're carrying out, just stop supporting them.

Your two-minute-and-thirty-second commentary was surrounded by a virtual cacophony of Gulf War propaganda.

Recall the comment of Jeff Greenfield, who used to be on *Nightline*. He explained why they wouldn't have me on. He said there were two reasons. First of all, I'm from Neptune. Secondly, I lack concision. I agree with him.

On both counts? Neptune also?

In my two minutes and thirty seconds, I must have sounded to a reasonable listener as if I were from Neptune. There was no context, no background, no evidence, and it was completely different from everything they were hearing. The rational response is, "This guy must be from Neptune." That's correct.

It leaves you with very simple choices: Either you repeat the same conventional doctrines everybody else is spouting, or else you say something true, and it will sound like it's from Neptune. Concision requires that there be no evidence. The flood of unanimous doctrine ensures that it will sound as if it's off the wall.

I came across this quote from George Orwell. He says, "Circus dogs jump when the trainer cracks his whip. But the really well-trained dog is the one that turns his somersault when there's no whip."

I suspect he was talking about intellectuals. The intellectual class is supposed to be so well trained and so well indoctrinated that they don't need a whip. They just react spontaneously in the ways that will serve external power interests, without awareness, thinking they're doing honest, dedicated work. That's a real trained dog.

What kind of suggestions would you make to people who are trying to decode the news?

The first thing is to be very skeptical. Begin by asking, "How is power distributed in society? Who decides what's going to be produced, consumed, and distributed?" You can figure that out in most places pretty easily. Then you should ask whether policies and the shaping of information reflect the distribution of power. You typically find you can explain quite a lot that way.

Take Iraq. One question is, "Why are the US and Britain bombing Iraq and insisting on maintaining sanctions?" If you look, you find answers that are given with near 100 percent agreement. You hear it from Tony Blair, Madeleine Albright, newspaper editors, and commentators. That answer is, "Saddam Hussein is a complete monster. He even committed the ultimate horror—namely, he gassed his own people. We can't let a creature like that survive."

As soon as anything's given with near unanimity, it should be a signal. Nothing is that clear. There happens to be an easy way to test it in this case: How did the US and Britain react when Saddam Hussein committed the ultimate horror? It's on the record. This was in April 1988, the gassing of the Kurdish town of Halabja. The second major gassing occurs in August, five days after the cease-fire when Iran basically capitulated. The US and Britain reacted by continuing—and, in fact, accelerating—their strong support for Saddam Hussein.

That tells you something right away: The gassing of his own people cannot possibly be the reason why the US and Britain are now trying to destroy him. He's a monster, he committed one of the ultimate horrors, and the US and Britain thought it was fine.

Elementary rationality is just not permitted. If anyone wants to test this, they can investigate how often that statement, "We have to bomb Saddam Hussein because he committed the ultimate horror," is followed by the three crucial words: "with our support."

When we look further, we find that a major and, indeed, conscious goal of those concerned with shaping thoughts and attitudes—the advertising and public relations industries and the responsible intellectuals who talk about how to run the world—is to regiment the minds of men as fully as the army regiments the body.

Secretary of Defense William Cohen kept his promise that he made in early 1998 after the public relations disaster at Ohio State: There will be no town meetings the next time we want to bomb Iraq.

They made a serious error that last time. In the buildup to the bombing of Iraq, they had arranged a very carefully planned town meeting, which looked very safe. It was in Columbus, Ohio. The questioners were selected in advance. They picked people they thought would be controlled. It looked like a nicely orchestrated propaganda exercise. But there was organizing in the background. Some of these polite people turned out to have some real questions. They asked them quietly and politely, but as soon as the first word of dissent broke through the uniformity, Cohen, Albright, and [National Security Adviser Sandy] Berger collapsed into gibberish. They couldn't respond. The audience reacted because the dissidence was right below the surface. It totally blew up. That was the context of Cohen's comment.

The bombing of Iraq last December was particularly striking. It was in flat violation of international law. The reason that the United States didn't go to the UN Security Council is perfectly obvious. It would not have permitted the bombing. So therefore the Security Council is another "hostile forum," and it's irrelevant. If the US and Britain want to use force, they will. Furthermore, they did it in as brazen a way as possible to demonstrate their contempt for the UN and international law. The timing was picked just when the Security Council was meeting in an emergency session dealing with this crisis. Other council members had not been informed. That's a way of saying as clearly as possible, "You're irrelevant. International law is irrelevant. We are rogue states. We will use force and violence as we choose."

That's a big change from, say, 1947, when the contempt for international law was hidden in secret documents, which would be released forty years later. Now it is clear and out in the open. It receives...you can't even say the "approval" of intellectual opinion, because it's so deeply taken for granted it's not even noticed. It's just like the air you breathe.

We're a violent, terrorist state. We have a big flag saying: International Law and the UN Charter Are Inappropriate for Us Because We Have the Guns and We're Going to Use Them. Period.

Incidentally, it's not reported here, but the world does notice. In India, for example, the Indian Council of Jurists is actually bringing a case to the World Court charging the US and Britain with war crimes. The Vatican called the bombing of Iraq "aggression." That got a little mention at the bottom of a page here and there. In the Arab world, it was widely condemned as aggression. In England, it was not as uniform as here. The *Observer* had a lead editorial condemning it as aggression.

One of the advantages of leaving the United States is to be exposed to different media. I was in Thailand in early January. The Nation *is one of their two English-language newspapers. There was a very critical article entitled,* "Containing America in the Post-Cold War Era." *It was by Suravit Jayanama, who wrote,* "While Washington talks about containing Saddam Hussein, what about the need to contain a superpower that zealously acts to protect its own interests?"

That's the attitude in much of the world, and with justice. When the world's only superpower, which has essentially a monopoly of force, announces openly, "We will use force and violence as we choose and if you don't like it, get out of the way," there's a reason why that should frighten people.

What about the legacies of this violence?

Look at Laos. It was saturated with probably hundreds of millions of pieces of ordnance. The US government conceded that most of this bombing had nothing to do with the war in Vietnam. At that time, it was the most intensive bombing in history, aimed at a completely defenseless peasant society. I know something about this. I was there and was able to interview some of the refugees—there were tens of thousands—who had just been driven off the Plain of Jars.

The most lethal bombardment was what they called Bombies, little colorful things. They were designed to maim and kill people—that was their only purpose. This region is just littered with maybe hundreds of millions—nobody knows how much—unexploded ordnance. The victims are mainly children and farmers. In fact, the one careful province survey that was done found that 55 percent of the victims were children. Kids are playing. They see these colorful things and pick them up, and they and anyone else around are dead. Farmers hit them if they're trying to clear the ground. That's going on right now. We're not talking about ancient history.

The first group to try to do something about it was the Mennonites. The Central Mennonite Committee has had volunteers working there since 1977, and they've been trying to publicize it and get people interested in it. They're trying to give people shovels. No high-tech equipment. There is a British volunteer group, a mine-detection group, professionals, but not the British government. And as the British press puts it, the Americans are notable by their absence.

According to the right-wing British press, the *Sunday Telegraph*, the British mine-clearance group claims that the Pentagon will not even give them technical information that would allow them to defuse the bombs. So the British mine clearers themselves are at risk because this is secret information. The US is now, after a lot of pressure, training some Laotians. There was a very proud article in the *Christian Science Monitor* about how the US is such a humane society because we're training Laotians to clear away mines which somehow got there.

Those mines didn't come from Neptune, where I came from. We know where they came from, and we know who's not there getting rid of them.

You, Edward Said, Howard Zinn, and Ed Herman recently issued a statement on Iraq, saying, "The time has come for a call to action to people of conscience. We must organize and make this issue a priority, just as Americans organized to stop the war in Vietnam. We need a national campaign to lift the sanctions." I know you're not against sanctions in all instances, for example, you cite South Africa as quite a separate case.

For clarity, the four of us signed that statement. But it was written, organized, and publicized by Robert Jensen at the University of Texas. That illustrates something that we know is true all the time: The people who really do the work are rarely known. What is known is somebody who stood up and said something or signed a petition.

The burden of proof is always on any imposition of sanctions. Can that burden of proof be overcome? Sometimes. Take South Africa. Two comments about that. One is that sanctions were supported by the overwhelming majority of the population, as far as anybody could determine. If the population is in favor of them, that's an argument, not a proof, that maybe they're a good idea. Two, it would have been a good idea if the US had observed the sanctions. The US undermined them. US trade and interactions with South Africa continued and I believe may have increased.

There was an AP report in mid-January 1999 about Israel. In response to criticism that Israeli security services use torture and excessive force when interrogating Palestinians, the government attorney, Yehuda Schaeffer, said, "In this, as in other matters, we are still a light unto the nations," referring to the century-old utopian Zionist slogan.

This has been a scandal even inside Israel. In fact, Israel does use torture, according to international standards. They're constantly condemned for this by human rights groups. Furthermore, they use it consistently. Arab prisoners who are often kept in administrative detention without charge are routinely tortured under interrogation. About ten years ago, this issue broke through to the public. A Druze military officer had been convicted for some crime. It turned out that he was innocent of the crime, and he had confessed to it. Immediately someone asked, "How come he confessed?" It turned out he had been tortured, and that became public.

For years, Palestinian prisoners when they came to court claimed that their confessions had been obtained under torture. The courts uniformly rejected that, all the way up to the High Court. They just dismissed that as false. After this Druze case, they had to recognize that, at least in this one instance, the confession was obtained under torture. Then came an inquiry. It turned out that they had been using torture routinely to interrogate. That was considered a huge scandal, not so much because they had used torture, but because the intelligence services hadn't told the court. It was kind of like Watergate. It was not bombing Cambodia that was a crime, but not telling Congress about it that's the real crime. Here, too, the High Court condemned the fact that the intelligence services were misleading them, which was a joke. Everybody outside, except for the justices of the High Court, knew that the confessions were being obtained under torture. Moshe Etzioni, one of the High Court justices, was in London in 1977 or so. He had an interview with Amnesty International, which asked why they were getting such a tremendously high rate of confessions. Everybody knows what that means. He said, Arabs tend to confess; it's part of their nature. Amnesty published it without comment.

There was no doubt that Israel was using torture, but the courts, including the High Court, decided to believe the intelligence services. So their claim that they had been misled is a little misleading. They chose to be misled. At that point, the Landau Commission was formed, which had secret meetings and came out with partially public but partially secret recommendations about the use of... they didn't call it "torture," but force or pressure or some euphemism. The Landau Commission said no, you shouldn't use this except... and then came up with a secret protocol. Nobody knows what's in it. It describes the methods you're allowed to use. You can tell what those methods are by what has happened to prisoners.

There are good ways of studying this. You can take independent testimony from prisoners who don't know each other but have been in the same place, and see if they describe exactly the same thing. The human rights groups have been doing this for years. Probably Israeli torture has been more systematically and carefully investigated than any other. The reason is, you have to have higher standards in the investigation. If you discuss torture in Pakistan, you don't need very high standards. Some prisoner tells you he was tortured—OK, headline. You say the same thing about Israel, you've got to meet the standards of physics. So when the Swiss League of Human Rights or Amnesty International or the London Insight team for the *Sunday Times* or some major newspaper did studies of torture in Israel, they were extremely careful. Still they couldn't get them reported here.

What do you say to those who hear your critique of Israel and its use of torture and ask, "Well, what about Syria? Why aren't you talking about Libya or Iraq? Aren't things much worse there?"

Sure, I mentioned Pakistan. Those countries are much worse. I would agree. I'm not really making a critique. I'm just quoting Human Rights Watch and Amnesty International. These are very conservative comments. I would take the same point of view they do, that we should keep to explicit US law, which bars aid to countries which systematically use torture. So I don't think we should be sending aid to Iraq. In fact, I protested strongly when we were doing exactly that in the 1980s. Of course, it's academic in the case of Iraq and Syria. But if you look at the leading recipients of US aid like Israel, Egypt, Turkey, Pakistan, and Colombia, they use torture. All that aid's illegal.

What's your understanding of the ongoing crisis in global capitalism?

We should begin by recognizing that for a good part of the population of the world, and probably the vast majority, it's been a crisis for a long time. It's now called one because it's starting to affect the interests of rich and powerful people. Up until then it was just starving people.

What has happened, point number one is: Nobody really understands. The Bank for International Settlements—the central bank of central bankers, it's sometimes called, the most conservative, respectable institution in the universe—produces an annual report. The last one stated: We have to approach these questions with humility, because nobody has a clue as to what's going on. In fact, every international economist who is semi-honest tells you, "We don't really understand what's going on. But we have some ideas." So anything that's said, certainly anything that I say, you want to add many grains of salt to, because nobody really understands.

However, some things are moderately clear and there's a fair consensus. Through the Bretton Woods era, that's roughly the Second World War up to the early 1970s, exchange rates were pretty close to fixed, and capital was more or less controlled. So there wasn't extreme capital flow. That was changed in the early 1970s by decision. Capital flow was liberalized.

The international economic system is patched together with scotch tape. There was a study by the IMF [International Monetary Fund]. It has about 180 members. From 1980 to 1995, it found that something like a quarter of the members had serious banking crises, sometimes several, and two-thirds had one or another financial crisis. That's a lot. There's debate about this, but it seems that since the liberalization of financial markets, they have been extremely volatile, unpredictable, irrational, lots of crises. Nobody knows when they're going to blow up.

You can say, "Well, we can handle it." Maybe. One of the leading international economists, Paul Krugman, has an article in *Foreign Affairs* called "The Return of Depression Economics," in which he basically says, "We don't understand what's happening. It's like the Depression. Maybe it'll be somehow patched together, but nobody can say. And nobody knows what to do."

There's one possibility that he rules out, and that is capital controls. He rules it out on theoretical grounds. He says capital controls lead to inefficient use of resources, and we can't have that. That's certainly true in a certain abstract model of the economy, the neoclassical model. Whether that model has anything to do with the real world is another question. The evidence doesn't seem to support it. Also one has to ask the question, "What is meant by 'efficient use of resources'?" That sounds like a nice, technical notion, but it's not. When you unpack it, it's a highly ideological notion. So you can efficiently use resources if it increases gross national product. But increasing gross national product may harm everybody. That's efficient by some ideological measure, but not by other measures.

Let me just give you one example to illustrate. The Department of Transportation did a study one or two years ago. It tried to estimate the effect of the decline of spending on maintaining highways. There's been a considerable decline since the Reagan era, so a certain amount of money has been saved by not repairing highways. They tried to estimate the cost. I forget the exact number, but the cost was considerably higher than the savings. However, the cost is cost to individuals. If your car hits a pothole, it's a cost to you. To the economy, it's a gain. That improves the efficiency of the economy. Because if your car hits a pothole, you go to the garage and you pay a guy to fix it, or maybe you buy a new car—something more produced. It makes the economy more efficient in two ways. You've cut down the size of government, and everybody knows that government drags down the economy, so you've improved it that way. And you've increased profits and employment and production. Of course, for you as a person, there was a loss. But for the economy, there was a gain by the highly ideological way efficiency is measured. This is a tiny case. It extends across the board. So when one hears words like "efficiency" used, reach for your gray cells. Ask, "What exactly does that mean?"

Is Social Security broken? Does it need to be fixed?

Even before getting to that, how come people are talking about it? Just a few years ago, this was called the third rail of American politics. You couldn't touch it. Now the question is, "How do you save it?" That's quite an achievement for propaganda.

If indeed the economy is going to undergo a historically unprecedented slowdown as far into the future as we can see, then the stock market is going to undergo a sharp slowdown, too. You can't have it both ways. This is not a particularly radical criticism. You can read it in *Business Week*.

The Social Security Act said, "We care if some other elderly person starves. We don't want that to happen." The idea of putting it in the stock market, though it's framed in all sorts of fraudulent gobbledygook, is to break down that sense of social solidarity and say, "You care only about yourself. If that guy down the street when he gets to be seventy starves to death, that's not your problem. It's his problem. He invested badly, or he had bad luck." That's very good for rich people. But for everyone else, it depends on how you evaluate the risk. Social Security's been very effective in that respect. Starvation among the elderly has dropped considerably.

Has the same kind of propaganda campaign been conducted on public education?

Very much so. There's a campaign under way to essentially destroy the public education system along with every aspect of human life and attitudes and thought that involve social solidarity. It's being done in all sorts of ways. One is simply by underfunding. So if you can make the public schools really rotten, people will look for an alternative. Any service that's going to be privatized, the first thing you do is make it malfunction so people can say, "We want to get rid of it. It's not running. Let's give it to Lockheed."

What about privatizing Medicare?

A private institution has one goal: maximize profit, minimize human conditions. That means you try to attract the patients who are least risky and are not going to cost you much, and you get rid of the rest.

Do you think that domestic issues like Social Security, public education, Medicare, and health care could be lightning rods to organize around and create popular movements?

If these issues are brought to the forefront and are discussed honestly, there could be a lot of problems. It's the reason NAFTA [North American Free Trade Agreement] was grossly distorted in the media coverage. After the fast-track fiasco a little over a year ago, the *Wall Street Journal* had an interesting article. They said that although it's a "no-brainer" that trade deals should be made by the president without any congressional input, nevertheless the opposition has what they called an "ultimate weapon": The population is against it, and it's really hard to keep the population out.

For organizers, it should be a bonanza. I remember at the time of the 200th anniversary of the signing of the Declaration of Independence, in one amusing poll, they gave people slogans of various sorts and asked them to say whether those statements were in the Constitution or not. One of the statements was, "From each according to his ability, to each according to his needs." About half the population thought that was in the Constitution. Speak of an organizer's paradise! If those sentiments aren't developed and used, then organizers are failing.

With the constant and ever-increasing demands on your time, how do you keep up with everything?

Badly. There's no way to do it. There are physical limitations. The day is twenty-four hours long. If you do one thing, you're not doing something else. You cannot overcome the fact that time is finite. So you make your choices. Maybe badly, maybe well, but there's no algorithm, no procedure to give you the right answer.

Do you have a time that you particularly like to work?

Virtually all the time.

You've been disdainful of spectator sports, arguing that they distract people from paying attention to politics. But last January, you knew not only which teams were in the Super Bowl, but also the outcome. Are you losing your grip?

I always read the front page at least of the *New York Times*. It said who won and what the score was. But it's even worse than that. I have a jock grandson who's finally helping me fulfill a secret dream to have an excuse to go to a professional basketball game. I don't know if I should admit it, but I'm actually going to my first game in around fifty years.

Eduardo Galeano
July 1999

Eduardo Galeano is one of Latin America's most distinguished writers, storytellers, journalists, and historians. His classic work is *Open Veins of Latin America: Five Centuries of the Pillage of a Continent* (Monthly Review Press, 1973). His other books include *Book of Embraces* (Norton, 1992), *We Say No: Chronicles 1963–1991* (Norton, 1992), and the award-winning trilogy *Memory of Fire*, reissued by Norton last year. His latest book, also published last year by Verso, is *Soccer in Sun and Shadow*.

Under the soft languid tones of Galeano's Uruguayan speech is a razor-sharp intellect infused with a poetic sensibility, a biting wit, and a commitment to social justice. He apologizes to Shakespeare and to any other native speaker for his English. But I found in listening to him that his creative and accented version actually made me hear more.

Born in Montevideo in 1940, he was a kind of prodigy. At thirteen, he was already submitting political commentary and cartoons to a local socialist weekly. Later, he was the editor of various journals and newspapers, including the daily *La Epoca*. In 1973, he went into exile in Argentina, where he founded and edited the magazine *Crisis*. He lived in Spain from 1976 to 1984 and then returned to Uruguay.

A scathing critic of the media and consumerism, Galeano writes in *We Say No*:

> The mass media does not reveal reality; it masks it. It doesn't help bring about change; it helps avoid change. It doesn't encourage democratic participation; it induces passivity, resignation, and selfishness. It doesn't generate creativity; it creates consumers.

In his book *Days and Nights of Love and War* (Monthly Review Press, 1982), he explains why he does what he does:

One writes out of a need to communicate and commune with others, to denounce that which gives pain, and to share that which gives happiness. One writes against one's solitude and against the solitude of others…To awaken consciousness, to reveal identity—can literature claim a better function in these times?

Galeano takes readers on a tour of Latin America—"the continent," as Isabel Allende describes it, "that appears on the map in the form of an ailing heart." His imaginative writing style supplies oxygen to patients in all hemispheres. Here's the mythic opening of *Faces and Masks*, part two of *Memory of Fire*:

> The blue tiger will smash the world. Another land, without evil, without death, will be born from the destruction of this one. This land wants it. It asks to die, asks to be born, this old and offended land. It is weary and blind from so much weeping behind closed eyelids. On the point of death, it strides the days, garbage heap of time, and at night, it inspires pity from the stars. Soon the First Father will hear the supplications, land wanting to be another, and then the blue tiger who sleeps beneath his hammock will jump.

Galeano was in Santa Fe in late April to receive the first $250,000 Prize for Cultural Freedom from the Lannan Foundation. In addition, another $100,000 was given to three alternative cultural institutions, designated by Galeano, in Uruguay. Lannan, an upstart in the foundation world, has progressive politics, though its wealth comes from a former director of the multinational company ITT (International Telephone and Telegraph). Lannan hit the news in March when it boldly stepped in to cover the printing costs for a bilingual children's book *Historia de los Colores: The Story of Colors* (Cinco Puntos Press, 1999), written by Subcomandante Marcos. The original funding from the National Endowment for the Arts was abruptly canceled when it learned the identity of the book's author.

At the reception following his prize ceremony, Galeano tried to whittle down our interview time by pleading a busy schedule. I told him it was for *The Progressive*. He relented. Now that's clout!

℘   ℭ

Open Veins of Latin America has sold more than a million copies. It's been translated into many languages. You wrote it in three months, which is a phenomenally short period of time. How did you generate such a burst of energy?

Coffee. The real author of this book was coffee. I drank oceans of it because at that time, 1970, I was working in the mornings at the university in Montevideo. I was the editor of university publications. In the afternoons, I was working for private publishers also as an editor, rewriting and correcting books on any subject you can imagine, like the sexual life of mosquitoes. Then, from seven or eight o'clock in the evening to five or six o'clock in the morning, I was writing *Open Veins*. I didn't sleep for three months. But it was an advertisement for coffee's virtues. So be careful with coffee if you don't want to become a left-winger.

What accounts for the book's staying power?

Perhaps masochism. I can't understand it. The book brings to the nonspecialized reader a lot of historical information. I didn't discover the facts I'm telling in *Open Veins*. I tried to rewrite history in a language that could be understood by anybody. Perhaps this is why the book has had such success. At the beginning, it had no success at all. But later, it opened its own road and went on walking, and it's still walking.

Perhaps the central idea of the book, which may work as a spinal cord, is that you cannot confuse a dwarf with a child. They have the same size, but they are quite different. So when you hear all the technocrats speaking about developing countries, they are implying that we are living in a sort of infancy of capitalism, which is not true at all. Latin America is not a stage on the way toward development. It is the result of development, the result of five centuries of history.

You could have had a comfortable life writing for magazines or teaching in universities, but a long time ago you decided to labor on behalf of the voiceless.

I don't feel there is anyone who is voiceless. Everybody has something to say, something that deserves to be heard by others. So I never shared this attitude of becoming the voice of the voiceless. The problem is that just a few have the privilege of being heard. I'm not a martyr, not a hero.

We all have the right to know and to express ourselves, which is nowadays very difficult as long as we are obeying the orders of an invisible dictatorship. It is the dictatorship of the single word, the single image, the single tune, and perhaps it's more dangerous than other dictatorships because it acts on a world scale. It's an international structure of power which is imposing universal values that center on consumption and violence. It means that you are what you have. If you don't have, you are not. The right to be depends on your ability to buy things. You are defined by the things you have. It's like you are driven by your car. You are bought by your supermarket. You are seen by your TV screen. You are programmed by your computer. We have all become tools of our tools.

Is there any end to this cycle?

If the consumption society imposes its values all over the world, then the planet would disappear. We cannot afford it. We don't have enough air, earth, or water to pay the price for such a disaster.

The model imposed on all of Latin America is not Amsterdam or Florence or Bologna; in these cities, cars are not the owners of the streets. These are cities with bikes, with public transport, with people walking. Cities that people feel they own. Cities that provide a common place. Cities were born from the human necessity of encounter. Cities were born as a result of, "I want to meet friends. I want to be with other people." Today, cities are places where machines encounter machines. We humans have become intruders.

And what do we want to become like? Los Angeles, a city in which cars own much more space than people. This is an impossible dream. We cannot become them. If the entire world has the same quantity of cars as the US with its one-person, one-car, then the planet will explode. We have poisoned the air, poisoned the earth, poisoned the waters, poisoned the human souls. Everything is poisoned.

When a Latin American president in his speech says, "We are becoming part of the first world," in the first place he's lying. Second, this is practically impossible. And in the third place, he should be in jail because this is an incitement to crime. If you say, "I want Montevideo to become Los Angeles," you are inviting the destruction of Montevideo.

A lot of people in the United States, when they think of Latin America, see a vast beach, a playground, from Cancún and Acapulco to Copacabana and Mar del Plata. Or they see a threatening and menacing face: narcotraffickers, leftist guerrillas, favelas, and shantytowns. What do you make of the US attitude toward Latin America?

I am astonished each time I come to the US by the ignorance of a high percentage of the population, which knows almost nothing about Latin America or about the world. It's quite blind and deaf to anything that may happen outside the frontiers of the US.

I was a professor at Stanford University three years ago. Once I was talking with an old professor, an important and cultured man. Suddenly, he asked me, "Where do you come from?"

I said, "Uruguay."

He said, "Uruguay?"

As I knew that nobody knows where Uruguay is, I quickly tried to change the subject and talk about something else.

But he was gentle enough to say, "Well, we have been doing terrible things there."

I suddenly realized that he was speaking about Guatemala because the *New York Times* had just published some articles about CIA involvement in Guatemala.

I said, "No, this is Guatemala."

"Oh, Guatemala."

"Yes, Guatemala."

This ignorance of what's happening outside the States implies a high degree of impunity. The military power can do whatever it wants because people have no idea of where Kosovo is or Iraq or Guatemala or El Salvador. And they have no idea that, for instance, centuries before New York was established, Baghdad had one million inhabitants and one of the highest cultures in the world.

The same is true for "our" America, the other America—we are not just echoes of the master's voice.

Or the shadow of his body.

Even the ruling classes in Latin America dream to become shadows and echoes. I'm always saying that our worst sin in Latin America is the sin of stupidity because we enjoy looking at our own caricature. For instance, when I meet Latin Americans here in the States, they say, "Now I am in America." Ah, you're in America now, because you are in the States. Before you were where? Greenland? Asia? Japan? We have accepted this distorted vision of ourselves looking at the mirror which despises and scorns us.

You write about the injustice of poverty.

In this world, you have injustice on such a broad scale. The difference, the gap, between rich and poor people in material terms has been multiplied in these thirty years since I wrote *Open Veins*.

The last UN report says that in 1999, 225 persons own a fortune equivalent to the total amount of what half of humanity earns. It's a very unjust distribution of bread and fishes.

But at the same time, the world is equalizing in the habits it imposes. We are condemned to accept the global uniformization, a sort of McDonaldization of the entire world. This is a form of violence against all the worlds that the world contains. I usually say that I reject the idea of being obliged to choose between two possibilities: Either you die of hunger or you die of boredom. We are practicing each day—and we don't notice it because it's invisible, it's secret—a sort of massacre of our capacity to be diverse, to have so many different ways to live life, celebrate, eat, dance, dream, drink, think, and feel. It's like a forbidden rainbow. Now we are being more and more obliged to accept a single way. And this single way is being mainly produced in US factories.

You took to radical politics at a very early age. Was it family influence?

No, it was my liver. Perhaps I'm still trying to organize indignation. My mind, which is not especially brilliant, is sometimes useful to organize my feelings, trying to make sense of them, but the process is coming from the feeling to the thoughts and not in the opposite way.

In politics, as in everything else, I am always seeking a perhaps impossible but desirable communion between what I think and what I feel, which is also an intention to develop, to win, to conquer, to discover a language able to express at once emotions and ideas, what Colombians in the small towns on the Caribbean coast call the "feel-thinking language." It's a language which is able to reunite what has been divorced by dominant culture, which is always breaking in pieces everything it touches. You have a language for ideas and another language for emotions. The heart and the mind divorced. The public speech and the private life. History and present, also divorced.

You say that history is not a sleeping beauty in some museum.

Official history is a sleeping beauty, sometimes a sleeping monster, in the museums. But I believe in memory not as an arrival place but as a point of departure, a catapult throwing you to present times, allowing you to imagine the future instead of accepting it. Otherwise it would be absolutely impossible for me to have any connection with history if history were just a collection of dead people, dead names, dead facts. That's why I wrote *Memory of Fire* in the present tense, trying to keep alive everything that happened and allow it to happen again as soon as the reader reads it.

Your trilogy, Memory of Fire, *is a dramatic departure from traditional history. You use an amalgam of poetry, news items, and scholarship. What inspired you to do that?*

I never accepted the frontiers of the soul, nor did I accept frontiers in the art of writing. When I was a child, I had a Catholic education. I was trained to accept that the body and the soul were enemies, that the body was the source of sin, guilt, pleasure, infecting the soul like the beauty and the beast.

It was very difficult for me to internalize this idea, this divorce. I always noticed the contradiction between what I really felt inside me and what I was receiving as revealed truth, coming from God. At that time I believed in him and I believed that he believed in me, so it was not easy to live this contradiction.

When I was ten or eleven, I had this terrible crisis. I felt this panic of feeling guilty about my body—associated, I suppose, with the fact that I was becoming sexual. My body was something like a source of perdition for me, condemning me to hell. Now I accept it. I know perfectly well that I'm going to hell, and I'm getting trained in warm tropical countries to accept the flames. It won't be so terrible.

When I began writing, I felt I had to respect the border separating essays and nonfiction from those other genres, like poetry or short stories or novels.

I hate to be classified. This world has an obsession with classification. We are all treated like insects. We should have a label on the front. So many journalists say, "You are a political writer, right?" Just give me the name of any writer in human history who was not political. All of us are political, even if we don't know that we are political.

I feel that I am violating frontiers, and I am very happy each time I can do that. I suppose I should be working as a smuggler instead of a writer, because this joy of violating a frontier is, indeed, revealing a smuggler inside me, a delinquent.

You recently received a prize from the Lannan Foundation, which was established from funds from a former director of International Telephone and Telegraph, ITT, a multinational corporation which you've written very critically about and which figured prominently in the overthrow of Salvador Allende in Chile.

I didn't receive the prize from ITT. I received the prize from the Lannan Foundation.

But the seed monies came from there.

It's a good trip from hell to heaven.

Why do you think the US is such a violent society?

I wouldn't say the US is a violent society. It contains also energies of beauty and democracy. I wouldn't fall in my own trap, saying, "The big bad guy in the world is the US." It would be too easy. Reality is much more complex.

There is a culture of violence, a military culture, *impregnando todo*, marking everything, spreading, permeating everything it touches. You have, for instance, the entertainment industry, which is thick with violence, oceans of blood coming from the TV or the big screens.

Everything is exploding all the time—cars, people. It is a sort of continuous bombing of everything. It is the old story of the chicken and the egg, which came first? The entertainment industry says, "We are innocent. A violent reality is reflected by the mirror of films or TV. We are not inventing violence. Violence comes from the streets." But in this circle, the media are having an influence.

So there is perhaps an invisible connection between Yugoslavia and Littleton, Colorado. Both are expressions of the same culture of violence. Wars are made in the name of peace, and military actions always are called humanitarian missions. We are receiving daily doses of violence through the news, films, and in the streets.

The world is a violent place. And it's very easy to condemn poor people who steal or kidnap or kill. It's like condemning drug addicts. But it's not so easy to find the roots and condemn the system which generates crime and the use of drugs. There is much anxiety and anguish that everybody is eating and drinking each day.

What about the Pentagon's role?

The huge US military budget is preposterous. Who is the enemy? It's like a Western movie. You need a bad guy. If he doesn't exist, then you invent him. In the States, you need new villains. Saddam Hussein this morning, Milosevic this afternoon. But you need a bad guy. What a poor God without a Satan to fight against!

One of the big paradoxes in this upside-down world is that the five countries empowered to take care of peace are also the five biggest producers of arms. Almost half of the total weapons in the world are made by the United States, followed by Great Britain, France, Russia, and China. These are the countries with the right of veto in the UN Security Council. The UN was born to bring peace to the world, but the five countries with this sacred, beautiful, poetic mission of peace are also the five ones conducting the business of war.

Uruguay is in the UN General Assembly. It's absolutely symbolic. The assembly can make suggestions, but the decisions are made by the five countries that own and control the world.

The twentieth century has been a century of wars—more than 100 million people killed. This is a great quantity of persons, a multitude. Each time I hear about wars in Yugoslavia, Iraq, Africa, and anywhere else, I always ask the same question, with no answer: "Who is selling the arms? Who is making profit from this human tragedy?" I have never found the answer in the media, and it's the main question you should ask when you hear about a war. Who is selling the arms? The five dominant countries that are taking care of peace. It's terrible, but it's a reality.

What can we learn from indigenous people?

A lot. First, the certitude of communion with nature. Otherwise you may confuse ecology with gardening. You may take nature for a landscape. Nature is you, me. We are part of nature, so any crime committed against nature is a crime committed against humanity. But I don't share the view that we're committing suicide because I'm not committing suicide. It's just 20 percent of the human population wasting natural resources and poisoning the earth; 80 percent are suffering the consequences.

When political leaders sometimes say, with hand on heart, "We are committing suicide," they are referring to a crime committed by the most profitable industries in the world. *Las que más dañan son las que más ganan*, those that damage the most, gain the most. And they are all green. When I was young, green were the valleys, *verdes valles*, green were the jokes, *chistes verdes*, and green were the old men pursuing girls, *los viejos verdes*. Now, everybody is green. The World Bank is green. The International Monetary Fund is green. The chemical industry is green. The automobile industry is green. Even the military industry is green. Everybody's green.

It's interesting because in the sixteenth and seventeenth centuries, when Europe conquered America, lots of Indians were punished or burned alive because they were committing the sin of idolatry. They were adoring nature.

Today, the system of power no longer speaks of nature as an obstacle that should be overcome in order to get profits. Conquering nature, nature as something to be vanquished—this was the old language. The new language now is about protecting nature. But in both cases, language is revealing the divorce. We human beings and nature are different.

We should learn from Indian culture the deep sense of communion. This is something for God to include in the Ten Commandments. It would be the eleventh commandment: "You should love nature, to which you belong."

How did you react to the collapse of the Soviet Union?

I never felt myself identified with the so-called socialism of the Soviet Union. I always felt it wasn't socialism at all. It was an exercise in bureaucratic power with no connection to people. They were acting in the name of people, but they despised them. They were paying tribute in their speeches and all the official language, but they were treating people as a minority, as children or sheep.

So I didn't feel that socialism was dead when the Soviet Union collapsed. That it collapsed in such an easy way was eloquent enough: There was almost no blood, no tears, no nothing. But socialism is not dead because it hasn't been born. It's something I hope that humanity may perhaps find.

The present situation—from the point of view of the poor countries, the outskirts of the world—is much worse than before because with the Soviet Union you had at least a certain balance of power. Now this balance of power has disappeared, and so we have no choices. The possibilities of acting with a sense of independence have narrowed.

Are there any hopeful signs you can point to?

There are a lot of signs of hope inside the US and Mexico, and inside other countries, as well. You have a lot of movements but most of them have no echoes in the media. They are more or less secret because they act on a local level. Sometimes they are very small. But they are incarnating an answer, looking for a different world, not accepting the present world as their destiny but living it as a challenge. You have a lot of small movements everywhere fighting for human rights, against sexual discrimination, against injustice, against exploitation of children, preserving and developing agricultural forms which are not damaging to the earth.

There is a popular movement in Mexico called El Barzón. Nobody knows about it outside Mexico, but it's very important. It's a spontaneous movement born from the necessity to resist the pressures of Mexican banks. In the beginning, it was no more than a hundred or so people defending what they had—their homes, their businesses, their farms—against the voracious financial powers. But it grew and grew, and now there are more than one million persons. They have become so important that when a delegation from El Barzón went to Washington, it was received by the vice president of the International Monetary Fund. I suppose this is such an important man he doesn't even speak to his wife, but he received El Barzón.

A lot of movements are telling us hope is possible, tomorrow is not just another name for today.

You make a distinction between charity and solidarity.

I don't believe in charity; I believe in solidarity. Charity is vertical, so it's humiliating. It goes from top to bottom. Solidarity is horizontal. It respects the other and learns from the other. I have a lot to learn from other people. Each day I'm learning. *Soy un curioso.* I'm a curious man, always devouring other people, their voices, their secrets, their stories, their colors. I'm stealing their words; maybe I should be arrested.

Explain the term abrigar esperanzas.

A beautiful Spanish expression, *abrigar esperanzas*, to shelter hope. Hope needs to be *abrigada*, protected.

Because it's fragile?

She's fragile, and a little delicate, but she's alive. I have friends who say, "I'm entirely hopeless. I don't believe in anything." But you go on living. How is it? I hope I never lose hope, but if that day comes and I'm sure that I have nothing to expect, nothing to believe in, and that the human condition is doomed to stupidity and crime, then I hope I will be honest enough to kill myself. Of course, I know that the human condition is something at once horrible and marvelous. *Estamos muy mal hechos, pero no estamos terminados.* We are very badly made, but we are not finished.

Edward Said
April 1999

I have talked with Edward W. Said many times over the last dozen years. I remember the first time I interviewed him in 1987. I was nervous, and my anxiety was not eased when he asked me at the outset if I had any good questions.

Said was born in Jerusalem, Palestine, in 1935 and attended schools there and in Cairo. He received his B.A. from Princeton and his M.A. and Ph.D. from Harvard. He is University Professor at Columbia and currently head of the Modern Language Association. He is the author of *Orientalism* (Routledge & Kegan Paul, 1978), *The Question of Palestine* (Institute for Palestine Studies, 1979), *Covering Islam* (Pantheon Books, 1981), *Culture and Imperialism* (Knopf, 1993), *Representations of the Intellectual* (Pantheon Books, 1994), *The Politics of Dispossession* (Pantheon Books, 1994), and *Peace and Its Discontents* (Vintage Books, 1996). His forthcoming books are *Out of Place: A Memoir* (Knopf, 1999), *Reflections on Exile* (Harvard University Press, 2000), and a work on opera. Currently, he writes a column for the Arabic newspaper *al-Hayat* in London.

"I have been unable," he writes in his memoirs, "to live an uncommitted or suspended life. I have not hesitated to declare my affiliation with an extremely unpopular cause."

The 1967 Arab-Israeli war stirred Said to political activism. A year later, his first political essay, "The Arab Portrayed," appeared. When Israeli prime minister Golda Meir infamously declared in 1969, "There are no Palestinians," Said decided to take on "the slightly preposterous challenge of disproving her, of beginning to articulate a history of loss and dispossession that had to be extricated, minute by minute, word by word, inch by inch," he writes.

For many years, he has been the main spokesman for the Palestinian cause in the United States.

"Palestine," he says, "is a thankless cause. You get nothing back but opprobrium, abuse, and ostracism. How many friends avoid the subject? How many colleagues want nothing of Palestine's controversy? How many *bien pensant* liberals have time for Bosnia and Somalia and South Africa and Nicaragua and human and civil rights everywhere on Earth, but not for Palestine and Palestinians?"

He has paid a price for his high profile on the Palestinian issue. He was vilified as "the professor of terror." The Jewish Defense League called him a Nazi. His office at Columbia was set on fire, and both he and his family "received innumerable death threats," he writes.

For more than a decade, Said was a member of the Palestine National Council, where he incurred the wrath of Arab nationalists because he advocated the "idea of coexistence between Israeli Jews and Palestinian Arabs" and because he recognized that "no military option exists," he writes. "I was also very critical of the use of slogan-clichés like 'armed struggle' that caused innocent deaths and did nothing to advance the Palestinian case politically."

Since resigning from the council in the early 1990s, Said has become one of the most public critics of Arafat and the so-called peace process. His was a rare voice of resistance amid all the euphoria when the Oslo Accords were signed on the South Lawn of the White House in September 1993. He understood instantly what Oslo meant and called it in these pages "a Palestinian Versailles."

"There was Clinton like a Roman emperor bringing two vassal kings to his imperial court and making them shake hands," he told me.

Parallel to his political activism is his enormous contribution to the humanities. With *Orientalism*, Said transformed the way we look at literary representations of Islam, Arabs, and the Middle East. He also explored the way knowledge is used to defend power. *Culture and Imperialism*, which came out in 1993, and *Orientalism* form the bookends to his great cultural work.

Somehow, in his spare time, this Renaissance man has time to play piano and write about music and opera. He loves to quote from an Aimé Césaire poem:

but the work of man is only just beginning
and it remains to man to conquer all
violence entrenched in the recesses of his passion.

And no race possesses the monopoly of beauty,
of intelligence, of force, and there
is a place for all at the rendezvous
of victory.

Poetry, incidentally, may have turned the trick for me that first time I interviewed him. As soon as I mentioned a couplet by Mahmoud Darwish, the great contemporary Palestinian poet, we began to hit it off. In the ensuing years, I did a series of interviews with Said, which resulted in *The Pen and the Sword*, a collection published by Common Courage Press in 1994.

Over the last few years, Said has been battling leukemia. I interviewed him in February, and we discussed his health, his current idea for a binational state, and his cultural collaborations with the pianist and conductor Daniel Barenboim.

80   08

In late 1998, you had occasion to speak in your mother's birthplace, Nazareth, which is now in Israel. I hear you spoke in an unlikely venue called Frank Sinatra Hall. What was that like?

Frank Sinatra was a great supporter of Israel. In the 1970s, he was prevailed upon to give money for a facility in Nazareth, which is a predominantly Arab town. It has some Jews living in it, particularly in Upper Nazareth. The idea was that this should be a kind of sports facility where young Arabs and young Jews could get together and play basketball. Over time, it evolved into a facility you could rent for the evening. Azmi Bishara, the Palestinian Israeli who is a member of the Knesset, arranged my visit. It was my first public encounter with Palestinians who are Israeli citizens.

I was asked to talk about the history of my political opinions and how I arrived at the positions I now hold. Then it was basically a free-for-all. They could ask any questions they wanted. I was very impressed. There was a kind of independent tone, an independent language, which reflected the fact that these people had had a different experience from all the other Arabs. They lived as Palestinians, as members of the Palestinian minority, within the Jewish state. So they're much more familiar with Israel than any other Arab group I've ever faced. Most of the questions were about the peace process. And, of course, everybody wants to know what's the alternative to the peace process, which is a difficult question to answer. But the main idea was to engage.

Everywhere I go, I notice a qualitative difference when it comes to generations. There's no question at all in my mind of a new courage and skepticism—an intellectual curiosity—to be found across the board in people who are at the most in their upper twenties. It's quite different from anything that I've experienced in people of my generation and the one that came right after it.

You recently wrote an article in the New York Times Magazine *calling for a binational state. Why have your views moved in this direction?*

I went to the West Bank and Gaza and Israel five times in the last year—the most since I left Palestine at the end of 1947. The more I go, the more impressed I am with the fact that Israeli Jews and Palestinians are irrevocably intertwined. The place is so small that you can't possibly completely avoid the other side.

Palestinians are employed by Israelis to build and expand West Bank and Gaza settlements. It's one of the greatest ironies of all. And the Palestinians are workers in restaurants inside Israel in places like Tel Aviv and Haifa. Of course, on the West Bank, the settlers and Palestinians interact, through antipathy and hostility, but physically they're in the same place.

This is something that can't be changed by pulling people back to separate boundaries or separate states. The involvement of each in the other—largely, I think, due to the aggressivity with which the Israelis have entered the Palestinian territory, and from the very beginning have invaded Palestinian space—suggests to me that some mode of arrangement has to be established that allows them to live together in some peaceable form.

And it's not going to be through separation. It's not going to be the way the Oslo process has forecasted, nor will it be the way I and many others used to talk about—namely partition, that there should be two states.

There is another factor which I think is very important: There is a younger generation—beginning with the Palestinians who are Israeli citizens—who are extremely aware of the difficulty that they face as an oppressed minority and are beginning to struggle in terms of civil and citizens' rights.

Interestingly, they are supported, implicitly, by secular Israelis who are extremely worried about the increased power of the clerics and the whole question of defining the laws of the state by religious means in this debate about "Who is a Jew?" A fairly important body of opinion that is secular has begun to talk about things like a constitution—since Israel doesn't have a constitution—and the notion of citizenship, which defines people not by ethnic but by national criteria. This would then have to include Arabs. That's very impressive to me. I've talked to groups from both sides, independently and together. The trajectory is unmistakable.

Then there is the demographic reality: By the year 2010, there will be demographic parity between the two, Palestinians and Israelis. The South Africans in a country twenty times bigger than Israel couldn't for long maintain apartheid. And it's unlikely that a place like Israel—which is surrounded on all sides by Arab states—is going to be able to maintain what, in effect, is a system of apartheid for Palestinians.

So although a binational state now seems like a totally long shot and completely utopian, not to say to many people a crazy idea, it is the one idea that will allow people to live with—and not exterminate—each other.

Your vision of inclusion and the one-state solution actually follows one of the old streams of Zionism.

As many Palestinians have, I've read the history of debates within the Zionist settlers' movement. There were people of a fairly important caliber, like Martin Buber, like Judah Magnes, who was the first president of Hebrew University, like Hannah Arendt, who realized that there was going to be a clash if the aggressive settlement policies and the ignoring of the Arabs pressed ahead. David Ben-Gurion actually said, "There's no case in history where a people simply gives up and allows another people to take their territory over."

So they knew that there would be a conflict, especially Magnes, who really was an idealist. He was a man way ahead of his time, and a remarkable spirit also. He said, "Let's try to think in terms quite morally and profoundly about the Arabs. Let's think in terms of their presence, not their absence."

That spirit is to be found in the work of the new Israeli historians, who have gone back over the national narrative of Israel and reexamined the myth of Israel's independence and discovered how much of it was based on the denial, or the effacement, or the willful avoidance of the Arabs. All that Israel has been able to do for the last fifty years is not, of course, to get security for itself. There is no security of that sort. But it has been maintaining a kind of holding operation by which the Arabs are simply kept out. Over time that can't work because of demographics and the fact that people don't give up if they're beaten down. They hold on even more resolutely and more stubbornly.

So there's a new climate of opinion. I think you could see it as coming out of Zionism. I don't want to appear negative or critical of it. A lot of it is an inter-Jewish debate, not something that's taking place between Palestinians and Israelis. It's taking place within—as it did in the case of Magnes and Arendt and Buber—the Zionist or Jewish camp.

People like myself, who luckily don't have to face the daily pressures of living in either Israel or Palestine, but have time to reflect at some distance, can play a role in terms of seeking out discussion and debate with their opposite numbers in the other camp. That's beginning to happen, more or less systematically. There are frequent dialogues, frequent conferences between Palestinians and Israeli intellectuals, not with an eye towards—as there have been for so many years—settling the problem in a governmental way, as an adjunct to the peace process. That's led nowhere.

This is a new kind of discussion, one that is based upon patient scholarship and scrupulous archival work. It's not carried out by people with political ambitions. It's mostly people who have a certain standing in their community as academics and intellectuals. It's quite a new phenomenon. I don't think it's been too focused on by the media, which is completely obsessed with the failing peace process.

It is clear that Yasir Arafat is not well. He shakes and looks drawn. What reports do you get on his health?

His loyal supporters—one of whom I saw last week quite by chance, we were on the same plane—say that he's in perfect health. He just has this little shake, this little tremor. Others, including a physician who lives in Gaza and has seen him, are convinced that he has Parkinson's disease. But everyone I've spoken to in the last year who's seen Arafat says he's considerably slowed down and he's not as alert or as perky as he once was. So I suppose that's true. The fact is, however, that he still is in command of everything. He signs every little piece of paper, including employees' vacation requests. Everything has to go past his desk. He's still a micromanager. He shows no sign of delegating authority in any serious way. Most of his employees bad-mouth him, including his ministers. But they're powerless to do anything.

I think it's important to note something that people may not be aware of: He is the largest single employer in the entire area. I include in that the Israeli government. His bureaucracy is now set by the World Bank at 77,000 people. That doesn't include the security apparatus, which is numbered at roughly 50,000. He employs more than 125,000 people—which, if you multiply by six or seven, roughly the number of dependents per head of household, you're talking about almost a million people. This is a very unproductive segment of the economy, but it accounts for the largest payroll. There is no serious investment in infrastructure. It's only about 3 percent. The situation is, in my opinion, getting worse every day, largely due to his methods, which are essentially to retain control and to make sure that there are no opponents or changes in the structure that is largely dictated to him by the Israelis and the US.

Your books were banned in Arafat's realm. Is that still the case?

It's very difficult to know, actually. You can buy them. They're available surreptitiously. To make matters even more ironic and peculiar, a year after the books were banned by order of the minister of information, whose name was affixed to the order, this same man sent me a letter asking me if they could enter into an arrangement with me whereby they could publish my books on the West Bank. You figure it out. I can't.

What about in Israel?

They're available.

And other Arab countries?

It depends. I haven't made a survey. They're mostly available in Egypt and Lebanon. I've heard reports that some of my books have been banned in Jordan and in various other countries of the Gulf. In Kuwait and Saudi Arabia, *Culture and Imperialism* is forbidden in Arabic. But that's the fate of everyone. We're talking about autocracies and despotisms. Somebody sees something that's offensive and they say, "We can't have this." So they ban it. Or they'll ban an issue of a newspaper or magazine. It's all very erratic.

After you visited Israel, you went to Egypt. Is there much interaction between Egyptians and Palestinians?

What you notice amongst Palestinians, whether inside Israel or on the West Bank and Gaza, is a sense of isolation. There's no question that they live under the shadow of Israeli power. What is missing is easy contact, natural contact, with the rest of the Arab world. You can't get to any place in the Arab world from Israel or the West Bank and Gaza without going through a fairly complicated procedure, which causes you to think three or four times before you do it: To cross the border, you need permits, and you go through endless customs. This is also true of me, and I have an American passport, but the fact that it says on it that I was born in Jerusalem means that I'm always put to one side. You're automatically suspect. So traveling and being in contact with Arabs in the Arab world is very, very difficult.

Hardly any Arabs who are not Palestinians come into the Palestinian territories, and hardly any at all, practically none, go to Israel. One of the themes of the nationalist and radical intellectuals of most Arab countries has been the opposition to what they call "normalization"— *tatbeea* in Arabic—the normalization of life with Israel and with the Arab states that have made formal peace with it. As an act of solidarity with Palestinians, these intellectuals have refused to have anything to do with Israel. The problem is that Palestinians—who are trying to build institutions, universities, newspapers, hospitals—are cut off from the kind of help they need from like-minded or counterpart

Arabs. Arab physicians from Egypt or Syria or Lebanon or Jordan could quite easily come and help Palestinians set up hospitals and clinics. They don't because of this stance against normalization.

The peace with Egypt and Jordan is a cold peace: Ordinary citizens, Jordanians or Egyptians, don't go to Israel, and they have nothing to do with Israelis. Israeli tourists go to Egypt and visit the pyramids. But beyond that, there's very little in the way of the kinds of intercourse—exchanges between universities, learned societies, businesses, and so on—that obtain between neighboring countries otherwise at peace in any other part of the world.

How do Arabs react when you urge them to go to Palestine?

When I now encounter Arabs and go to these Arab countries, I say to them, especially to the Egyptians, "You can go to Palestine. You can go through Israel because Israel and Egypt are at peace. You can take advantage of that and go help them, speaking, being there for some time, training them."

"No," they say, "we can't possibly allow our passports to be stamped. We won't go to the Israeli embassy and get visas. We won't submit to the humiliation of being examined by Israeli policemen at the border."

I find this argument vaguely plausible on one level but really quite cowardly on the other. It would seem to me that if they took their pride out of it, if they did go through an Israeli checkpoint or barricade or border, they would be doing what other Palestinians do every day and would see what it's like.

Second, they wouldn't be recognizing Israel or giving it any credit. On the contrary, they would be demonstrating solidarity with Palestinians. For example, as Israeli bulldozers destroy houses for settlements, it would be great if there were a large number of Egyptians and Jordanians and others who could be there with Palestinians confronting this daily, minute-by-minute threat.

Are there other reasons Arabs are not coming to Palestine?

It's not only parochialism. There is also a kind of laziness, a kind of sitting back and expecting somebody else to do it. I think that's our greatest enemy, the absence of initiative. They could be helping

Palestinians and actually dealing with Israel, not as a fictional entity but as a real power that is in many ways negatively affecting Arab life.

In no university that I know of in the Arab world is there a department of Israeli studies, nor do people study Hebrew. And this is true even of Palestinian universities—where again, you can understand it as a kind of defense against this great power that has intervened in all of our lives, that we don't want to have anything to do with it. But for me, I think the only salvation is to encounter it head-on, learn the language, as so many Israeli political scientists and sociologists and Orientalists and intelligence people spend time studying Arab society. Why shouldn't we study them? It's a way of getting to know your neighbor, your enemy, if that's what it is, and it's a way of breaking out of the prison which suits the Israelis perfectly to have Arabs in.

Alas, this passivity, this provincialism, extends not just to Israel. There is very little attention paid to India, Japan, China, to the great civilizations of the rest of the world. You go to a university like that of Amman. I can guarantee you won't find anybody studying Africa or Latin America or Japan. And it's a sign of delinquency, our weakness, our state of intellectual quiescence, that we are so uncurious about these other parts of the world. We have to break out of our self-constructed, mind-forged manacles and look at the rest of the world—deal with it as equals. There's too much defensiveness, too much sense of the aggrieved. This, in part, accounts for the absence of democracy. It's not just the despotism of the rulers, not just the plots of imperialism, not just the corrupt regimes, not just the secret police. It's our intellectuals' lack of citizenship, in the end. The only way to change a situation is oneself doing it, reading, asking, encountering, breaking out of the prison.

One of the things you stress is the need for Israelis to acknowledge what they did to your people, the Palestinians. Why is that so important?

Because so much of our history has been occluded. We are invisible people. The strength and power of the Israeli narrative is such that it depends almost entirely on a kind of heroic vision of pioneers who came to a desert and dealt not with native people who had a settled existence and lived in towns and had their own society, but rather with nomads who could be driven away. The construction of the figure of the nomad was a very complex procedure, but it was certainly used by the Zionists to deal with us as a people.

Wherever you go in Israel, the road signs are written in English and Hebrew. There's no Arabic. So if you're an Arab and you can't read Hebrew or English, you're lost. That's by design. That's a way to shut out 20 percent of the population.

The formation and education of Israeli citizens in the 1950s and the 1960s was precisely to construct this shutting out of the Palestinians. It's a very difficult thought to accept—that you are there not because you're a great, heroic figure escaping the Holocaust, but you are there largely at the expense of another person whom you've displaced or killed or driven away.

It seems to me, therefore, absolutely crucial that to achieve any kind of real normalization—where Israelis can become part of the Middle East and not an isolated sanctuary connected to the West exclusively and denying, and contemptuous of, and ignorant of the Palestinians—Israelis must be forced intellectually and morally to confront the realities of their own history.

There is a part to be played by the new Israeli historians, but I think it's also important that Palestinians do it directly to Israelis and say, "This is the reality." At this late date, we can begin to talk about Palestinian and Israeli history together—separate histories that can be seen as intertwined and counterpointed with each other. Without that, the Other is always going to be dehumanized, demonized, invisible. We must find a way.

That's where the role of the mind, the role of the intellectual, the moral consciousness is crucial. There has to be a way properly to deal with the Other and render that Other a place, as opposed to no place. So it's very far from utopian. A utopia means no place. So this is a placing of the Other in a concrete history and space.

Moshe Dayan made a famous remark in the middle 1970s. He said every Israeli town and village had a former Arab occupant. He was able to see it, and he said it. But subsequent generations—partly through the effects of the closeness of the US and the diaspora American Jewish community—have eroded the possibility of that sensibility.

I think it's important for those of us who have freed ourselves from the constraints of dogma and orthodoxy and authority to take those steps and to show those places as they really are. And it's important for Arabs to understand, too, that Israeli Jews are not like Crusaders or imperialists who can be sent back somewhere. It's very important for us also to insist, as I often do, that the Israelis are Israelis. They are citizens of a society called Israel. They're not "Jews," quite simply, who can be thought of once again as wanderers, who can go back to Europe. That vocabulary of transitory and provisional existence is one that you have to completely refuse.

Daniel Barenboim is a world-famous pianist and conductor who was born in Argentina and grew up as an Israeli. You've had some interesting interactions with him. How did you get to know him?

We met seven or eight years ago and quite surprisingly we've become very close friends. He travels a great deal, as do I. Sometimes our paths have crossed. We've tried to do things together. We've had public discussions, not political ones so much, because he's not a politician any more than I am, but we talk about things like music and culture and history. He's very interested, as a Jewish Israeli musician, in the work of people like Wagner, who is, you might say, the total negation of Jews but was a great musician. So he's interested in the process whereby culture and music work in parallel and contradictory ways at the same time. We're doing a book together based on that theme.

But he's also very dissatisfied, as am I, with the prevailing orthodoxy in his own community. He hasn't lived in Israel recently, and last year he refused to do anything with the Israeli Philharmonic for the fiftieth anniversary of Israel. He is very much opposed to the occupation of the West Bank and Gaza. He speaks openly about a Palestinian state. He's a man of courage.

Music connects us, but also the facts of biography. He arrived in Tel Aviv roughly about the time that my family was evicted from Palestine. I arranged recently for him, for the first time ever, to play a recital at the leading West Bank university, Bir Zeit, which he did. It was a great gesture on his part.

The concert was a fantastic success, one of the great events of my life. This was a humane act of solidarity and friendship. Barenboim was offering his services, which God knows in any concert hall in the world would be in tremendous demand and are very costly. He's at the very top of the musical profession as a great pianist and a conductor. But he was there simply as an individual to play.

All of that gave the evening a very high emotional cultural resonance that was lost on absolutely no one there. Zubin Mehta came, a great friend of Daniel's. He's the conductor of the Israeli Philharmonic. He's an Indian, but he's fanatically pro-Israeli. He'd never been to the West Bank. But he came. Tears were streaming down his face. It was an event of considerable importance precisely because it wasn't political in the overt sense. Nobody was trying to make a killing, score a point.

Barenboim's position is that if Israel is going to continue to exist, it has to exist in relations of friendship and equality with Arabs and Muslims. He's desperately anxious to learn Arabic. He's a very remarkable man. There aren't too many of them around.

Perhaps I should also mention that he and Yo-Yo Ma are doing something in Weimar this summer. We have this idea where we would bring gifted, mostly Arab, but some Israeli musicians between the ages of eighteen and twenty-five to Weimar for about ten days. Weimar, interestingly, is about an hour away from Buchenwald. So there's that history. Plus, of course, it's the city of Goethe and Schiller and Wagner, the summit of German culture. So the idea is to have master classes with Daniel and Yo-Yo and musicians from the Berlin State Opera, which Daniel is the conductor of, and in the evening have discussions led by me on the relationships between culture, politics, history, and especially music. We've accepted some wonderful young musicians. It promises to be quite an exhilarating experience for all of us. The good thing about it, for me, at any rate, is that there is no program. Nobody is going to sign a declaration at the end. What we are interested in is the power of music and discussion and culture to create a sense of equality and fellowship otherwise unavailable to us in the anguish and tension of the polarized life of the Middle East.

Your critique of what is called popularly the "peace process" has been unrelenting since Oslo, September 1993. For years, the mainstream media, at least in the United States, pretty much studiously ignored you. However, recently there's been a surge in terms of your visibility—articles in Newsweek *and the* New York Times, *appearances on NPR, PBS, and other venues. What accounts for that?*

It's difficult for me to tell. There's a form of censorship here in the US, which is that you're marginalized. You can't appear in the mainstream media. But my stuff is published in the Arab countries, and then it appears on the Internet. It's picked up and people read it. When I got a request to write an article for the *New York Times Magazine* about my idea of a solution, a binational state for Palestinians and Israelis, that was because an editor there had read me on the Internet. Plus, there's the fact that it was clear, he told me, that the peace process wasn't working, and neither, he said, was Zionism. For those reasons, they turn their attention.

But I don't think it's anything more than just a token kind of side look. "We want to be inclusive so we might as well include him." I think that's really what it is.

In general, the old discourse, the old clichés, the old stereotypes are absolutely in place, untouched by reality or fact. It's quite striking. I was on *Charlie Rose* on PBS, and he kept repeating the conventional wisdom and didn't let me finish my sentences. What I was saying was so outrageous that he couldn't allow it to be said.

It's been about eight years now since, during a routine check on your cholesterol, you discovered that you had leukemia. People want to know about your health. How are you feeling?

I have had bad periods of time. For the first three years, I didn't need any treatment. Suddenly, in early spring of 1994, I began treatment, first chemotherapy and later radiation. All of which led to various kinds of infections and debilitating consequences which, during 1997 and 1998, were very, very difficult for me. I was sick most of the time. I lost a lot of weight. I have a wonderful Indian doctor who is taking care of me. During the course of all of this, I discovered to my dismay that I have a very rare form of leukemia called refractory leukemia, which resists all the known chemotherapies. Last summer, I did a twelve-week experimental treatment, called a monoclonal antibody, which was incredibly difficult to go through. I was sick the whole time, for twelve weeks. I did it three or four times a week. Happily, I have what is now called a temporary remission. It's not a cure. The disease comes back, but at least it's been able to give me six months so far without major treatment and general good health. I'm feeling good about it.

As they say in Arabic, inshallah, *may you be with us for a long time to come.*

Taylor Branch
May 1998

Taylor Branch is the author of *Parting the Waters* (Simon & Schuster, 1988), winner of the Pulitzer Prize. His new book, *Pillar of Fire* (Simon & Schuster, 1998), covers the years 1963 to 1965 and is the second volume in his trilogy on the civil rights movement. *At Canaan's Edge* will be the final installment. Though he discusses other historical figures, it is to Martin Luther King, Jr. that he returns almost as a polestar. April 4 marked the thirtieth anniversary of Martin Luther King's assassination, and Branch remains fascinated with the man. Though he details King's personal foibles, he stands almost in awe of this historic figure.

Branch and his wife, Christina Macy, incidentally, are both linked to the First Family. Branch befriended Clinton in 1972 when they were both involved in the George McGovern presidential campaign in Texas. Branch helped write both Clinton inaugural addresses and has served as one of the president's advisers. Macy is a speechwriter for Hillary Rodham Clinton.

Branch is a soft-spoken man who writes clearly and breathes life into his subjects. With *Pillar*'s publication, Branch writes that he has now "emerged from almost nine years in a cave of research and writing." I caught up with him between book signings and readings in the Denver area.

※　※

You're the son of a dry cleaner who grew up in Atlanta. How did that lead you to a career as a historian?

I guess my only connection with the race issue, as an oblivious kid growing up in segregated Atlanta in the 1950s, was that most of my father's employees were black. I knew them all.

My father and his cleaner, Peter Mitchell, had a running bet on the baseball games of the Atlanta Crackers, which was the local minor-league team in Atlanta. The three of us would sometimes go to the games when I was only eight or nine. When we got to the ballpark, Peter would have to go sit in the colored section because the ballpark itself was segregated. That was the only time I remember as a child hearing my father, who used to laugh and tease and banter with Peter all day, complain about segregation and say, "This isn't right." It was very hard to figure out how to get back together at the end of the game.

He'd make those comments but he would not invite conversation from me. He wouldn't invite me to talk about it because it was like the weather. There was nothing you could do about it. He didn't want me to think that there was.

Peter died when I was about ten years old. I went to the funeral. We were the only white people in the church. I'll never forget it. They were carrying people out who were getting happy in church. I was astonished by all this. They invited my father to speak, and he broke down crying. It was the first time I ever saw him cry, at Peter's funeral. So I have indelible memories of race, but not of it as a political issue, but as a cultural divide with emotional reality on both sides. The question of why we didn't have a more equal or different social relationship when there was that much emotional intensity was never really discussed.

Were you aware of the political undercurrents in Atlanta at that time?

I wasn't aware of any of that. All I was aware of was football and girls until the civil rights movement started and I saw on television some of the demonstrators and began to say, "Wait a minute. These are people who don't think this is the weather, who don't shy away from this emotional gulf that everybody's afraid of even dealing with."

When I saw the dogs and the fire hoses loosed on elementary school children on television when I was in high school, that had a very powerful effect on me, both because I couldn't explain why it was happening, and because I could feel that what was making the kids stand up to it was very, very powerful. It was a primeval storm that I didn't understand. They were singing these freedom songs, and the dogs were attacking them, and they would keep going. These were little kids doing this in the face of not only the dogs and the fire hoses but the gigantic policemen in motorcycle boots.

So this was something very powerful and made me interested in it. A few years later in college, I dropped all my premed courses in favor of political courses to try to catch up with where this had come from. I've been doing it ever since.

Do you recall when you first became aware of King?

I never was that curious about him until 1963 and the Birmingham demonstrations. I intensely remember where I was the moment he was killed. I was in college at the University of North Carolina at Chapel Hill. I was with my mother. Lyndon Johnson had just announced he wasn't going to run. We had had a symposium at Carolina on China and the West. Jesse Helms, the local TV commentator, had called me a communist for having a symposium on China. He said we already know all we need to know about China, which is that it's communist. We had scholars from all over the world there. My mother was trying to support the fact that we were doing this.

We had just finished this incredible week that began with Johnson announcing he was going to resign. We were in a restaurant. A waiter started running through the restaurant, an all-white restaurant, saying, "Dr. King's been shot in Memphis." We aborted our meal and went out to try to find more news.

Why do you evoke biblical images as titles for your books?

The book of Exodus is the great freedom story. It's the reason why most African American churches to this day draw their names, like Ebenezer and Shiloh, from these places in the Old Testament, in the Jewish scripture, where you have the march of freedom of people out of slavery. Pillar of Fire is the incandescent period when they think they're going to go to the Promised Land. Instead, they go into the wilderness. Where I want to leave it when I finish the third book is at Canaan's edge, where Moses overlooked the Promised Land but didn't get there.

Parting the Waters concludes with a chapter entitled "Crossing Over: Nightmares and Dreams." You write, "Layers of intrigue were piling up against King within the secret chambers of the federal government." Did King know what was going on?

I think only very imperfectly. Justice Department officials—Burke Marshall and John Doar and those people—were his contacts. I don't think they knew everything that was going on inside the FBI. I know they didn't. But they did know that J. Edgar Hoover considered King and the entire civil rights movement to be a nuisance at best and an enemy threat at worst. They also knew that, politically, Bobby Kennedy and the president were very ambivalent about how far they could push their Southern constituency because they didn't believe that a Democratic president could stay in office without the support of a solid Democratic South. That was a political reality that it's hard for us to connect to today. They were constantly trying to use this issue as a way of controlling King: "Don't make more trouble. Don't have more demonstrations because Hoover says you're vulnerable."

In fact, I feel one of the most poignant moments in *Pillar of Fire* is when Bobby Kennedy said—in his own secret oral history that would not be released until his death—that he never had a conversation with Martin Luther King on any topic other than communists and what to do about them. That's terribly tragic. Here's Bobby Kennedy, a historic figure, in the middle of his growth period as to what he understands about history and race relations and peace and international affairs, saying that he's been interacting with Martin Luther King, another figure of great history, and confessing that all of his conversations were about essentially trying to control Dr. King.

Robert Kennedy seemed to be deeply conflicted. You write that there was a "Faustian undertow in Kennedy's dilemma." What was his dilemma?

Kennedy's dilemma was that he was responsible for his brother, for one thing, and his brother was always in trouble, including with women. And the same techniques that J. Edgar Hoover used to find out about Martin Luther King's affairs he had used for the president's affairs. Bobby Kennedy needed Hoover's goodwill to protect his brother in this ugly world of blackmail and politics. He also needed to protect his brother politically.

But every time he would, he was always offered the choice where you can protect yourself with Hoover and you can protect your brother with the Southerners, but to do that you have to undermine the civil rights movement. He would do it, and he would feel guilty about it and try to do something to make up. He would get somebody out of jail. He would make a gesture to Dr. King. Then it would cause him political problems.

So he was a tumbling, existential character through this period. I enjoy writing about it, but it's somewhat painful. He was open. He was not protected. He was not cool, not aloof emotionally the way his brother was. He didn't have that coldness. He would go one way and then the other.

Have you looked at the public consequences of private behavior? We see that with Bill Clinton, with JFK, with Martin Luther King.

I personally think that the way that's debated is childish right now. On one side, people say there's absolutely no connection between private life and public life. On the other hand, you have people saying that one slip in your private life can invalidate your entire public posture and what it means. Take the second one, it seems absurd, because you've had slips from people of all political persuasions, and therefore it would have invalidated every political persuasion from right to left.

King felt a certain affinity, you suggest, with JFK, not necessarily with Lyndon Johnson.

I think that he felt a kinship with Kennedy in the sense that Kennedy had charm and charisma and King had oratory. He felt that there was some sort of public-presence kinship that they had. I think he felt politically that he could deal with Johnson and didn't have this huge blister between him and Johnson early on, through the Civil Rights Bill period, that he had with Kennedy over communists.

It was a great breath of fresh air the first time King met Johnson. All they talked about was how to get this bill passed. LBJ would say, "Dr. King, I'm going to do everything I can." Johnson would actually be talking, have King in his office, a phone call would come in, and he'd put whoever called on the phone with Dr. King. He was open. He was aggressive about civil rights in a way that Kennedy never was. When King went to Kennedy's office, if somebody called, Kennedy wanted to make sure that whoever his caller was wouldn't know that Dr. King was there, whereas Johnson would put King right on the phone.

Five days after Kennedy is assassinated, Johnson announces that he's going to push through the Civil Rights Act. Less than eight months later, it's enacted and signed.

With LBJ shaking hands with Martin Luther King, who had been a partner all through that. Although in the lobbying period it is true that there were elements in the Johnson administration who were telling King, "You don't need to demonstrate anymore. It hurts us. We're going to pass this bill." King was telling them, "You're wrong. I have to have demonstrations because a lot of Americans think we don't need the Civil Rights Bill anymore." He went to St. Augustine, Florida, which he said was the most violent town he ever worked in, just to keep suffering enough to make people know that the need for the Civil Rights Bill was still there.

Johnson came in with a burst of energy on the issues themselves: "What are we going to do about segregation? I don't care about the Southern base. If I have to give it up, I'm going to do it for the Civil Rights Bill." At the beginning at least there was a tremendous liberation from the pinched worries about communism, worries about, "Am I going to lose the South?" This volume has a political King in alliance with Johnson making decisions. "How are we going to get this bill through? How can we get to the Voting Rights Act?" It's more building on the spiritual King. The potentialities of that are thrilling, and make it all the more tragic that all of that went down the tubes over Vietnam.

You write that Hoover "loathed" King. What's the evidence for that?

It runs all through, from the beginning to the end. No criticism from King was too small for it to rocket up to Hoover's attention, no matter what else he was doing running an entire FBI. Anything King did that was noble or democratic they ignored. Anything they could misconstrue as nasty they would trumpet inside the bureau as evidence that he was an opportunist, that he wanted money. There was no slander on King that was not embraced by the FBI's own internal memos.

They were constantly getting death threats against Martin Luther King. Hoover's resentment of King was such that he ordered that King never be advised when there was a threat against him. In other words, if a death threat came in against Roy Wilkins, the FBI would call up in an ingratiating but also a dutiful way and say, "Mr. Wilkins, we have a threat against your life. We're on it, and we're going to try to do what we can. We've notified the police." If a threat came in on Martin Luther King, Hoover's orders were that King was not to be notified. It was that vindictive.

Hoover is a perfect Madisonian lesson that you shouldn't leave somebody in power for fifty years, holding that kind of power, operating a secret agency that works on informants and wiretaps. It's a formula for disaster. If we understood our Constitution better, we wouldn't have done that.

But Americans worshiped J. Edgar Hoover. He was a more popular figure than FDR. It ought to be taken as a warning, first of all, that we still do have monarchist tendencies in our psyche that we've got to warn ourselves against, and second, that the FBI shouldn't be put to political uses. I still don't think we've faced that issue as far as the FBI is concerned.

You devote quite a bit of the second volume to Malcolm X and the Nation of Islam. Why did you do that?

Partly because Malcolm has become a cultural icon. He has an amazing presence around the world on par with Muhammad Ali and Martin Luther King himself. I didn't have very much about him in *Parting the Waters*.

This is the period of his incandescent ministry, when he was stalked and killed and when he really comes to public attention. So I knew that I wanted to have some Malcolm X when I started.

Then, when I began doing the research, it became clear first of all that there was an extraordinary gangland battle here that was just good journalism, even though it was not public. But secondly, it had a religious quality that I think gives it historical significance. Malcolm was killed in part for trying to establish out of the Nation of Islam,

which was a bastardized version of Islam, a legitimate and even a noble
or democratic and multiracial Islam. That was his goal. I stuck with
it because I think there's a lot of evidence that in our time Malcolm's
goal, the one he died for, has been realized. There are now somewhere
between two and three million African American Muslims who are
of the variety of Islam that he wanted. There are more Muslims in
America than Presbyterians and Episcopalians.

We don't see this phenomenon because of our preoccupation with
Louis Farrakhan, who represents about one out of every 300 Muslims
in America, a tiny and declining, irrelevant speck. He's the mouse
that makes us jump up on the chair in the kitchen and keeps us blind
to the fact that this very, very significant religious development has
taken place.

*Malcolm X was openly critical of King, denouncing him as an "Uncle
Tom" and ridiculing his commitment to nonviolence. What kind of
change occurred in their relationship?*

They never had anything like a real rapprochement. They never had
a partnership. They met only once. They sent signals back and forth
to one another. Naturally, King did not like the separatist philosophy
of the Nation, nor did he like the ridicule of nonviolence because
he saw it as a teaching tool for change. He also saw that if the black
movement became violent it might feel good for a minute but it would
lose its moral form and any potential for teaching. So it was mostly
over nonviolence. Malcolm went to Selma at the end, right before he
was killed, when King was in jail, toward the end of the book.

Nonviolence was an easy target for Malcolm. Essentially, what he
says is, "Americans are not nonviolent. Their movie heroes are Gary
Cooper. There are people who say, 'I don't want to be violent but I
will be when I have to.'" He's just saying, "That's the measure of the
distance in race relations." But if he says it in the context of America,
America jumps up and down and says he's a fanatical, violent person.

King was saying it's perfectly understandable for black people to
want to be normal, to want to be like Gary Cooper, but we have to
recognize that if we want to be teachers in America, teachers of what
America's own values ought to be, we have to use nonviolence as a

tool. We have to be willing to make that sacrifice. Malcolm resented the sacrifice.

Violence is sort of the conclusion of Pillar of Fire. *LBJ, in late February 1965, dispatches the first ground units to Vietnam, and Malcolm X is assassinated.*

And Jimmy Lee Jackson was killed in Selma. The Selma campaign had gone on for two months, and, like the Birmingham campaign against segregation two years earlier, appeared to be on the brink of failure. Because of the reaction to this murder of a young black man in a nonviolent march by state troopers, they planned to have the march from Selma to Montgomery. So violence is there.

The movement responds to the violence of Jimmy Lee Jackson with a nonviolent mass gesture that does teach and goes into history and produces the Voting Rights Act. The non-movement sources in Vietnam react to violence with more violence, which in this case leads only to tragedy. Johnson and Vietnam are running all through here. On the same day, you'll see him deal with finding the bodies of civil rights workers killed in Freedom Summer and with the Gulf of Tonkin episode. Then Bob Moses at the memorial service for one of the people killed in Freedom Summer stands up and says, "Are we fighting for the same freedom in Vietnam that James Chaney died for in Mississippi?"

The private Johnson record on Vietnam will change the history of the Vietnam War. It wasn't about the best and the brightest. Johnson knew all the criticisms of the Vietnam War. He knew that we didn't have very good prospects there. He knew that we didn't have much support.

But he could not bear to walk away from the war because he feared that he'd be run out of office and, possibly worse, called "chicken." He couldn't stand that. He says as much in these meetings that have been declassified and in some of the phone conversations.

The popular Dr. King is frozen in time at the Lincoln Memorial in Washington, DC, in August 1963 with "I have a dream." I would like to suggest that his speech at Riverside Cathedral in New York on April 4, 1967, was truly a remarkable transformation.

Exactly one year before he was killed. He was killed a year later, April 4, 1968. Naturally, it was not the first speech he ever made against Vietnam. In fact, he made speeches as early as February 1965 on Vietnam. But he backed off and said that he made a mistake.

The speech at Riverside was the first public one in which he announced that the future of his ministry would be to oppose the Vietnam War, regardless of the consequences to the civil rights movement because, he said, a prophet cannot choose his causes. That's what he said privately.

There was tremendous opposition within the movement and even more ferocious opposition in the media, from the *New York Times* and the *Washington Post.* They blistered him for this. But he said, essentially, in one of the famous lines, "My own country I lament is the greatest purveyor of violence in the world today." That speech was a watershed for him that he knew would unite his racial opponents with his patriotic war opponents into a hatred of him that I'm afraid culminated in his assassination.

It triggered an immediate national response. It was like a whole political organism felt invaded by a bacillus and mobilized against it. Roy Wilkins denounced him. The movement people denounced him. The national media denounced him. And unfortunately, Hoover said, "See? What I've always been telling you is this guy's no good. We've got to get rid of him." It mobilized the FBI and the federal government. Johnson, who had a paranoid side, was manic. He loved Dr. King or he hated him. Because he was in such torment on the Vietnam War, he wanted to believe that there had to be some sort of nefarious, scapegoat, communist explanation behind why Dr. King would do that. So Johnson turned on him, too, So he was a very, very lonely figure for the last year of his life.

There's also a sense of the promises of the Great Society, the War on
Poverty being sacrificed at the altar of Vietnam. King called it a "cruel
hoax." Then he denounced the giant triplets of racism, materialism, and
militarism.

He did that also in his Nobel Peace Prize speech, which, unfortunately, was not taken very seriously. People just thought that it was great that he got the Nobel Prize. King was not taken seriously in his lifetime very much as a thinker. Intellectuals tended to patronize him as somebody who read the "turn the other cheek" part of the Bible and was a Baptist minister who got carried away with it and produced a nonviolent movement. But he was saying things that were prophetic all through his career. That's one reason why I respect him, and the depth of his experience, much more now than I did when I started fifteen years ago.

The longer I study King the more I think you can see in his own sermons that he's almost pushing himself. He knows that he's not as good privately as people think he is. He says so and he says, almost, "We need to redeem ourselves in public for our failures. I may not be perfect as a man or at home, but I know that this country has problems to right, and if I have to give my life to do that, I will." You see almost a furnace there, an engine, doing penance.

Eqbal Ahmad
November 1998

Eqbal Ahmad, activist scholar, was born in India probably in 1934. He is not quite sure. In 1947, he left with his brothers for the newly created state of Pakistan. He came to the United States to study at Princeton in the 1950s. He then went to Algeria. He worked there with Frantz Fanon during the revolt against the French. He was active in the civil rights movement in the United States and the anti–Vietnam War movement. In 1971, he was prosecuted—along with the Berrigan brothers and several others—on the trumped-up charge of trying to kidnap Henry Kissinger. The case was dismissed.

Ahmad has long been active on the issue of Palestinian sovereignty. This work brought him into a close friendship with Edward Said, who dedicated *Culture and Imperialism* to him. It also brought him to the attention of Yasir Arafat, who met him several times but never took his advice, Ahmad says.

In the 1960s, Ahmad taught at Princeton, the University of Illinois, and Cornell. After making a speech to a group of students about the Six Day War between Israel and the Arab states in 1967, in which he argued that the conflict was more complicated than the media were portraying it, he found himself ostracized in the academy. "A large majority of the faculty at Cornell took great exception to that talk," he told me. "For the next year, I found myself increasingly so isolated that sometimes I would sit at the lunch table and large numbers of people would be lining up for a table and nobody would sit at mine."

Ahmad left Cornell, did some freelance work, and helped found the Transnational Institute in Amsterdam, which is affiliated with the Institute for Policy Studies in Washington, DC. From 1982 to 1997, he taught a semester each year at Hampshire

College in Amherst, Massachusetts, and he still returns there as professor emeritus.

But now he spends most of his time in Islamabad, Pakistan, where he is trying to establish an alternative university. He also writes a weekly column for *Dawn*, Pakistan's oldest English newspaper. His work in Pakistan consists chiefly of trying to bridge differences with India on the issues of Kashmir and nuclear weapons. Both countries tested nuclear weapons in May, and in September the prime ministers of both countries announced their willingness to sign the Comprehensive Test Ban Treaty.

The first time I ever interviewed Ahmad was in the early 1980s in his apartment on New York's Upper West Side. It was memorable. On my way home, I thought, "Wow, I've got a great interview!" But when I sat down to listen to it, the tape was blank. I had failed to turn the machine on. With considerable embarrassment, I explained to Ahmad what had happened. He invited me over the next day, and we did another interview, and that time, I pressed the right button.

The current interview is the product of two marathon sessions in his small apartment in Amherst. The last session began in the afternoon and ended with an Urdu poem at two o'clock in the morning. It was punctuated by a couple of wonderfully spicy meals and a hike around nearby Mount Holyoke.

        ℘ ℛ

How did you react when Pakistan tested its own nuclear weapons shortly after India?

As a Pakistani citizen, I should say that the testing was a mistake. It was not necessary. We should begin by recognizing that Pakistani and Indian rulers are caught in medieval, militaristic minds. They are no more modern than the Clintons and the Bushes, who see power in terms of military prowess. We are living in modern times and are dominated by medieval minds.

Do you think Pakistan had a choice?

Of course it had a choice. Just because India had done it and Indian leaders had made provocative statements does not mean that one should be provoked. I don't believe in nuclear weapons. I believe in unilaterally not having to compete with India in the nuclear arms race.

What do you make of the claim by a reporter in the New York Times *that Pakistan had fulfilled a long-held plan to build "an Islamic bomb"?*

The reporter is talking about Zulfikar Ali Bhutto [Pakistan's prime minister in the early 1970s], who never said an "Islamic bomb." This is a misquotation that began somewhere about fifteen or twenty years ago. It has continued to spread. What Bhutto reportedly did say is that everybody has a bomb. The Jewish people have a bomb. The Christian powers have a bomb. Now India, seeing itself as a Hindu power, is developing a bomb. Why shouldn't Muslims also develop their own bomb? He came close to talking about an Islamic bomb, but that's not exactly the phrase that he used.

I doubt that the Pakistani bomb is Islamic. Among other things, it hasn't been circumcised.

This bomb has to do with Pakistan, and not with Islam. It has to do with Pakistan's fears and competition with India, and not with anything else. If India had not tested its bomb in 1974, Pakistan probably would never have started work on its. I think these are all childish acts, not acts of national security.

What triggered India's decision to set off underground nuclear explosions last May?

The only way you can explain India's decision to test its nuclear weapons is the particular brand of nationalism that the BJP [Bharatiya Janata Party], the Hindu nationalists, represent. They tested to become equals of the other nuclear powers. They tested in the expectation of joining this silly abstraction called the "nuclear club." What the privileges are of its membership are not clear to me or to anyone else. India, rationally speaking, should not have done this testing. But it did so.

Why do you say it was irrational?

Here's why: After more than thirty years of failure to improve relations with China following the India-China war of 1962, India's relations with China were improving rapidly. This was the greatest single achievement of Indian foreign policy in the last ten years. In a single day, the BJP leadership destroyed this achievement and turned China once again into an adversary. India cannot afford an arms race with China. It will be disastrous for India, just as Pakistan cannot afford an arms race with India.

Secondly, this testing has brought India's projected rate of economic growth down from 7 percent to 4 percent. What India needs most at the moment is to feed its poor—400 million people are living below the poverty level. Why did they hurt themselves?

Thirdly, India has ambitions to be a regional power. One basic principle for a regional power is that it should have better relations with its neighbors. By exploding this bomb, India has increased tension in this region and frightened its neighbors. If there is a nuclear war in South Asia, Indians and Pakistanis will not be the only ones to die. South Asia is an ecological unit. A bomb would hit everybody because the wind blows every which way, and the distances are short.

You, personally, saw the beginnings of the tensions between Pakistan and India when you were young. How did that affect you?

Witnessing the partition of India had a very lasting impact on me because what I saw then was the ease with which humanity, perfectly good humanity, can descend into barbarism. I saw the extent to which ideas, ideology, political affiliations change human behavior.

And what about the murder of your father?

That played an important role because in addition to leaving a very deep scar on me as a child, it made me unconsciously absorb certain conclusions about life. One is that property is more dear to people than friendship or blood ties. Some relatives of my father were involved in his murder because they felt their property rights were being threatened by his politics.

Was he involved in the Gandhian movement?

Yes, he was involved with the Indian National Congress, and he was giving away some of his land to the poor.

Were you with him when he was killed?

We were sleeping in the same bed. He tried to protect me and obviously succeeded. I'm still sitting here.

When you look back at Gandhi and the movement to free India from colonial rule, was there any way to prevent the partition of India into two countries and the bloodbath that followed?

I think so. When two communities have actually coexisted with each other for 700 years, it is impossible not to find ways out of separation. I just don't understand why the leadership of India—both Muslim and Hindu, including Gandhi—failed to ensure that its two communities, one Hindu and the other Muslim, could continue to live side by side. There were tensions in this relationship, as there are tensions in, frankly, all relationships. But by and large, these two peoples had lived collaboratively with each other. A civilization had grown; a new language, Urdu, had emerged; new art, architecture, music, and poetry also developed.

Partition could have been avoided, but it could not have been avoided unless Indian anti-imperialist movements also understood the necessity of avoiding the ideology of nationalism. Nationalism is an ideology of difference, and Gandhi is at least as responsible for contributing to the division of India as anyone, if not more. Lest Gandhi is understood as sort of a Hindu communalist—which is the Pakistani nationalist line against him, a line I do not share—I should say that he was, above all, an anti-imperialist opportunist. It is that streak of opportunism in Gandhi that led him to pursue a politics that spiritualized and sectarianized the politics of India. Gandhi began to take on Hindu symbols because they were the symbols of the majority people. They had the most capacity, the most power as mobilizing symbols. In the process, the Muslim community got very frightened that its own cultural traditions were being shunted aside. Gandhi would do anything within the framework of his nonviolent philosophy that would mobilize the masses.

What about Britain's role?

World War II exhausted Britain's imperial will. When the war was over, Britain halfheartedly engaged in a holding pattern and then kind of suddenly gave up. The British were careful only to not renounce their energy holdings. They doggedly controlled the areas where energy resources were concentrated—in World Wars I and II, they had come to a rather deep, respectful realization of the importance of oil. They cared about places like India much less. They seemed to care about two things: oil and English people. Wherever there was a large English colony, such as Kenya, they hung on to it. Where there was oil, they hung on to it. The rest of it—they were almost irresponsible.

I was a child of about twelve. I have this vivid memory of my brothers, all nationalists, talking in 1946 about the worst that can happen would be the British pulling out prematurely. They did not even have the staying power to ensure an orderly withdrawal. I think what we witnessed in 1947 in India and then again in 1948 in Pakistan were hurried, unthought-out, irresponsible, and, frankly, cowardly withdrawals.

There are some who say Pakistan today is being recolonized by the forces of globalization: the multinational corporations, the International Monetary Fund, and the World Bank. Do you agree?

I have one difficulty with the argument. We are always reinventing the wheel in which we have been caught for a long, long time. We never really went through the process of decolonization. The British ruled India with the help of three institutions: the army, the bureaucracy, and the feudal landlords. The army and the bureaucracy had top commanders who were English. Top civil servants were often English. And just below them there was a large number of Indians serving them. Our economy was tied to the Western economy. We produced to supply Britain. We bought our consumer goods mostly from Europe.

Now take a look at Pakistan for the last fifty years. It's exactly that situation. A British-trained army, a British-trained bureaucracy, and the same feudal landlords. We buy almost all our armaments from America. We produce very little on our own. Most of our big products come from industrialized countries. Previously it was only Britain.

Now it is mostly America, plus Japan and Germany. Globalization is only the increase in the number of buyers and sellers in our countries. Nothing else has changed. The economic and political realities have not changed. Pakistan never became a decolonized country. Never.

You were in Pakistan when the United States bombed Afghanistan and the Sudan. What did it look like to you?

The United States is a superpower that claims to be judge, accuser, and executioner. You don't allow that in your system. We don't allow it in our system. But we are allowing it on a world scale. Why didn't the United States go to international forums and present the evidence that it had against bin Laden before bombing Afghanistan and the factory in Khartoum? There is increasing evidence now that the factory was not producing any chemical weapons. The camp they hit in Afghanistan I visited in 1986. It was a CIA-sponsored camp. The United States spent $8 billion in producing the bin Ladens of our time.

What do you mean by that?

He was socialized by the CIA and trained by the Americans to believe deeply that when a foreigner comes into your land, you become violent. Bin Laden is merely carrying out the mission to which he committed with America earlier. Now he is carrying it out against America because now America, from his point of view, is occupying his land. That's all. He grew up seeing Saudi Arabia being robbed by Western corporations and Western powers. He watched these Saudi princes, this one-family state, handing over the oil resources of the Arab people to the West. Up until 1991, he had only one satisfaction: that his country was not occupied. There were no American or French or British troops in Saudi Arabia. Then even that small pleasure was taken away from him during the Gulf War and its aftermath.

What is the background of the CIA role in Afghanistan?

After the Soviet Union intervened in Afghanistan, an Islamic fundamentalist dictator in Pakistan, Zia ul-Haq, promoted, with the help of the CIA, the mujahideen resistance. Now what you had was Islamic fundamentalists of a really hard-core variety taking on the Evil Empire. They received $8 billion in arms from the US alone. Add another $2 billion from Saudi Arabia under American encouragement. And, more than that, American operatives went about the Muslim world recruiting for the jihad in Afghanistan. This whole phenomenon of jihad as an international armed struggle did not exist in the Muslim world since the tenth century. It was brought back into being, enlivened, and pan-Islamized by the American effort. The United States saw in the war in Afghanistan an opportunity to mobilize the Muslim world against communism. So the United States recruited mujahideen from all over the Muslim world. I saw planeloads of them arriving—from Algeria, the Sudan, Saudi Arabia, Egypt, Jordan, and Palestine. These people were brought in, given an ideology, told that the armed struggle is a virtuous thing to do, and the whole notion of jihad as an international, pan-Islamic terrorist movement was born.

They were trained and armed by the CIA. The militants of the Islamic movement almost everywhere have all been trained in Afghanistan. The CIA people now call it "Islamic blowback."

Why do you think the West is so ready to treat Islam as the enemy?

After the cold war, the West had no viable threat around which it could organize its policies. All powers, all imperial powers—especially democratic ones—cannot justify their uses of power only on the basis of greed. No one will buy it. They have needed two things: a ghost and a mission. The British carried the white man's burden. That was the mission. The French carried *la mission civilisatrice*, the civilizing mission. The Americans had, first, manifest destiny, and then found the mission of "standing watch on the walls of world freedom," in John F. Kennedy's ringing phrase. Each of them had the black, the yellow, and finally the red peril to fight against. There was a ghost. There was a mission. People bought it.

Right now, the United States is deprived of both the mission and the ghost. So the mission has appeared as human rights. It's a very strange mission for a country that for nearly one hundred years has been supporting dictatorship, first in Latin America and then throughout the world. And in search of menace, it has turned to Islam. It's the easiest because the West has encountered resistance here: Algeria, then Egypt, Palestinians, the Iranian revolution. And a portion of it is strategically located: It's the home of the oil resources for the West.

What is your view of the Taliban of Afghanistan?

The Taliban is as retrograde a group as it is possible to find. Last year, I spent two weeks in Afghanistan. One day, I heard drums and noises from the house where I was staying. I rushed out to see what was going on. There was a young boy who couldn't have been more than twelve years of age. His head was shaved. There was a rope around his neck. He was being pulled by that rope. There was one man behind him with a drum. He slowly beat the drum.

I asked, "What has the boy done?"

People told me he was caught red-handed.

"Doing what?" I asked.

"He was caught red-handed playing with a tennis ball."

I went off to interview one of the Taliban leaders. He said, "We have forbidden boys to play with balls because it constitutes undue temptation to men." So the same logic that makes them lock up women behind veils and behind walls makes them prevent boys from playing games. It's that kind of madness.

These people are anti-women, anti-music, anti-life, and some of the highest officials of the United States have been visiting them and talking to them. The general impression in our region is that the US has been supporting them.

Why would the United States do that?

When the Soviet Union fell apart, its constituent republics became independent. The Central Asian republics, whose majority population is Muslim, happen to be oil-rich, gas-rich states. Their gas and oil used to pass through the Soviet Union. Now a new game starts: How is this oil and gas going to get out to the world?

At this point, American corporations move in. Texaco, Amoco, Unocal, Delta Oil—all of these are now going into Central Asia to get hold of these oil and gas fields. They don't want to take any pipelines to Iran because Iran is, at this moment, boycotted. It's an enemy of America. So Afghanistan and Pakistan become the places through which you lay pipelines. And you cut the Russians out. Just look at the story here: President Clinton makes personal telephone calls to the presidents of Uzbekistan, Kazakhstan, Tajikistan, and Azerbaijan, urging them to sign pipeline contracts. And the pipeline has to go through Afghanistan. In this game, both Pakistan and the US get into the business of saying who will be the most reliable conduit to ensure the safety of the pipelines. And they pick the most murderous, by far the most crazy, of Islamic fundamentalist groups, the Taliban, to ensure the safety of the pipelines.

In this situation, the US concern is not who is fundamentalist and who is progressive, who treats women nicely and who treats them badly. The issue is, who is more likely to ensure the safety of the oil and gas resources.

What's behind the rise of fundamentalism not just in the Islamic world but also in the United States, Israel, Sri Lanka? What gives power to these movements?

There are a number of factors. The first is the fear of—and reaction to—homogenization. Globalization of the economy, the shrinking of spaces through modern technology, the power of the media in creating common tastes, everybody eating McDonald's hamburgers or wearing jeans—all this has made a whole lot of people uncomfortable with what is receding from their own way of life. That discomfort is used by right-wing ideologues to say, "Come to us. We will return you your old-time religion. Come to us. We will give you back your old ways, your old memories." And people who don't know any better often follow.

There is a second factor, and that is a disappointment with modernism, a sense of disillusionment with life as it is constructed in our time. It seems empty, void of meaning. It feels like families are breaking up but there is no substitute for the proximities, the comfort, the security of family life. These are changes that occur from technology and from the expansion of the tentacles of capitalism into every aspect of human life. In many ways, advertisers are deciding the color of underwear that we wear, the kind of sexual advances that we make to our wives and lovers. Once that starts happening, people feel a loss of individual autonomy. In search of autonomy, we look for some specific, unique way of relating to ourselves. Fundamentalism offers that. Old-time religion offers that. New-time religion also offers that.

The media critique of fundamentalism seems to be very selective in its targets. What about Saudi Arabia?

This is a very interesting matter you are raising. Saudi Arabia's Islamic government has been by far the most fundamentalist in the history of Islam until the Taliban came along. Even today, for example, women drive in Iran. They can't drive in Saudi Arabia. Today, men and women are working in offices together in Iran. In Saudi Arabia, they cannot do that. Saudi Arabia is much worse than Iran, but it has been the ally of the US since 1932, and nobody has questioned it. But much more than that is involved. Throughout the cold war, starting in 1945, the US saw militant Islam as a counterweight to communist parties of the Muslim world.

You mentioned the Iranian revolution. Is there a parallel between Iran in the 1970s, which looked like an impregnable US fortress, and Saudi Arabia in the 1990s?

I think it was 1981 or 1982 that a fairly senior CIA official who had either retired already or was on the brink of retiring wrote a very interesting article in the *Armed Forces Journal*. The article was entitled "The American Threat to Saudi Arabia." His argument primarily was that the policies that the US government and corporations were pursuing out of greed were going to turn Saudi Arabia into a model of Iran, a totally dependent state and extremely vulnerable to revolution.

Osama bin Laden is a sign of things to come. The US has no reason to stay in Saudi Arabia except exploitation and greed. Saudi Arabia is not threatened with invasion by anyone that we know of. Any potential aggressor, such as Saddam Hussein, has already been knocked out from any capability of invading Saudi Arabia. And the Americans demonstrated in 1991 that they are capable of mobilizing against any attack on an ally in the Middle East. So what's the justification of an American military presence, an intelligence presence, a massive presence in every other area in Saudi Arabia?

Every ministry is infiltrated with American advisers. It's creating deep discontent there.

The answer is money. Money in ten different ways. The Saudis' oil is essentially controlled and marketed by American interests. Saudi wealth is invested in the US and Europe. And the Saudis, since the early 1980s, went into the arms market, so the US dumped something like $100 billion worth of armaments in that place.

The Saudi people are going to be discontented. But Saudi discontent shouldn't be seen only as Saudi. Unlike Iran, Saudi Arabia is an Arab country, part of an Arab world. The Saudis are the guardians of our Muslim holy places, and they have been unable to guard them. The Arabs are, at the moment, an extremely humiliated, frustrated, beaten, and insulted people. If you look at the situation from the standpoint of the Arab as a whole, this is a most beleaguered mass of 200 million people. What is actually uniting them at the moment is a sense of common loss, common humiliation.

This people has only two choices now, as its young people see it: It's either to become active, fight, die, and recover its lost dignity, lost sovereignties, lost lands, or to become slaves. Terrorism is not without a history. All social phenomena have historical roots, and nobody here is looking into the historical roots of terror.

What do you think is the future of Israel?

In the short run, seemingly bright and powerful. In the long run, very dark. Israel is losing its chance to make peace with its Arab neighbors. For decades, Israeli officials talked about wanting to be recognized. Now every Arab government, plus the PLO, recognizes Israel's right to exist. But the Israelis are continuing to take Palestinian lands, set up settlements, and occupy Lebanon and Syria. Their policies are convincing the Arabs that no matter what they are willing to give, Israelis want peace on their terms, and their terms are more territory and more humiliation of Arabs. It can't last that way. Israel is a small country, 5.5 million people. The Arabs are many. They are, at the moment, weak, disorganized, and demoralized. Their leaders are a bunch of country sellers. It's not a permanent condition. Someday, the Arabs will organize themselves. Once they do that, you will see the beginning of a different history, and it won't be pretty. In fact, I'm scared of it.

What do you make of the PLO and Yasir Arafat these days?

They are thugs collaborating with Israel. Right now, in the moment of greatest thuggery, the Western media is saying nothing about them. They have suddenly become good guys.

The BBC did a documentary about your return to India, and there's a wonderful poem that you inject by Faiz Ahmed Faiz. What was your idea for putting that in?

I know of no third world poet other than Faiz who was so prescient in catching the mood of disillusionment in postcolonial states. He wrote this poem about six months after India and Pakistan were independent:

> These tarnished rays, this night-smudged light
> This is not that dawn for which,
> ravished with freedom,
> we had set out in sheer longing for
> so sure that somewhere in its desert
> the sky harbored a final haven for the stars
> and we would find it…
> Did the morning breeze ever come?
> Where has it gone?
> Night weighs us down.
> It still weighs us down.
> Friends, come away from this false light.
> Come, we must search for that promised dawn.
> [As translated by Agha Shahid Ali]

You've traveled an extraordinarily long distance literally in terms of miles, as well as intellectually. What are your thoughts on your journey?

What were my choices? Essentially, I had two choices. I could have lived a very comfortable, boring, selfish, quiet existence as a regular academic or a corporate executive. Instead, I chose to live a life that has been very rich spiritually and intellectually and rather poor materially. But look, I have friends from Calcutta to Casablanca, from Algiers to San Francisco, and students, of course. I have the simple satisfaction of knowing that we have tried—did the best we could, didn't always succeed, but tried—to change where change seemed necessary.

Vandana Shiva
September 1997

Vandana Shiva is a burst of creative energy and intellectual power. Born in India in 1952, she is one of the third world's most eloquent and passionate voices on the environment, women's rights, and sustainable development. She directs the Research Foundation for Science, Technology, and Ecology in New Delhi. In 1993 she received the Right Livelihood Award, also known as the alternative Nobel Prize.

A trained physicist, she did her Ph.D. on the foundations of quantum theory. She gave up her academic career to be an activist. Solving social problems "is as challenging as solving an elementary-particle physics equation," she told me. "And it's more fulfilling. It's more satisfying. I'll do physics again when I'm sixty years old and can't run around like I do."

Shiva has supported grassroots organizations in India and around the world in their struggles against clear-cutting of forests, large-scale dams, the industrialization of aquaculture, and the invasion of multinational agribusiness. One of the first organizations she was involved with was the Chipko movement, a group of women who were defending their forests with acts of civil disobedience. Her recent work in India has focused on the protection of farmers' rights to their own seed stock.

She is a determined foe of globalization, which she sees as the latest phase of the North's ongoing quest to subjugate the South.

Shiva is a contributing editor to *Third World Resurgence*, a leading journal of opinion from Malaysia. Among her many books are *Staying Alive* (Zed Books, 1988) and *Monocultures of the Mind* (Zed Books, 1993). Her new book, published by South End Press, is *Biopiracy: The Plunder of Nature and Knowledge* (1997). I talked with her first in Boulder in April and then again in

Denver in June during the Other Economic Summit, where she was a featured speaker.

ꙅꙩ   ꙭ

How did you become an activist?

My personal background is actually very unusual for the kind of career I chose. I didn't meet anyone who had ever done physics in my life. I grew up in the Himalayan forests. My father was a forest conservator, which meant that if I wasn't in school I was in the forests with him. That has been very largely responsible for my ecological inclinations.

One particular spark was when I went back to my favorite spot in the mountains where my father always used to take us before my graduate studies in Canada and finding that the stream I had gone swimming in wasn't there. The forest had been converted into an apple orchard with World Bank financing. The entire place, literally, had changed.

A second trigger for me was when I did a study on social forestry. It turned out that the World Bank was basically financing the conversion of food-growing land to timber-growing, pulp-growing land with huge subsidies. That study created a whole movement. The peasants and farmers reacted. They started to uproot eucalyptus. It created a major discussion of industrial forestry, and it was the first major challenge to a World Bank project in India. This was way back in 1981.

The director of the institute where I was working apologized about these young, enthusiastic researchers when the World Bank visited because he was afraid the institute would lose the World Bank consultancies. That's the day I decided that I had to follow my mind and heart. I couldn't be working for the bosses who were apologizing for the fact that I was following my conscience.

I went back home and started the Research Foundation for Science, Technology, and Ecology—an extremely elaborate name for the tiny institute that I started in my mother's cowshed. My parents handed over family resources and said, "Put them to public purpose." That's how I survived.

How did you get involved with the Chipko movement?

The Chipko activists have always been close to my parents, since my father was among the few forestry officials who supported them within the bureaucracy. And I was involved with the Chipko movement in my student days. It started up in the Alakananda Valley, in the Himalayan foothills. The women were protesting against logging, which was destroying their fuel and fodder base, and making their springs disappear. They were walking longer distances to collect water. It was creating a very direct threat to their lives because landslides were occurring and floods were increasing. In the 1970s these women would go out in the hundreds and thousands and say, "You will have to chop us up before you chop this tree." These actions spread village to village.

In 1978 we had a huge flood. An entire mountain slipped into the Ganges River, formed a four-mile-long lake, and when that lake burst, we had a flood in the Gangetic basin all the way down to Calcutta, where homes were under one or two feet of water. It became quite clear that these were not illiterate village women just acting out of stupidity—which is what it was made to look like in the early days. Delhi, the central government, realized that what the women were saying had something to it. We got a logging ban in the mountains as a result of that.

You write that the Chipko movement flew in the face of the traditional paradigm of a charismatic leader.

Absolutely. It was ordinary women who created this ingenious strategy and said, "We'll block the logging by embracing the trees." And the message spread from village to village, literally by word of mouth. There was no organized external leadership doing this. People like me came in to support the movement long after it had been given its articulation by the women.

A particular incident stands out very clearly in my mind. The government realized that the women were getting too strong. Their slogan was, "Why all these profits to these contractors and timber merchants?" The officials thought what they would do was put in place logging cooperatives made of local men. Then the government would get the revenue. They said, "We'll cooperatize this sector. We'll make it into a state sector. We won't have private contractors." They sent out the logging teams. In a particular village the logging unit was being headed by the chief of the village, and the protest against logging was headed by his wife, Bachni Devi. It was a tremendous conflict. The women were saying, "To us, it's the destruction of our forests. It doesn't matter who holds the axe. We want these trees to live."

You wrote a book in the late 1980s with the German sociologist Maria Mies called Ecofeminism. *Do you still use that term?*

Ecofeminism is a good term for distinguishing a feminism that is ecological from the kind of feminisms that have become extremely technocratic. I would even call them very patriarchal.

I saw some women had written that the cloning of Dolly was wonderful since it showed that women could have children without men. They didn't even understand that this was the ultimate ownership of women—of embryos, of eggs, of bodies—by a few men with capital and control techniques, that it wasn't freedom from men but total control by men.

One of the things you talk about is stri shakti, *women's power. What's that about?*

It's about the power that women of Chipko have. It's the power the women of the Narmada Valley have when they stand there and say, "Narmada is our *mata* [mother]. We will not let you either dam her or displace us." It's the *shakti* in the women who are blocking the industrial shrimp farms on the coasts of India. That amazing power of being able to stand with total courage in the face of total power and not be afraid. That is *stri shakti.*

Tell me about your mother.

My mother was a tremendous woman. I was just cleaning up old trunks and I found a book with her notes written during the war years, in the 1940s. She was studying in Lahore, which became Pakistan. She was writing about how women alone could bring peace to the world, that the men with all their greed and egos were creating all these tensions and violence. I always knew she was a feminist, ahead of her time. She brought us up that way, to the extent that we never felt that we had to hold ourselves back because we were girls. She didn't put pressure on us because she had spent her life removing that pressure from herself. In her day she was highly educated. She was among the few women in her community who became a graduate. She was an inspector of schools in the education department.

When partition took place in 1947, she came to India and decided to leave a highly privileged career and become a farmer. She spent some time doing politics on the side to build a new India. By the 1960s she had reached saturation with politics and did a lot of writing on spirituality in nature. She has always been a major influence for me in never feeling second-rate because you're born a woman, never feeling afraid of any circumstance in life. I never saw her afraid, and yet, with all that, she was so deeply compassionate. She taught that if anyone needs you, you should be available to them.

You often invoke Mahatma Gandhi. Why is he so important to you?

I have a deep connection with him, partly because my mother was a very, very staunch Gandhian and brought us up that way. When I was six years old, and all the girls were getting nylon dresses, I was very keen to get a nylon frock for my birthday. My mother said, "I can get it for you, but would you rather—through how you live, and what you wear, and what you eat—ensure that food goes into the hands of the weaver or ensure that profits go into the bank of an industrialist?" That became such a touchstone for everything in life. We used to always wear *khadi* [handspun or handwoven cloth] as children. The fact that I still find so much beauty in a handicraft is because my mother taught us to see not just the craft as a product but the craft as an embodiment of human creativity and human labor.

My links with Gandhi now are very political links because I do not believe there is any other politics available to us in the late twentieth century, a period of a totalitarianism linked with the market. There is really no other way you can do politics and create freedom for people without the kinds of instruments he revived. Civil disobedience is a way to create permanent democracy, perennial democracy, a direct democracy.

And Gandhi's idea of *swadeshi*—that local societies should put their own resources and capacities to use to meet their needs as a basic element of freedom—is becoming increasingly relevant. We cannot afford to forget that we need self-rule, especially in this world of globalization.

You write a lot about biodiversity. What do you mean by that?

It's basically the diversity of all life forms around us: the plants, the animals, the microorganisms, both the cultivated and the wild. We have a very old conservation movement, particularly in the United States, which has focused on campaigns to protect endangered species: the spotted owl, the old-growth forest. But usually it stops there. To me, biodiversity is the full spectrum. Species conservation is not only about wilderness conservation. It's also about protecting the livelihood of people even while changing the dominant relationship that humans have had with other species. In India, it's an economic issue, not just an ecological one.

How is globalization affecting India?

American firms are beginning to reproduce non-sustainable systems, to force the elite of India to become energy consumers of the kind that the US has become. That's what globalization is about: Find markets where you can. If China has markets, rush there. If India is an emerging economy with millions of new consumers, sell them the Volvo. Sell them the Cielo car. Sell them whatever you can, hamburgers and KFCs. It's the middle classes who have moved into being able to own a car, a refrigerator. For them there is this mantra that the General Electric refrigerator is better than some other model, that the Cielo car is fancier than our own Ambassador.

Because of these new car models there is suddenly on the streets of Delhi a new intolerance by the motorists for both the cows and the cyclists. So for the first time, the sacred cow in India, which used to be such a wonderful speed breaker, is now seen as a nuisance. For the first time, I've seen cows being hit and hurt. These guys just go right past, and if the cow is sitting on the road, they don't care. We can't afford to have a sacred car rather than a sacred cow.

The other thing they're working very hard at doing is to try and make cyclists—including all the people who do servicing and sell vegetables on every street—declared illegal because they're getting in the way of the fast cars. It means robbing the livelihood of millions of people who are more ecological, who are helping save the climate for all of us. I hope that in the next two months I'll be able to work with some of these cyclists and vendors who are being made illegal on the streets of Delhi.

The United States, with some 3 percent of the world's population, consumes about 25 percent of its resources. Why is no one talking about restructuring the economic system, the patterns of consumption?

Amory Lovins has said that the only reason Americans look efficient is that each has 300 energy slaves. Those 300 energy slaves will now be reproduced among the elite of India.

The poorest of families, the poorest of children, are subsidizing the growth of the largest agribusinesses in the world. I think it's time we recognized that in free trade the poor farmer, the small farmer, is ending up having to pay royalties to the Monsantos of the world. It's not that Monsanto is making money out of the blue. It's making money by coercing and literally forcing people to pay for what was free. Take water, for instance. Water has always been free. We've never paid for drinking water. The World Bank says the reason water has been misused is because it was never commercially priced. But the reason it's been misused is because it was wasted by the big users—industry, which polluted it.

Today you have a situation where now the prescription is: People who don't have enough money to buy food should end up paying for their drinking water. That is going to be the kind of situation in which you will get more child labor. You will get more exploitation of women. You're going to get an absolutely exploitative economy as the very basis of living becomes a source of capital accumulation and corporate growth. In fact, the chief of Coca-Cola in India said: "Our biggest market in India comes from the fact that there is no drinking water left. People will have to buy Coca-Cola." Something is very, very wrong when people don't have access to drinking water, and Coke creates its market out of that scarcity.

Everything has been privatized: seeds, medicinal plants, water, land. All the land reforms of India are being undone by the trade liberalization. I call this the "anti-reform reform."

You mentioned Monsanto, a major US-based multinational corporation.
You write that "the soya bean and cotton are now Monsanto monopolies."
How did that happen?

If you read Wall Street's reports, they don't talk of soya bean as originating in China. They don't talk of soya bean as soya bean. They talk of Monsanto soya. Monsanto soya is protected by a patent. It has a patent number. It is therefore treated as a creation of Monsanto, a product of Monsanto's intelligence and innovation.

Monsanto makes farmers sign a contract for Roundup Ready Soya because the soya bean has been genetically engineered to tolerate high doses of herbicide, which means that it will allow increased use of Roundup by farmers. It's projected to reduce chemical use, but it will increase Roundup use. The reason Monsanto's done this is because the patent on Roundup runs out in a few years, and it's their biggest selling commodity. They sell $1 billion a year of Roundup, the herbicide. The contract with farmers forces them to use only Roundup. They cannot use any other chemical. Monsanto can come and investigate the farms three years after planting to see if farmers have saved the seed. Saving the seed—having even one seed in your home—is treated as a crime in which you are infringing on Monsanto's property.

The kind of capitalism we are seeing today under this expansion of property into living resources is a whole, new, different phase of capitalism. It is totally inconsistent with democracy as well as with sustainability. What we have is capital working on a global scale, totally uprooted, with accountability nowhere, with responsibility nowhere, and with rights everywhere. This new capital, with absolute freedom and no accountability, is structurally anti-life, anti-freedom.

A majority in the United States opposed NAFTA [North American Free
Trade Agreement] and GATT [General Agreement on Tariffs and Trade].
But this didn't stop those agreements. Why do you think that is?

That's the most significant crisis in the world today. We have reached a stage where governments and political processes have been hijacked by the corporate world. Corporations can within five hours influence the vote in the US Congress. They can influence the entire voting patterns of the Indian parliament. Ordinary people who put governments in power might want to go in a different direction. I call this the phenomenon of the inverted state, where the state is no longer accountable to the people. The state only serves the interests of corporations.

Governments have a favorite phrase: "lean and mean." But they've been made very, very fat from corporate interests. Look at the way your Patent Office is increasing in size. It's an arm of government. It's not getting thin. But to create the protection for the corporations, government is actually growing bigger than ever before, in every part of the world. Yet it's growing extremely thin as a protector of people.

GATT today is in my view the counterpart of the Papal Bull [the 1493 edict that legitimized European conquest of the world]. Renato Ruggiero, who is the director general of the World Trade Organization that came out of GATT, basically said that GATT is the world constitution. It's interesting that the people were not involved in writing this constitution. Do you want a world constitution whose only yardstick and measure is freeing up capital and commerce from any limits, whether it is social responsibility, the rights of workers, or restrictions on either exploitation of resources or dumping of toxins? And the free-trade treaty that we have is a treaty for the annihilation of life on this planet if we don't very, very quickly change the terms of politics and economics in the world.

The slogan "Think globally, act locally" isn't enough for you. Why?

For me, both thinking and acting have to be local and national and global all the time. That's why I travel across oceans, miss flights, and sit at airports—for the simple reason that I believe the only way globalization can be tamed is by a new internationalism which recovers the local and recovers the national.

It looks like you have a lot of fun, even though you carry on an exhausting schedule.

I do have fun. Even when I'm fighting I'm enjoying it, for two reasons: I think there's nothing as exhilarating as protecting that which you find precious. To me, fighting for people's rights, protecting nature, protecting diversity are constant reminders of that which is so valuable in life. That is recharging. But frankly, I also absolutely get thrills from taking on these big guys and recognizing how, behind all their power, they are so empty. I just keep going at it. Each of these balloons does deflate. I've seen a lot of balloons get deflated in my life.

Howard Zinn
July 1997

Howard Zinn is a model of the activist scholar. His classic work *A People's History of the United States* (HarperCollins, 1980) has sold more than half a million copies and is widely used in college and university classrooms. A project to develop *A People's History* into a TV series is under way.

Zinn grew up class-conscious in a poor immigrant family. "We were always," he recalls, "one step ahead of the landlord." There were no books or magazines at home. The first book he remembers reading was *Tarzan and the Jewels of Opar*. He found it in the street, the first ten pages ripped out. But it did not matter to him. When his parents discovered his interest in books, they took advantage of a newspaper offer and ordered the complete works of Charles Dickens. Later they got him a used Underwood No. 5 typewriter. The rest is history.

Even though he earned a Ph.D. from Columbia, Zinn learned of the Ludlow Massacre in Colorado only by hearing a Woody Guthrie song about the event. That omission in his education taught him a lot about what is included and excluded in conventional textbooks.

Zinn is an excavator and memory retriever. He recovers valuable and hidden aspects of the past. The lessons inform us, and they inspire us to social action.

He also has a keen interest in the arts. His play *Emma*, on the life of Emma Goldman, has been performed in New York, Boston, London, Edinburgh, and Tokyo. His most recent play is *Marx in Soho*.

At seventy-five, Zinn is as active as ever. The professor emeritus at Boston University is in great demand as a speaker all over the country. But in characteristic fashion, he does not just speak. He acts as well. He recently was arrested in Everett, Massachusetts, in support of Salvadoran women workers at a curtain factory.

Zinn is one of the most beloved figures in the progressive movement. And he is proof that you can be radical and have a sense of humor. I talked with him in the offices of the Harvard Trade Union Program in Cambridge.

წ   G

In your memoir, you write of an incident in Times Square that had a big political impact on you.

I was a seventeen-year-old kid living in the slums of Brooklyn. Living on the same block were these young communists who were older than I and seemed very politically sophisticated. They asked me to come to a demonstration at Times Square. I had never been to a demonstration, and going to Times Square sounded very exciting. I went along.

It seemed like nothing was going on. But my friend said, "Wait." The clock on the *New York Times* building said ten. Suddenly, banners unfurled all around me. People started marching down the street. It was very exciting. I wasn't even sure what it was all about, except that vaguely I thought that it was against war.

At some point there were two women in front of us carrying banners. This was before the age of feminist consciousness, even among leftists. My friends said, "We mustn't let these two women carry this banner. You take one end. I'll take the other end." It was like Charlie Chaplin picking up that red flag, a railroad signal flag, and suddenly there's this army of unemployed people marching behind him in this demonstration.

Then I heard these sirens. I thought there must be a fire somewhere around. But no. The mounted police arrived, driving their horses into the crowd, beating the people. It was a wild scene. Before I knew it, I was spun around by the shoulder, hit, and knocked unconscious.

I woke up, I don't know how much later, in a doorway. Times Square was back as it was before. It was very eerie, as if nothing had happened. My friend was gone. The demonstration was over. The police were gone.

I was nursing not only a hurt head, but hurt feelings about our country. All the things these radicals had been saying were true. The state is not neutral, but on the side of the powerful; there really is no freedom of speech in this country if you're a radical. That was brought home to me, because these people were engaging in a nonviolent demonstration, presumably protected by the Constitution and—zoom!—the police are there beating heads and breaking up the demonstration.

The title of your memoir is You Can't Be Neutral on a Moving Train. *Why did you pick a title like that?*

To confuse people, so that everybody who introduces me at a lecture gets it all wrong, like, You Can't Be Training in a Neutral Place. The title came out of my classroom teaching, where I would start off my classes explaining to my students—because I didn't want to deceive them—that I would be taking stands on everything. They would hear my point of view in this course, that this would not be a neutral course. My point to them was that in fact it was impossible to be neutral. You Can't Be Neutral on a Moving Train means that the world is already moving in certain directions. Things are already happening. Wars are taking place. Children are going hungry. In a world like this—already moving in certain, often terrible directions—to be neutral or to stand by is to collaborate with what is happening. I didn't want to be a collaborator, and I didn't want to invite my students to be collaborators.

Was your job at Spelman College in Atlanta a radicalizing experience for you? I presume you lived in a black neighborhood near the college.

Actually, the first year we were there, 1956, we lived in a white, working-class neighborhood on the edge of Atlanta, which was an interesting experience in itself. We weren't far from Stone Mountain, which is a Ku Klux Klan gathering place. One of the first things that happened when we were there is we heard all this noise. We went outside. There was a main street about a block from our house. There was a parade of people with white hoods, KKK, marching to Stone Mountain.

We moved to the Spelman College campus, which was surrounded by a black community. We lived in the black community for the next six years. Probably that time at Spelman College was the most intense experience of learning in my life. Talk about social change: I could see social change happening all around me. I was writing about it, observing it, participating in it. My Spelman College students— especially young black women—were being trained to take their obedient places in the segregated society. Trained to pour tea and wear white gloves and march into and out of chapel.

Then suddenly I saw them break away from this after they watched the sit-ins taking place in Greensboro and Rock Hill and Nashville, and I saw them getting together and planning the first sit-ins in the spring of 1960 in Atlanta.

This was remarkable—this growth of courage and getting arrested, going to jail. I saw my students literally leaping over that stone wall that surrounded Spelman College campus and doing what they weren't supposed to do.

I saw Marian Wright Edelman, my student at Spelman, go to jail. A photo of her appeared in the newspapers the next day showing this very studious Spelman student behind bars reading a book which she brought along with her so she wouldn't miss her homework.

I participated in sit-ins, and I saw the atmosphere around us in Rich's department store suddenly change from friendly to hostile when four of us—two black and two white, my wife and I and two black students from Spelman—sat down at this lunch counter. Suddenly it was as if a bomb had been dropped or a plague had been visited on it. The people gathering around us were shouting and cursing. I got an inkling of what it is to be black and be subject all your life to the thought that if you step one foot out of line you'll be surrounded by people who are threatening you.

I saw the South change in that time. White Southerners getting used to the idea that the South was going to change and accepting it.

I learned a lot about teaching, too. I learned that the most important thing about teaching is not what you do in the classroom but what you do outside of the classroom. You go outside the classroom yourself, bring your students outside, or have them bring you outside the classroom, because very often they do it first and you say, "I can't hang back. I'm their teacher. I have to be there with them." And you learn that the best kind of teaching makes this connection between social action and book learning.

Do you miss teaching?

I miss the classroom and the encounter with students. But I'm not completely divorced from that situation, because now that I'm not teaching in a formal way, I do go around the country and speak to groups of young people, and do a kind of teaching. I love to speak to high school students. As a result, I don't miss teaching as much as I might have if I simply retired from teaching and played tennis.

Why do you think so many of your colleagues want to just busy themselves with their scholarship and churn out papers and attend conferences? I'm not saying that doesn't have any value. But when it comes to being "out there," to being engaged with what's happening in the streets, in society, they don't feel it's appropriate.

In our society, there's a powerful drive for safety and security. Everybody is vulnerable because we are all part of a hierarchy of power. Unless we're at the very, very top, unless we're billionaires, unless we're the president of the United States, unless we're the boss, and very few of us are bosses, we are somewhere on some lower rung in the hierarchy of power. If somebody has power over us, somebody has the power to fire us, to withhold a raise, to punish us in some way.

Here in this rich country, so prideful of the economic system, the most clear-cut thing you can say is that everybody is insecure. Everybody is nervous. Even if you're doing well, you're nervous. Something will happen to you. In fact, the people who are doing fairly well, the middle class, are more nervous than the people at the bottom, who know what to expect. The academic world has its own special culture of conformity and being professional. Being professional means not being committed.

It's unprofessional to be a teacher who goes out on picket lines, or who invites students out on picket lines, unprofessional to be a teacher who says to students, "Look, instead of giving you a final exam of multiple-choice questions asking you who was president during the Mexican War, your assignment is to go out into the community and work with some organization that you believe in and then do a report on that."

And you will stand out. You will stick out if the stuff you write is not written for scholarly journals but is written for everybody. Certainly the stuff written for scholarly journals is deliberately written in such a way that very few people can read it. So if you write stuff that an ordinary person can read, you're suspect. They'll say you're not a scholar, you're a journalist. Or you're not a scholar, you're a propagandist, because you have a point of view. Of course, scholarly articles have a point of view. They have an agenda. But they may not even know they have an agenda. The agenda is obedience. The agenda is silence. The agenda is safety. The agenda is, "Don't rock the boat."

Have you noticed any changes in your profession, history?

No question there have been changes. Not changes enough to say that the teaching of history has changed. But obviously enough changes to alarm the right wing in this country, to alarm the American Legion, to alarm senators, to alarm Lynne Cheney, Robert Dole, William Bennett, Gertrude Himmelfarb, and to alarm all these people who are holding on to the old history.

The story of Columbus has changed now, not in the majority of schools around the country, but in thousands. This is alarming. What? Young kids are going to begin to think of Columbus as not just an adventurer, but as a predator, a kidnapper, an enslaver, a torturer, a bad person, and think maybe that conquest and expansion are not good things and that the search for gold is not something to be welcomed? Kids, be happy! Gold has been found!

And maybe, let's take a look at the Indian societies Columbus came upon. How did they live? How did they treat one another? Columbus stories told in the schools don't usually tell about how the Indians were living on this continent.

Somebody sent me a letter reminding me of the work of William Brandon. He has done research for decades about Indians and their communities in this hemisphere before Columbus came and after. It's an amazing story, and one that would make anybody question capitalism, greed, competition, disparate wealth, hierarchy. To start to hint about that, telling a new kind of Columbus story, a new kind of Native American story, is subversive.

Also, the Reconstruction period is being told in a new way. Eric Foner's book *Reconstruction* is marvelous. It's a very different treatment of Reconstruction than when I was going to graduate school in the 1950s, where incidentally they did not put on my reading list W. E. B. DuBois's *Black Reconstruction*, which is a vital predecessor to Eric Foner's book.

So a lot of history teaching has changed. Not enough. But just enough to frighten the keepers of the old.

Some years ago, speaking to a gathering of university presidents, John Silber, the chancellor of Boston University, talked darkly about those teachers who "poison the well of academe." His two chief examples? Noam Chomsky and Howard Zinn.

I guess Silber thinks that there is some kind of pure well, then along come people like Chomsky and me and ruin it. That is the kind of accusation now being made in a larger sense about education by the right wing in this country, who claim that education was wonderful before the multiculturalists came in, before we had feminist studies and black studies and Native American studies and Chicano studies. The well was pure before students had to read *The Autobiography of Malcolm X* alongside Thomas Hardy, before they were given *I, Rigoberta Menchú* alongside Tolstoy and Rousseau.

But it was not a very pure well. It was pure only in the sense of the racial purity that was so talked about during the fascist years—a well that I would argue was itself poisonous. It perpetuated an education that left out large numbers of the world's people.

Here's an easy one: How does social change happen?

Thanks, David. I can deal with that in thirty seconds. You think I know? What I try to do is look at historical situations and extrapolate. You see change happening when there has been an accumulation of grievance until it reaches a boiling point. Then something happens. What happened in the South in the 1950s and 1960s? It's not that suddenly black people were put back into slavery. It's not as if there was some precipitating thing that suddenly pushed them back. They were, as the Southern white ruling class was eager to say, making progress. It was glacial progress, extremely slow. But they were making progress. But the ideal in the minds of the black people was, "We have to be equal. We have to be treated as equals." The progress that was being made in the South was far from that. The recognition of that gap—between what should be and what is—existed for a long time but waited for a moment when a spark would be lit.

You never know what spark is going to really result in a conflagration. After all, before the Montgomery bus boycotts there had been other boycotts. Before the sit-ins of the 1960s, there had been sit-ins in sixteen different cities between 1955 and 1960 that nobody paid any attention to and that did not ignite a movement.

But then in Greensboro, on February 1, 1960, these four college kids sit in, and everything goes haywire. Then things are never the same.

I think this is an encouragement to people who do things not knowing whether they will result in anything. You do things again and again, and nothing happens. You have to do things, do things, do things; you have to light that match, light that match, light that match, not knowing how often it's going to sputter and go out and at what point it's going to take hold. That's what happened in the civil rights movement, and that's what happens in other movements. Things take a long time. It requires patience, but not a passive patience—the patience of activism.

When I was in South Africa in 1982, it was very, very interesting. We know about books being banned; there, people were banned. They couldn't speak. They couldn't go here or there. The secret police were everywhere. Just before I arrived at the University of Capetown, the secret police of South Africa had broken into the offices of the student newspaper at the University of Capetown and made off with all of their stuff. It was the kind of thing that happened all the time. There was an atmosphere of terror. You would think, perhaps, that nothing is going to happen here. But having come from that experience in the South, I was aware that underneath the surface of total control things were simmering; things were going on. I didn't know when it would break through, but we saw it break through not long ago. Suddenly Mandela comes out of Robben Island and becomes president of the new South Africa.

We should be encouraged by historical examples of social change, by how surprising changes take place suddenly, when you least expect it, not because of a miracle from on high, but because people have labored patiently for a long time.

When people get discouraged because they do something and nothing happens, they should really understand that the only way things will happen is if people get over the notion that they must see immediate success. If they get over that notion and persist, then they will see things happen before they even realize it.

Let's talk about the American Left and its values. What are left values to you?

When I think of left values I think of socialism—not in the Soviet sense, not in the bureaucratic sense, not in the Bolshevik sense, but socialism in the sense of Eugene Debs and Mother Jones and Emma Goldman and anarchist socialists. Left values are fundamentally egalitarian values. If I had to say what is at the center of left values, it's the idea that everyone has a fundamental right to the good things in life, to the necessary things of life, that there should be no disproportions in the world.

It doesn't mean perfect equality; we can't possibly achieve that. I notice that your sweater is better than mine. But we both have a sweater, which is something.

The Declaration of Independence—the idea that everybody has an equal right to life, liberty, and the pursuit of happiness—to me is a remarkable statement of left values. Of course, in the Declaration of Independence it was all men. It had to be extended as the feminists of 1848 did when they created a new Declaration that added "women" to it. Now it has to be extended internationally.

One of the crucial values that the left must embrace is a value of international solidarity and equality across national lines. That's very important, because it changes everything if you begin to understand that the lives of children in other countries are equivalent to the lives of children in our country. Then war is impossible.

Just speaking around the country, presenting what I think are left values, I talk about the equal right of everybody to these things and about extending the principles of the Declaration of Independence all over the world. I find that people everywhere I go—and these are not captive audiences of just left-wing people; these are assemblies of people, a thousand high school students who are assembled forcibly to hear me—they agree with this. It makes sense. It seems right. It seems moral.

They find themselves then accepting what they didn't accept before, for instance, the fact that you might say the dropping of the bomb on Hiroshima can be a controversial issue within the limits of discussion that have generally been set in our society. But if you change those limits by simply introducing the idea that the children of Japan have an equal right to life with the children of the United States, then suddenly it is impossible to drop a bomb in Hiroshima, just as it would be impossible to drop a bomb on the children of New York, even in order to end World War II faster.

Talk about the idea of equality of opportunity, which is a big theme, versus equality of condition and then the outcome.

The conservatives, and sometimes the liberals, make a big thing of, "Oh, well, what we just want to give people is equality of opportunity. We'll give them an education, and we'll send them out into the world and see what happens." Basically that's it. "We've done our best. And now let the fittest survive." It's a Darwinian idea. Our values should be that people should have health care and housing and work and food and an education, the fundamental things they need, and that should be guaranteed. To say we're giving people opportunity consigns to poverty those people who don't have, let's say, moneymaking skills, moneymaking intelligence: the special kind of qualities that enable some people to become millionaires. These people may be poets or musicians, or they may just be decent people, or they may be carpenters, and so on. But they won't have a chance. So it's very important to rid ourselves of the notion that it's sufficient to give people so-called equality of opportunity.

You've said, "We can't go on with the present polarization of wealth and poverty." Why not?

I don't know how long we can go on, but I know we can't go on indefinitely. That growing, growing gap between wealth and poverty is a recipe for trouble, for disaster, for conflict, for explosion. Here's the Dow Jones average going up, up, up, and there are the lives of people in the city. The Dow Jones average in the last fifteen years has gone up 400 percent. In the same period, the wages of the working population have gone down 15 percent. Now the richest 1 percent of the population owns 43, 44 percent of the wealth. Up from the usual maybe 28 percent, 30 percent, 32 percent, which is bad enough and which has been a constant throughout American history. When they did studies of the tax rolls in Boston in the seventeenth century, they concluded that 1 percent of the population owned 33 percent of the wealth. If you look at the statistics all through American history, you see that figure, a little more, a little less, around the same. Now it's worse and worse. Something's got to give.

So despite what the pundits are telling us about the population being passive and quiescent, you think there's an audience there for dissidence?

Absolutely. Five hundred people come to hear me in Duluth, Minnesota. They're not people who are already aficionados of the Left and of radical messages. They come maybe out of curiosity. Their interest has been piqued by an article in the newspaper or whatever, and they come to hear me.

Then I deliver what I believe is a radical message: This is what's wrong with our economic system. This is what's wrong with our political system. It's fundamental. We need to redistribute the wealth in this country. We need to use it in a rational way. We need to take this enormous arms budget and not just cut it slightly but dismantle it because we have to make up our minds we're not going to war anymore. We're not going to intervene militarily anymore. If we're not going to go to war any more, then we have $250 billion. We don't have to worry about Medicare, Social Security, child care, universal health care, education. We can have a better society.

I say things which, if you mentioned them on *The NewsHour with Jim Lehrer*, they would say, "That's a little too much for our listeners." It's not too much. You tell people what makes common sense. It makes common sense that if you're a very, very rich country that nobody should be hungry. Nobody should be homeless. Nobody should be without health care. The richest country in the world. Nobody should

be without these things. We have the resources but they're being
wasted or given somewhere to somebody. It's common sense. So there
are people all over this country, millions of people, who would listen
to such a message and say, "Yes, yes, yes!"

Ben Bagdikian
April 1997

B en Bagdikian has just about done it all. He is the winner of almost every top prize in American journalism, including the Pulitzer. His career as a reporter and editor spans more than fifty years. At the *Washington Post*, Bagdikian was instrumental in getting the *Pentagon Papers* published. He then went from the newsroom to the academy, becoming dean of the Graduate School of Journalism at the University of California at Berkeley. Now retired, he is a leading critic of his own profession.

Bagdikian is perhaps best known for his landmark book *The Media Monopoly* (Beacon Press), which first came out in 1983. The book described the increasing concentration of media ownership. Reviewers chastised him for being an alarmist and for not trusting the market to correct itself. But, if anything, Bagdikian understated the problem: Media conglomeration has accelerated in the last decade, and the 1996 Telecommunications Act gave an additional push toward merger mania.

Bagdikian was born to an Armenian family in 1921 at the tail end of the genocidal Turkish attack against the Armenians. His childhood escape to America is movingly recounted in his memoir, *Double Vision*.

Bagdikian picked me up from the subway station near his home in the Berkeley hills. We sat down on his living-room sofa and started chatting. He told me that once, when he was in pursuit of a story, he had used my last name as an alias. Clearly, we were destined to do an interview together.

&) CR

In the first edition of The Media Monopoly, *you identified fifty corporations that control most of the media in the United States. What's the current situation?*

The new actors are bigger than ever before and have subsumed some of the old actors. What we have now is a small number of companies. Each has far more communications power than anything in the past. You have Disney-ABC, which has major newspapers, a television network, movies, studios, books. It controls every step in the process: the creation of content, control of the delivery system nationally, and the wire into the home. It's a closed circuit. Nobody gets on that circuit that you don't want.

How does this affect the First Amendment?

The First Amendment was based on the assumption that everyone was free to speak in the village green or to pay a printer a few pennies to publish some posters you could tack up in the tavern or on a local tree. And if people didn't agree with what you said, they could stand on a soapbox in another corner of the park, and they could say something else.

We don't have villages where most people live any more. We have these huge urban complexes, and we don't have everything decided by people gathering in a town hall where they hear the arguments pro and con.

The First Amendment says, in effect, that you or I or the woman next door are free to create a $100 million metropolitan newspaper or a $50 billion TV network or an international publishing house if we wish. All we need is unlimited money and credit.

More and more cities have seen their second papers disappear. What effect does this have?

We have about 1,500 cities in the country with daily papers. In most of them, there's only one paper. So, for all practical purposes, we have one paper per city, but we have more and more cities without daily papers. People on one side of Town A—which may be 100 miles in diameter and include ten or twelve different communities—will see news from a community on the other edge of that area. It's homogenized news and the cheapest news. Local news is expensive.

You have to pay a reporter a salary, benefits, and a pension plan. Whereas if you have a lot of fluff and entertainment and syndicated stuff, you have a machine that produces at negligible cost. If it weren't for alternative radio and alternative weeklies, there would be very little differentiation in voice and content.

Newspapers are constantly talking about their need to cut costs. Why is that?

This is the economics of the fat man at the heavily laden dinner table who doesn't have a choice of three different kinds of roast beef. In good times, the average profit of the daily newspaper industry is four times the average profit in all of manufacturing. In recessions, it is only two or three times higher.

Is Wall Street driving the trend to smaller and smaller newsrooms?

Yes, it's not whether the customers are happy; it's whether the Wall Street analysts are happy and what's happening to the stock. Decisions used to be made by editors. They're now made by the Wall Street analysts. Also, when you get a local publisher who has stock options, and in many cases the local top editor has stock options, the money they save on the news is money in their pocket. They get rewarded for giving the community as little real news as possible.

Corporate lawyers are casting longer and longer shadows in newsrooms. There was that incident last year involving 60 Minutes and Brown and Williamson, the tobacco giant. CBS was going to broadcast an interview. The lawyers said, "Back off." What do you think about that?

It was shameful. CBS didn't want to go to court to defend putting on the air someone who could show that the tobacco companies lied; it didn't want to go to court and say, "This company suing us kills people." Not a bad case, but that takes money.

And tobacco companies have diversified. While they no longer advertise on television, they own big food companies that do advertise. They're our only killer with a huge advertising budget.

The one thing which is sacrosanct in American standard news is the corporate system. Not necessarily any particular corporation, because particular corporations get into court suits and get into spectacular evil doing and get caught in the glare. But if you point to the system that rewards that evil doing and makes most of it almost inevitable— that is hard to get in print and almost impossible to get on the air.

Talk about access to power as a form of journalistic control. Erwin Knoll, the late editor of The Progressive, *told me he once asked Lyndon Johnson a very critical question at a press conference. In subsequent press conferences, he was never called upon again. If your beat is the White House or the state house and the president or the governor never returns your calls or responds to your questions, your editor is not going to be very happy and you soon might be looking for another job.*

That depends on the integrity of the editor. I don't think it's so important that you don't get called upon because you ask too many penetrating questions. There are plenty of present correspondents whose stock in trade is to ask a question in the manner of a prosecutor— the Sam Donaldson question, the accusatory question. That is usually not of great substance. It is manner more than substance.

I remember the first press conference that John Kennedy held. It was right after the Bay of Pigs fiasco. The regular reporters were asking questions, as usual, of strategy. Should there have been more air cover? Should there have been a different kind of craft used on the landing? Could there have been better intelligence? Dick Dudman, a friend and colleague, got called on. He said, "Mr. President, should you have invaded Cuba in the first place or should you have resisted?" All the guys in the front row, the networks, the wire services, turned in indignation that he had asked this irreverent question, which was the crucial question, because as usual they were concerned with the strategies and the tactics and the margins, not the core. The number of crucial questions that are not asked at presidential press conferences would fill a book.

What do you make of the celebrity status that a lot of journalists, particularly the network anchors, have achieved?

"Anchoritis" is a dread disease. I think the worst thing that can happen to a journalist is to become a celebrity You can become corrupt. You can become destroyed. The honest job of the journalist is to observe, to listen, to learn. The job of the celebrity is to be observed, to make others learn about him or her, to be the object of attention rather than an observer of some object.

Then the garden clubs will pay them $5,000, $10,000, $20,000 to come and impart their Washington wisdom. We have all gone to these sessions in communities around the country where celebrity journalists bring the word to the provinces. The amount of pontification and frivolous information is appalling. Journalists should be read and not seen.

What accounts for the growth and seeming popularity of TV and radio talk shows, the so-called shout shows where the various participants are engaged in yelling matches?

It comes essentially from the commercials themselves. The rule of thumb on most commercial television is that the screen cannot stay unchanged for more than two or three seconds. So if you have jumped images—bang, bang, bang, bang—on the screen all the time, you're much more likely to absorb passively and uncritically the commercial that comes on—bang, bang, bang—telling you you're going to have a gorgeous bedmate if you use the right kind of deodorant, or you'll stay young forever if you drink Pepsi-Cola. That's absurd, of course. But it's not absurd if it's in a setting which encourages passive acceptance of the absurd.

That's one reason why highly popular programs, like *Roots,* for example, which had an enormous audience, don't make much money. Most of the advertisers don't want to advertise on that because the audience is in too serious a mood, and to try to tell them at that point that you use this cosmetic and you're going to get the best bedmate you ever saw in your life, that doesn't come out of serious thinking. You just laugh at it.

So people who advertise on television want what they call a "good atmosphere" for the ad. And that determines the nature of the noncommercial part of the program. The whole content is forever under pressure to be degraded socially, intellectually, and every other way.

In most polls, when Americans are asked to rate public institutions, the media rank among the most unpopular entities in the United States. Why is that?

A lot of it is with good reason, but a lot of it is an injustice to good journalists. Someone in a spectacular case—a sex case, an O. J.-type of case—comes out of a courthouse, and he's mobbed by these piranhas. Everybody's sticking their microphones and cameras in his face, not to get real information, but to get the sound bite for their station and asking crude questions which are asked mostly for the questions rather than for the answers. It's a pretty disgusting scene.

The public sees that and says, "Look, if that's journalism, I don't want it on my front lawn."

Gradually, over the years, what's become important is how your hair looks and not what's operating underneath your hair. What's become important is your personality projection rather than your ability to ask good questions about relevant situations and give clear answers.

The present people who run the networks want it quick and dirty. It's a matter of intent. They can make more money more quickly by a story about a bloody accident. So it is a reflection of the greed in television, not of a lack of ability.

One of the most damaging stereotypes in journalism is that people are not interested in serious subjects. That's nonsense. They are intensely interested in serious subjects that affect their personal lives in a serious way. There is absolutely no question about it.

The guy who is in danger of losing his job in the buttonhook industry will read and listen to something about what's happening in the buttonhook industry. The person who's afraid that he's not going to keep up his payments on his mortgage because credit has dried up and he may be losing his job, he's very concerned about interest rates.

The person who has a kid in school who is excited to be there and then suddenly half the courses which excite him are going to be cut out is intensely interested in educational policy.

If you know that and if you respect it, you can put out a good radio program, a good newspaper. You can deal with serious things. You don't need to be 100 percent solemn, but you can put out things that really mean something to people's lives, and they will pay attention.

You've practiced and taught journalism for years. How did you impart to students your notions of objectivity and balance?

Objectivity isn't a word I use. It's misleading. Journalism by its nature is not objective. Journalism is looking upon a social, political, economic scene, a human scene, and deciding what in this extremely complex scene you're going to report. Real objectivity is a kind of uniformity. What I like better is fairness and balance, but also consciousness of social significance.

What about a subject close to your heart, like Armenia? Some scholars continue to deny that a genocide ever took place in Turkey. How would you report that?

You report what they say, and then you provide the evidence. The United States supports Turkey in suppressing this information because we want Turkey as a buffer against other countries and because, among other things, our tobacco companies have a very big interest in Turkey—not only as a market but as a source for tobacco. But basically it's because the US, for geopolitical reasons, sees Turkey as the bulwark, what used to be the bulwark against the Soviet Union. Now it's the bulwark against highly anti-Western, religious fundamentalist Islam.

So Turkey gets away with murder, with a history of murder, and with denying it happened. The most it will say is there was a civil war between the Armenians and the Turks. It's unfortunate that most of the people killed were Armenians, of course, but *c'est la guerre.*

So you would include all of this information in your report.

I would certainly include what the Turks say and what they give as their explanation. I believe in that John Stuart Mill precept: Let the arguments contend. But let both sides contend.

But aren't you then contributing to the legitimacy of this debate by putting out both sides?

In this case, what you are doing is contributing an answer which up to now pretty much hasn't existed. The Turks have a free ride in this country. They have US government support for what they say, for their country itself, and the US government refuses to condemn Turkish involvement in genocide. It isn't as though you're creating an audience for the Turkish side that didn't exist. The Turks have full-page ads. They have a very large PR machine. There are pro-Turkish professors at American universities. And the opposite side simply doesn't get heard very often. The Armenians are not a huge bloc in the American electorate. It isn't as though I would take the initiative to publicize the Turkish argument. I would take the initiative to publicize the answer to the Turkish argument.

Let's say someone starts the Flat Earth Society. They have meetings and publish scholarly books and magazines and have TV and radio shows. You report on the activities of the Flat Earth Society. I, as a consumer of news, all of a sudden have this doubt planted in my mind. Oh, I thought the Earth was round. Maybe there is another point of view.

I think it works this way: If there were, let's say, such a thing as a Flat Earth Society, what you do is say: "You're hearing from many authorities that the Earth is flat. They're wrong. Let me tell you why they're wrong and how we know that they're wrong. When you see a ship sailing toward the clear horizon, it doesn't disappear all at once. What disappears first? The bow. Then the bottom of the mast. Then the top of the mast."

I do believe every generation must re-create the reality against certain kinds of illusions. There will be illusions. They come out of innocence in human affairs; they come out of the venality in human affairs. You have to answer them. You have to answer them and answer them and answer them. You have to propagate rationality, humanism, what we have learned in the history of the human race, and that's never over. You have to do it every single generation.

What kind of steps should we take to improve the media?

First of all, I would repeal that Telecommunications Act, which is not only an outrageous giveaway to big corporations but also doesn't solve any of the basic problems. It said it would open up competition between the telephone companies and the cable companies, but the first thing they've done afterward is to become joint ventures and join each other in a monopoly.

I would require all holders of licenses to devote a significant percentage of their air time to public community needs.

I would push low-power TV, neighborhood TV. What does that mean? Neighborhoods can talk about their own neighborhood problems: school, trash collection, playground problems. And the little dry cleaner and the mom-and-pop pharmacy can advertise on it.

I would say for the two months before every election, every significant candidate must be given ample prime time to use as he or she wishes, but in fifteen-minute segments, not one-minute segments. Absolutely free. And when I say significant candidates, that can be handled. It's done in all kinds of ways. People who get 5 percent or more in a previous election or who are running for the first time and have so many signatures get free time. I would ban all paid political advertising from American television.

These are doable things. These exist in other countries. In Western European democracies, for example. In Japan.

I would do something else, too. I would create not just one public-broadcasting channel, but numerous channels that would be noncommercial. Let them be amateurish. People don't mind an amateurish production if it's on a subject they care about. If they want to argue whether their local school should have a factory built next to it, you don't need fancy sets and elocutionists. On local issues, you don't have to have a lot of high-pressure, high-cost accoutrements. You don't have to have dulcet-voiced announcers. You can have ordinary people doing it. Very often, ordinary citizens are absolutely eloquent about what they really care about in their own neighborhood. That's what we're missing on television now. And on radio for the most part.

So there's no lack of things that could be done.

And I would work at changing the basic system. We have a commercially corrupted system, and we've got to change it both from the bottom—locally—and at the top, where the decisions aren't being made by the American public, they're being made by the big industrial lobbies.

People haven't been told for a long time that the public owns those airwaves, and the people who hold those licenses do so on condition of their good behavior. We aren't seeing much good behavior. So we have to rouse people. It's a very hard job.

How is that going to happen?

The media is going to be affected more by outside events than by anything within the media. Those outside events will, I hope in my lifetime, mean the emergence of new, progressive, socially conscious parties. You need grassroots organization. All over the country this is happening. It's happening in something called the New Party. It's happening in something called the Alliance. I would hope that in ten or fifteen years we will have political forces that will change the media. The media will not change all by themselves.

Index

A

abortion rights, 111–12
Abu-Jamal, Mumia, 83
Act of War: The Overthrow of the Hawai'ian Nation (Trask), 91
affirmative action, 88
Afghanistan, 20–23, 25–26, 39, 42–46, 52, 180–84
After the Dance (Danticat), 1, 6, 8–9
Ahab, Captain (protagonist in *Moby Dick*), 54–55
Ahmad, Eqbal: on Afghanistan, 181–84; on Arafat, 186–87; on colonialism, 180–81; on father's murder, 178–79; on fundamentalism, 184–85; on globalization, 180–81, 184; media critique by, 175, 184; on nuclear weapons, 177–79; personal notes, 175–76, 178–79, 187–88; Said and, 175
AIDS, 4, 6, 7, 27, 30
Akbar, Emperor, 58
al-Hayat (London), 147
al-Maarri, 45–46
Al Qaeda, 19–20, 22, 25–26, 43
Albright, Madeleine, 123–24
Algebra Project, 27
Ali, Agha Shahid, 187
Ali, Muhammad, 169
Ali, Tariq: on history, 42–43; Khomeini opera, 41; personal notes, 41–42; US as warlike, 43–47; works by, 41
All Our Relations (LaDuke), 115

Allende, Isabel, 136
Alternative Radio, 110
American Civil War, 65
American Humanist Association, 16
American Indians, 94, 98, 111, 144–45, 204–5
Amnesty International, 23, 28, 121, 127–28
Amoco, 183
Angola, 29
apartheid, 81, 121, 126, 150–52, 163–64, 171, 202. *See also* racism
"The Arab Portrayed" (Said), 147
Arafat, Yasir, 148, 153, 175, 186–87
Arendt, Hannah, 151, 152
Armed Forces Journal, 185
Armenia, 211, 217–18
Ashcroft, John, 6
Asimov, Isaac, 16
assimilation, 97–98, 103–4. *See also* Hawaii; languages
At Canaan's Edge (Branch), 163, 165
Atlanta Crackers, 164
Australia, 37, 64, 84
The Autobiography of Malcolm X (Malcolm X), 205
Azerbaijan, 184

B

Bagdikian, Ben: on celebrity, 214–15; on fundamentalism, 217; media critique by, 211–16, 218–19; works by, 211–12
Bandit Queen, 72

Bank for International Settlements, 129
banking, 129–30, 145–46
Barenboim, Daniel, 149, 158–59
Barrios Unidos, 32
Bay of Pigs invasion of Cuba, 214
BBC, 187
Beloved, 27
Ben-Gurion, David, 151
Bengal famine (1943), 59–60, 65
Bennett, William, 204
Berger, Sandy, 124
Berrigan brothers, 175
Berry, Halle, 31
"Beyond Vietnam" (King), 28, 172–73
Bhutto, Zulfikar Ali, 177
bilingual education, 101–3
bin Laden, Osama, 29, 43, 51–52, 55, 181, 185
biodiversity, 194
Biopiracy (Shiva), 189
Bishara, Azmi, 149
"Bitter River" (Hughes), 31
BJP (Bharatiya Janata Party), 62–63, 177
Black Caucus, 29
Black Panther Party, 81
Black Reconstruction (DuBois), 205
Blair, Tony, 33–35
blood quantum classification, 97
Blue Legacies and Black Feminism (Davis), 82
Bluebeard (Vonnegut), 12
Boggs Center, 32
Book of Embraces (Galeano), 135
The Book of Saladin (Ali), 41
Booker Prize, 69–70
Boukman (Haitian rebel), 4–5
Branch, Taylor: on biblical images, 165; on civil rights movement, 164–73; on Hoover, 166, 168–69, 172; on Johnson, 165, 167–69, 171–73, 214; on the Kennedy brothers, 166–68; on King, 163, 165–70, 172–73; on Malcolm X, 97, 169–71; personal notes, 163–64; on violence, 170–71; works by, 163, 165–66, 169, 171
Brandeis, Louis, 117
Brandon, William, 204
Brazil, 29
Breakfast of Champions (Vonnegut), 11–12

Breath, Eyes, Memory (Danticat), 1
Brecht, Bertolt, 7
Bretton Woods era, 129
Brown, John, 30
Brown and Williamson, 213
Buber, Martin, 151, 152
Buchanan, Pat, 112
Bush, George H. W., 34
Bush, George W.: abuse of power, 7, 12, 46, 176; advisors, 14, 33–38, 45, 54, 70

C

Canada, 99
capital flow, 129–30
Capital (Marx), 65
capitalism, 50, 65, 129, 184, 196, 204
caste, 69, 75
Cat's Cradle (Vonnegut), 11
CBS, 213
celebrity, 70, 78–79, 82, 89, 214–15
censorship, 33–34, 44, 61, 128, 160, 214–16
Center for Science in the Public Interest, 109
Center for the Study of Responsive Law, 109
Central Mennonite Committee, 125
Césaire, Aimé, 148–49
Chaney, James, 171
charity, 146
Charlie Rose, 160
Cheney, Dick, 35, 37
Cheney, Lynne, 204
China, 21, 61, 177–78
Chipko movement, 189–92
Chomsky, Noam: on brevity, 122; on Britain's terrorism policies, 45; on critical thinking, 122–24; on international banking, 129–30; on Medicare privatization, 131; personal notes, 119–21; on public education, 131; on Social Security, 130–31; on "speaking truth to power," 120; on sports, 120, 132–33; on torture, 126–28; on US as violent, 124–26; works by, 119; Zinn and, 205
Christian Science Monitor, 126
CIA (Central Intelligence Agency), 181–82

Cicero, 117
citizenship, 6, 34, 104–5, 107–8, 151, 157–58
civil disobedience, 189, 193–94
civil rights movement, 28, 111, 164–73, 175, 205–6. *See also* racism
The Clash of Fundamentalism: Crusades, Jihad, and Modernity (Ali), 41
class, 13, 57, 59–60, 69, 75, 83
Clinton, Bill, 35–36, 45, 94, 167, 184
Clinton, Hillary Rodham, 163
cloning, 192
Coca-Cola, 195
Cohen, William, 123–24
Colombia, 29, 121, 128, 141
colonialism: decolonization, 96–98, 104, 108, 180–81; famines under, 57, 61; Haiti under, 4–5; Hawaii under form of, 91, 94–95; India under, 178–79; Kenya under, 180; Pakistan and, 180–81; psychological aspects of, 96–98, 104–6; Puerto Rico under form of, 104–8; stripping wealth and resources, 4, 65, 180
The Color Purple, 27
Columbus, Christopher, 204–5
commonwealth, 105. *See also* colonialism
communism, 52, 81–82, 165–68, 172, 182, 185, 200
communitarianism, 58–59
Comprehensive Test Ban Treaty, 112–13, 176
Congress of Industrial Organizations (CIO), 16
Constant, Emmanuel, 2
corporate welfare, 109, 111, 115–17
corporations: cloning and, 192; government as serving interests of, 115, 116–17, 196–97; media, 37, 212–14, 218; multinational, 69, 75–77, 115–17, 142, 180–81, 189, 195–96
Corrections Corporation of America, 84
The Cost of Living (Roy), 70
Crisis, 135
Cuba, 6, 85, 113, 214
Culture and Imperialism (Said), 147–48, 154

D

Daily Mirror (London), 35–37
Daily Telegraph (Pakistan), 19
dams, 70, 72–75
Danticat, Edwidge: on Aristide, 7; on colonial Haiti, 1–6; on masks, 8–9; on Vodou, 4–5; works by, 1, 6; on writing, 8
Darwish, Mahmoud, 149
Davis, Angela: Black Panther Party member, 81; on death penalty, 83, 86–87; on prisons, 81–88; student activism, 89; works by, 81–82
Dawn (Pakistan), 176
Dayan, Moshe, 157
Days and Nights of Love and War (Galeano), 135–36
Death of a Nation: East Timor (Pilger), 33
death penalty opponents, 28–29, 83, 86–87, 105
Debs, Eugene, 15, 207
decarceration strategies, 84. *See also* prisons
decolonization, 96–98, 104, 108, 180–81
Decolonizing the Mind (Ngugi), 97–98
Dellinger, Dave, 114
Delta Oil, 183
democracy: civil disobedience as, 193–94, 202; defined, 33; famines prevented by, 57, 61–62; globalization and, 45–46; in India, 62–63, 75; Pilger on American, 33
Democracy Now (radio), 101
Dessalines, Jean-Jacques, 4
detentions, 6–7, 26, 28–29. *See also* prisons
Deterring Democracy (Chomsky), 119
Development as Freedom (Sen), 57, 60
Devi, Bachni, 192
Devi, Phoolan, 72
The Dew Breaker (Danticat), 1–2
Dickens, Charles, 199
Discipline and Punish (Foucault), 86
disease, 94–96
Disney-ABC, 212
dispossession, 94, 194
Dispossessions and Punishments (Davis), 82
District of Columbia, 107–8
DNA technology, 86

Doar, John, 166
Dole, Robert, 204
Dominican Republic, 3
Donaldson, Sam, 214
Dostum, Abdul Rashid, 23
Double Vision (Bagdikian), 211
drug war, 24–25, 84, 143
"Drum" (Hughes), 30
DuBois, W.E.B., 83, 205
Dudman, Dick, 214

E

Ecofeminism (Mies), 192
Edelman, Marian Wright, 202
Eden, Anthony, 43
education, public, 88, 101–3, 131, 199, 201–5
Egypt, 47, 128, 154–55, 182–83
El Barzón, 145–46
election ads, 219
Emma (Zinn), 199
"The End of Imagination" (Roy), 70
Enron, 14, 70, 75–76
Environmental Protection Agency, 109
La Epoca, 135
equality, 64, 67–68, 208–10
Etzioni, Moshe, 127

F

Faiz, Faiz Ahmed, 187
famines, 57, 59–62, 65
Fanon, Frantz, 97–98, 105–6, 175
Far Eastern Economic Review, 19
farming, 24, 76, 189, 195–96
The Farming of Bones (Danticat), 1, 3
Farrakhan, Louis, 170
The Fast Runner, 31
Fateful Triangle (Chomsky), 119
Fates Worse Than Death (Vonnegut), 12
Faulkner, William, 2
FBI (Federal Bureau of Investigation), 81, 104, 166, 168–69, 172
Fear of Mirrors (Ali), 41
fertility and women's literacy, 64
First Amendment, 200–201, 212
Foner, Eric, 205
Foreign Affairs, 129
forestry, social, 190–92
Foucault, Michel, 86
Franks, Tommy, 21
FRAPH (Front for the Advancement

and Progress of Haiti), 2
free association, 108
freedom, defined, 59, 67, 117
Freedom of Information Act, 109
Freeh, Louis, 104
From a Native Daughter (Trask), 91
The Front Page, 17
Fugard, Athol, 27
fundamentalism, 41, 76–77, 184–85, 217

G

Galeano, Eduardo: on banking, 145–46; on being heard, 137–38; on classification, 140–42; on collapse of Soviet Union, 145; on consumer society, 137–38; on culture of violence, 142–44; on El Barzón, 145–46; on ignorance of US population, 139; on indigenous people, 142–44; on Lannan Prize, 142; personal notes, 135–36, 140–42; on poverty, 140; on uniformization, 138, 140, 184; works by, 135–37, 140–41
Gandhi, Mahatma, 58, 178–79, 193–94
GATT (General Agreement on Tariffs and Trade), 196–97
General Motors, 109
Global Crossing, 14
globalization: abuses due to, 45–46, 66–67, 69, 75–77, 140, 189, 194–95; as colonial power, 180–81; definitions of, 64–65, 69, 181, 194; democracy at risk from, 46, 193–94; non-sustainable systems, 11, 24, 76, 189, 194–96; prison models and, 84; uniformization and, 138, 140, 184, 212
Glover, Carrie M., 30
Glover, Danny: on death penalty, 28–29; on military tribunals and detentions, 28–29; personal notes, 27, 30; on reparations for slavery, 29; screen career, 27–28, 31–32

The God of Small Things (Roy), 69, 71–73, 79
Goering, Hermann, 12
Goldman, Emma, 199, 207
Gonzalez, Juan: on language, 101–2, 106–8; works by, 101–2, 104
Goodman, Amy, 101
Gore, Al, 35
Green Party, 82, 110–15
Greenfield, Jeff, 122
Guam, 95
Guantanamo Bay, 26, 29
Gulf War, 43–44, 51, 121–22, 181
Guthrie, Woody, 199

H

Haiti, 1–3, 6
Halliburton, 14
Hand, Learned, 116
Hapgood, Powers, 16
Harlem Renaissance, 30
Harper's Ferry, 30
Harvest of Empire (Gonzalez), 101, 102, 104
Hawaii: cosmology of, 96–97; language, 97–98; military presence in, 91, 94; sovereignty movement in, 90, 94–99; tourism, 91–93, 95, 98
Heart of Darkness (Conrad), 53
Helms, Jesse, 165
herbicides, 92, 196
Herman, Ed, 126
Hilliard, Earl, 29
Himmelfarb, Gertrude, 204
Hiroshima, 13, 99, 208
Hispanic Academy of Media Arts and Sciences, 102
Hispanic Business, 102
Historia de los Colores (Galeano), 136
Hitler, 42–43
homogenization, social, 138, 140, 184. *See also* globalization
homosexual rights, 111
Hoover, J. Edgar, 166, 168–69, 172
Hughes, Langston, 30–31
Human Rights Watch, 23–24, 87, 128
"humanitarian intervention." *See* war
Hussein, Saddam, 14, 39, 43, 47, 113, 123–26, 143, 185

I

I, Rigoberta Menchú (Menchú), 98, 205
immigration holding centers, 6. *See also* detentions
imperialism, 33, 47, 65–66. *See also* colonialism
In These Times, 11, 101
India: BJP (Bharatiya Janata Party), 62–63, 177–78; China, war with, 177–78; dam study, 73–75; democracy in, 62–63, 75; non-sustainable systems, 194–95; nuclear testing by, 177–78; Pakistan unrest and, 21; partition, 178–79, 193; privatization and, 75–77, 195–96
indigenous peoples, 5, 84, 91–99, 142–44. *See also* American Indians
Indigenous Women's Network, 98
Indonesia, 3, 26, 64, 75
Industrial Workers of the World (IWW), 33
insecticides, 92
Institute for Policy Studies, 175
International Monetary Fund (IMF), 129, 146
International Security Assistance Force (ISAF), 19–20, 22–23, 25–26, 43
International Settlements Bank, 129
International Telephone and Telegraph (ITT), 136, 142
International Women's Week, 92
internationalism, 197
invisible people: displaced people, 73–74; indigenous peoples, 84, 91–99, 142–44, 205; lacking usefulness to the West, 39, 129; the lower classes, 13; the nomad, 156–58; Palestinians as, 156–57; the powerless, 75; starving people, 129; the underdog, 33; untouchables, 73; voiceless, 137–38. *See also* indigenous peoples; racism
Iran, 21, 51, 113, 123, 183, 185–86
Iraq: aggression toward, 7, 14, 34–36, 47, 123–24; Hussein, 14, 39, 43, 47, 113, 123–26, 143; sanctions against, 51, 112, 123, 126; threat to Israel, 46–47; torture by, 128; US aid to, 113, 128
Irish famine, 60
Irish Republican Army (IRA), 45

Islam: hijacked, 50, 52, 181–85, 217; ignorance about, 52–55; "Islamic blowback," 182; "Islamic bomb" misquote, 177; Koran parody, 46; Nation of Islam, 169–70; portrayed, 41, 52, 54, 148, 182

Israel: apartheid in, 150–52; Arabs visiting, 154–57; binational state, 49, 148, 150–51, 158–60; citizenship, 151, 157–58; dialogue in, 149–52, 155–57; fundamentalism, 151, 184; future of, 151–52, 186–87; history of, 152; Iraq and, 46; Jews critical of, 158–59; Palestinians and, 52–53, 148, 151–52, 154–60, 186; provincialism, 156; settlements, 52, 186; Six Day War, 175; torture of prisoners, 127–28; US and, 36, 46–47, 51–52, 128

J

Jackson, Jimmy Lee, 171
Jackson, Robert, 14
Jailbird (Vonnegut), 12
James, C.L.R., 4
Japan, 99
Jayanama, Suravit, 125
Jensen, Robert, 126
Jewish Defense League, 148
jihad, 182
Jihad (Rashid), 19
Johnson, Lyndon B., 165, 167–68, 171–73, 214
Jones, James Earl, 12
Jones, Mother, 207
Jones Act of 1917, 104
Jordan, 182
journalism, 33, 37–39, 101, 126, 211–12, 214
Justice Policy Institute, 88

K

Ka Lahui Hawai'i, 91, 94
Karzai, Hamid, 19–20, 22–23
Kashmir, 26, 176
Kazakhstan, 184
Kennedy, John, 166–68, 182, 214
Kennedy, Robert, 166
Kenya, 180
KGNU radio, 120

Khalilzad, Zalmay, 20–21
Khan, Ismail, 23
Khomeini, Ayatollah, 41
King, Martin Luther, Jr., 28, 97, 163, 165–73
Kissinger, Henry, 46, 175
KKK (Ku Klux Klan), 201
Knesset, 149
Knoll, Erwin, 214
Koran parody, 46
Krauthammer, Charles, 44
Krik? Krak! (Danticat), 1–2
Krugman, Paul, 129

L

labor, 60, 65–66, 85, 115
Labour Party (Britain), 34–36
LaDuke, Winona, 98, 115
Landau Commission, 128
landmines, 125–26
languages: Arabic, lacking in Israel, 157; English as official, 97–98, 101–3, 106–8; euphemisms, 14, 37–38; feeling-thinking, 141; Hawaiian, 97–98; Modern Language Association, 147; about nature, 144; passive voice use, 37–38; Spanish, 101–3, 106–8
Lannan Foundation Prize, 136, 142
Latin America, 137–45
Lebanon, 186
left values, 207–8
Legal Services for Prisoners with Children, 88
"Let America Be American Again" (Hughes), 30
Lethal Weapon movies, 27
Libya, 128
life imprisonment, 86–87
Light in the Crevice Never Seen (Trask), 91
logging, 190–92
London Insight team, 128
London *Sunday Times,* 128
L'Ouverture, Toussaint, 4
Lovins, Amory, 195
Ludlow Massacre, 199
Lumumba, Patrice, 31
"Lumumba's Grave" (Hughes), 31
Luxemburg, Rosa, 98

M

Ma, Yo-Yo, 159
Mackandal (Haitian rebel), 4
Macy, Christina, 163
Magnes, Judah, 151–52
Malcolm X, 97, 169–71, 205
mana, 97
Mandela, Nelson, 206
Manufacturing Consent (Chomsky), 119
Maori women, 98
Marcos, Subcommandante, 136
Marshall, Burke, 166
Marshall Islands, 99
Marx, Karl, 16, 41, 58, 65
Marx in Soho (Zinn), 199
Master Harold and the Boys (Fugard), 27
McCarthy era, 31
McDonald's, 76, 140, 184
McGovern, George, 163
McKinney, Cynthia, 29
McVeigh, Timothy, 15
media: accuracy of news, 43–44, 132,
    135, 175, 212–14; advertising,
    184, 215, 219; censorship
    and, 33–34, 44, 61, 128, 160,
    214–16; corporate control of, 37,
    212–14, 218; critiques of, 37–39,
    43–44, 175, 212–16, 218–19;
    false stereotypes by, 215–16;
    journalism, 33, 37–39, 101, 126,
    211–12, 214, 217; "objectivity"
    of, 33, 38, 217–18; radio, 101,
    110, 120–21, 160; suggestions
    for, 218–20. *See also* newspapers;
    television
The Media Monopoly (Bagdikian),
    211–12
Medicare, 131
Mehta, Zubin, 159
Meir, Golda, 147
Memory of Fire trilogy (Galeano),
    135–36, 141
Menchú, Rigoberta, 98, 205
Mia, Kader, 58–59
Mies, Maria, 192
military: in Afghanistan, 21–22; culture
    of violence, 142–44, 176; in
    Hawaii, 91, 94; occupation of
    Palestine, 36; tribunals, 28–29
military-industrial complex, 113
Mill, John Stuart, 58, 217
Milosevic, Slobodan, 43

mines, land, 125–26
Mitchell, Peter, 164
Moby Dick (Melville), 54–55
Modern Language Association, 147
Monk, Thelonius, 82
Monocultures of the Mind (Shiva), 189
Monsanto, 195–96
Monsoon Wedding, 31
Moonies, 37
Moses, Bob, 27, 171
Mother Jones, 207
multinational corporations, 69, 75–77,
    115–17, 142, 180–81, 189, 195–96
Multinational Monitor, 109
Murdoch, Rupert, 37
Musharraf, General Pervez, 26

N

Nader, Ralph: on abortion rights,
    111; on globalization, 115;
    on government serving
    corporate interests, 109, 111,
    115, 116–17; Green Party
    presidential candidate, 110–11;
    on homosexual rights, 111; of
    Lebanese descent, 116; on None-
    of-the-Above law, 114; on nuclear
    testing, 112–13; on proportional
    representation, 114; on wages,
    115; *Unsafe at Any Speed,* 109
NAFTA (North American Free Trade
    Agreement), 109, 132, 196
Nagasaki, 13, 99
Narmada Bachao Andolan (NBA), 70,
    72–75, 192
Nasser, Gamal Abdel, 42–43
Nation of Islam, 169–70
Nation (Thailand), 125
nation-within-a-nation status, 94
National Congress for Puerto Rican
    Rights, 101
National Endowment for the Arts, 136
National Public Radio (NPR), 121, 160
National Traffic and Motor Vehicle
    Safety Act of 1966, 109
nationalism, 22, 76–77, 177, 179
NATO (North Atlantic Treaty
    Organization), 45
NBA (Narmada Bachao Andolan), 70,
    72–75, 192

"The Negro Speaks of Rivers" (Hughes), 30
Nehru, Jawaharlal, 74
Netherlands, 84
"neutrality," 201–4
New Left Review, 41
The New Military Humanism (Chomsky), 119
New Republic, 54
The New Rulers of the World (film by Pilger), 33
New Statesman, 120
New York Daily News, 101
New York Times, 111, 133, 139, 160, 172, 177
New York Times Magazine, 150, 160
News Corporation, 37
newspapers: banned, 20; democracy and, 61; outside US, 20, 125, 147, 154, 176, 206; profitability, 212–13; self-censorship, 128, 216. *See also* media; *individual newspapers by name*
Newsweek, 23, 160
NGOs (non-governmental organizations), 67
Ngugi Wa Thiongo, 97–98
Nightline, 122
1984 (Orwell), 38
Nobel Prizes, 57, 173, 189
the nomad, 156–58
non-people. *See* invisible people
non-sustainable systems, 24, 76, 189, 194–97
None-of-the-Above law, 114
nonviolence, 75, 170, 179, 200–201
nuclear weapons, 63, 70, 76–77, 99, 112–13, 176–77

O

objectivity, 33, 38, 201–4, 217–18
Observer (London), 54, 124
Ohio State town meeting, 123–24
oil: British control of, 180; pipelines, 21, 183–84, 186; Suez War and, 42; US control of, 46–47, 51, 181–83, 186
Omar, Mullah, 20
On Suicide (Marx), 41
Open Media Fund for Afghanistan, 19, 147

Open Veins of Latin America (Galeano), 135–37, 140
Orientalism (Said), 54, 147–48
Orwell, George, 33–34, 37–38, 122
Oslo Accords, 148, 150
the Other Economic Summit, 190
Out of Place: A Memoir (Said), 147
L'Ouverture, Toussaint, 4
Oxford Committee for Famine Relief (OXFAM), 57

P

Pacific Radio, 101
Pakistan: Al Qaeda connection, 25–26; Ashcroft on terrorism from, 6; globalization, 180–81; India tensions with, 178–79; nuclear weapons, 63, 76, 176–78; oil pipelines, 21, 183; Taliban connection, 42; torture in, 128
Palestine Is Still the Issue (Pilger), 33
Palestine National Council, 148
Palestinians: Arafat, Yasir, 148, 153, 175, 186–87; and binational state, 49, 148, 150–52, 158–60; Darwish and, 148; demographics, 151, 152; dialogue, 152–56; Egyptians, 154–56; history, 147, 156–58; Israel and, 52–53, 151–52, 154–60, 186; Meir on, 147; as the Nomad, 156–58; normalization opposed, 154–55; Said as spokesperson in US, 49, 147–48; Sharon and, 33, 36; sovereignty struggle, 150–51, 157–58, 175; torture of, 127–28
Paris Commune, 65
Parting the Waters (Branch), 163, 166, 169
Pashtuns, 21–23, 25
"Pax Americana: Hawai'i 1848" (Trask), 95–96
Paying the Price: Killing the Children of Iraq (Pilger), 33
PBS (Public Broadcasting Service), 33–34, 160
Peace and Its Discontents (Said), 147
The Pen and the Sword (Barsamian), 149
Pentagon Papers, 211
A People's History of the United States (Zinn), 12, 199

Perle, Richard, 35
pesticides, 72, 92, 144
pharmaceuticals, 113
Philippines, 26, 95
Physicians for Human Rights, 24
Pilger, John: censorship, 33–34;
        on journalism, 33, 37–39; on
        language, 37–38; on US as
        warlike, 33–38; works by, 33
Pillar of Fire (Branch), 163, 165–66, 171
pipelines, 21, 183–84
Places in the Heart, 27
Plain of Jars, 125
poi, 96
"Politics and the English Language"
        (Orwell), 37
The Politics of Dispossession (Said), 147
pollution, 72, 92, 144, 195–96
poverty, 57, 59–62, 64, 67–68, 140, 173,
        208–9. *See also* invisible people
Poverty and Famines (Sen), 57, 60
Powell, Colin, 24
Power, Politics, and Culture (Said), 49
"Power Politics" (Roy), 70
prisoners of war, 23–24
prisons: abolition of, 83, 85; detentions,
        6–7, 26, 28–29; health care in,
        88; number in, 15, 84; prison-
        industrial complex, 81–83, 85,
        87; race and, 84, 87–89; reform,
        86–87; South Africa, 206; torture
        in Israeli, 127–28; voting rights,
        87; war prisoners, 23–24, 127–28;
        women's, 84–85, 87–88
privatization, 75–77, 131, 189, 195–96
Prize for Cultural Freedom, 136, 142
Profit Over People (Chomsky), 119
Progressive, 136, 214
Progressive Caucus, 29
proportional representation, 114
prostitution, 93
provincialism, 14, 39, 42–43, 51–55,
        139, 156
Public Broadcasting Service (PBS),
        33–34, 160
Public Citizen, 109
public education, 88, 101–3, 131, 199,
        201–5
Public Interest Research Group, 109
Puerto Rico: citizenship, second class,
        104–5, 107–8; commonwealth of,
        95, 105, 107–8; cultural identity

of, 106–8; decolonization of, 108;
        laws thwarted by US, 105–6
Pulitzer Prize, 163, 211
punishment, role of, 85

Q

The Question of Palestine (Said), 147

R

racism, 83–84, 87, 93, 97, 121, 150–52,
        164, 205. *See also* apartheid
radio, 101, 110, 120–21, 160
Rand Corporation, 21
rape, 72
Rashid, Ahmed: on Dostum, 23;
        on Karzai, 20, 22–23; on
        Khalilzad, 20; on lack of anti-
        terrorism strategy, 20–22; on
        Musharraf, 26; personal notes,
        19; on Taliban, 19–20, 22–25; on
        torture, 23–24; on war against
        drugs, 24–25; on women in
        Afghanistan, 24; works by, 19
reading, as a skill, 14
Reagan, Ronald, 35, 52, 81, 130
Reconstruction (Foner), 205
Redemption (Ali), 41
Reflections on Exile (Said), 49, 147
reparations, 27, 29
Representations of the Intellectual (Said),
        147
Research Foundation for Science,
        Technology, and Ecology, 189–90
"The Return of Depression Economics"
        (Krugman), 129
Ricardo, David, 65
Rich, Adrienne, 98
Right Livelihood Award, 189
Robinson, Randall, 27
Roe v. Wade, 112
Roll Down Your Window (Gonzalez),
        101
Roosevelt, Franklin D., 14
Roots, 215
Roundup, 196
Roy, Arundhati: on caste, 69, 75;
        on dams, 70, 72–75; on
        fundamentalism, 76–77;
        on globalization, 69, 75–77;
        on marriage and women's
        rights, 70–72; on nationalism,

76–77; on NBA, 70, 72–75; on nuclear testing, 70, 76–77; on powerlessness, 75; on privatization, 76; works by, 69–73, 79
The Royal Tenenbaums, 28
Ruggiero, Renato, 197
Rumsfeld, Donald, 35, 45

S

Sacco, Nicola, 16
sacred cows, 194–95
Safire, William, 111
Said, Edward: Ahmad and, 175; on binational state, 151–52, 158–60; on Islam, 52–55; on the Palestinian/Israeli crisis, 149–57, 159–60; personal notes, 49–50, 147–49, 160–61; on sanctions, 126; on terrorism, 50–55; works by, 49, 54, 147–48, 154
The Saint of Fort Washington, 27
sanctions, 36, 51, 112, 123, 126
Saudi Arabia, 47, 181–82, 185–86
Savimbi, Jonas, 29
Schaeffer, Yehuda, 127
School of the Americas, 5
seeds, 24, 76, 189, 195–96
segregation, 81, 163–64, 168, 171, 202. *See also* racism
Sen, Amartya: on BJP, 62–63; on causes of famines, 57, 59–62; on colonialism, 65; on communitarianism, 58–59; on democracy in India, 62–63; on gender equality, 64; on globalization, 66–67; on inequality, 64, 67–68; on labor, 60, 66; on nuclear testing, 63; on women's rights, 64; works by, 57, 60
Senegal, 29
Sentencing Project, 87
September 11 attacks, 12, 28, 35, 50–51, 53
Sermon on the Mount, 15–16
Serrano, José, 104
Shadows of the Pomegranate Tree (Ali), 41
Shah, Zahir, 21, 43
Sharon, Ariel, 33, 36

Shaw, George Bernard, 15
The Sheik, 54
Shirzai, Gul Agha, 23
Shiva, Vandana: on biodiversity, 194; Chipko movement, 190–92; on civil disobedience, 189, 193–94; on democracy, 193–94; on globalization, 193–95; internationalism, 197; on power of corporations, 196–98; on privatization, 189, 195–96; on social forestry, 190–92; works by, 189; World Bank impact on, 190
shrimp farms, 192
Silber, John, 205
Sinatra, Frank, 149
sit-ins, 202–3, 206
Six Day War, 175
60 Minutes, 213
Slaughterhouse-Five (Vonnegut), 11, 13–14
slavery, 3–4, 9, 13, 16, 29, 65, 165
Smith, Adam, 58, 65
Soccer in Sun and Shadow (Galeano), 135
social change phenomenon, 190–92, 202–4, 205–10
social forestry, 190–92
Social Security, 130–32, 209
socialism, 16, 145, 207
The Souls of Black Folk (DuBois), 83
South Africa, 29, 64, 84, 121, 126, 151, 206
South End Press, 115, 119, 189
Soviet Union, 42, 52, 61–62, 145, 181, 183, 207
soya bean, 196
Spanish language, 101–3, 106–8
"speaking truth to power," 120
Special Rapporteur on Violence Against Women, UN, 87
Spelman College, 201–2
sports, 120, 132
Sri Lanka, 184
statehood debates, 107–8
Staying Alive (Shiva), 189
The Stone Woman (Ali), 41
Street Soldiers (Oakland), 32
stri shakti, 192
Sudan, 182
Suez War of 1956, 42
Sun, 37

swadeshi, 193–94
Sweden, 84
Swiss League of Human Rights, 128
Syria, 46, 71, 127–28, 155, 186

T

Tagore, Rabindranath, 57–58
Tahiti, 99
Tajikistan, 184
Tajiks, 22–23
Taliban (Rashid), 19
Taliban, 19–20, 22–25, 42–44, 183–85
Telecommunications Act (1996), 211, 218
television: advertising, 215–16; critique of, 34, 43–44, 160, 211–16, 219; Murdoch and, 37; power of, 13, 54, 164, 212–16
territories. *See* colonialism
terrorism: Afghanistan, 20; Al Qaeda, 19–20, 22, 25–26, 43; bin Laden, 29, 43, 51–52, 55, 181, 185; Haiti, 2–3, 6; jihad, 182; root causes, 35–36, 46, 51, 186; September 11, 12, 28, 35, 50–51, 53; South Africa, 206; strategies lacking against, 20, 26, 34–36, 45, 47, 51; US support of, 121, 124. *See also* violence, cultures of
Texaco, 183
Third World Resurgence, 189
Thomas, Norman, 15
"three strikes," 86
tobacco, 213, 217
Tomei, Marisa, 12
torture, 2, 121, 127–28, 204
tourism, 91–93, 95, 98, 155
"town meeting" fiasco, 123–24
TransAfrica Forum, 27, 29
Transnational Institute, 175
Trask, Damien, 93
Trask, Haunani-Kay: Hawaiian language, 97–98; indigenous sovereignty movement, 91–99; Ka Lahui Hawaii, 91, 94; on nuclear-testing, 98–99; on oppression of tourists, 92–93, 95, 98; sisters of, 81, 93–94, 97; works by, 91, 95–96
Trask, Mililani, 81, 94, 97
triumphalism, 52
Trujillo, Rafael, 3

truth in sentencing, 86
Turkey, 47, 75, 128, 211, 217–18
Turkmenistan, 21

U

Ukraine famine, 61
ul-Haq, Zia, 181
United Arab Emirates, 47
United Nations (UN): on blood quantum, 97; on decolonization, 108; Development Program, 27; Human Development Index, 57; peace purpose of, 143; poverty report, 140; rule of international law and, 50; Security Council, 121, 124, 143; standard minimum rules for prisoners, 85; US contempt for, 37, 43–47, 52, 124–25, 181; violence against women report, 87
United States (US): apartheid, 164; colonies of, 94–95, 104–8; contempt for international law by, 37, 43–47, 52, 124–25, 181; drug war, 24–25, 84, 143; foreign aid, 20, 26, 121, 128; hypocrisy of, 51, 123, 126, 181; ignorance of citizens of, 14, 39, 42–43, 51–55, 132, 136, 139, 215; international image of, 51–52, 123, 181; Israel and, 36, 46–47, 51–52, 128; Latino populations in, 103–4
Unocal, 21, 183
Updike, John, 16
uranium mining, 99
Urban Peace Award, 32
Uruguay, 135–36, 139, 143
Uzbekistan, 184

V

Valentino, Rudolph, 54
Vanzetti, Bartolomeo, 16
the Vatican, 124
Vietnam War, 13, 28, 97, 125–26, 168, 171–73, 175
violence, cultures of, 52, 87, 124, 142–44, 170–71, 176, 182. *See also* terrorism; torture; war
Vodou, 4–5

Vonnegut, Kurt: on Bush, 12, 14; on ethics, 16; influence of Shaw on, 15; on reading, 14; works by, 11–14

voting rights, 87, 105, 114, 168, 171

W

wages, 60, 65–66, 85, 115
Wake Island, 95
Walker, Alice, 12, 91
Wall Street Journal, 132
war: century of, 143–44; civil war, 29, 65, 120; cold, 125, 182, 185; crimes, 14, 23–24, 33, 124; against drugs, 24–25, 84, 143; famine and, 60; Gulf War, 43–44, 51, 121–22, 181; India/China, 177–78; India/Pakistan, 21; King on, 28, 172–73; language of, 37; media critiques and, 12, 44, 144; for oil, 42, 46–47; populace against, 35, 44, 207, 209; preventing, 207, 209; Six Day War (Arab/Israeli), 147, 175; town meeting about, 123–24; Turkey/Armenia, 217; Vietnam War, 13, 28, 97, 125–26, 168, 171–73, 175; World War II, 12, 31, 180, 208. *See also* terrorism
Washington, Denzel, 31
Washington Post, 32, 172, 211
Washington Times, 37
water, 76, 191, 195
We Say No (Galeano), 135
Wilkins, Roy, 169, 172
WNET television, 34
Wolfensohn, James D., 72
Wolfowitz, Paul, 35
women: abortion rights, 111–12; cloning and, 192; fertility rates, 64; marriage and, 70–72; power of, 73, 98, 189–93, 202, 207; in prison, 84–85, 87–88; rights of, 64, 71–72, 111–12, 185, 207; violence against, 72, 87; in the workforce, 24, 64
Women, Culture and Politics (Davis), 81
Women, Race and Class (Davis), 81
Woodard, Alfre, 12
Wordsworth, William, 4
World Bank: on Arafat's employees, 153; impact of, on Shiva, 190;

Narmada River Valley dams and, 72–73; Pakistan "colonized" by, 180; pollution, 72, 144, 195; practices of, 190; on pricing of water, 195; Sen lectures at, 57
World Conference on Racism, 29
world constitution, 197. *See also* GATT (General Agreement on Tariffs and Trade)
World Orders Old and New (Chomsky), 119
World Trade Organization (WTO), 109

Y

You Can't Be Neutral on a Moving Train (Zinn), 201
Young Lords, 101, 106

Z

Zinn, Howard: on equality, 208–10; on left values, 207–8; on Ludlow Massacre in Colorado, 199; memoir, 201; on neutrality, 201–3; on sanctions, 126; Silber on, 205; on social change, 202–4, 205–10; Spelman College, 201–2; on teaching, 202–5; Times Square incident, 200–201; works by, 199

About David Barsamian

David Barsamian is a radio producer, journalist, author, and lecturer. He is founder and director of Alternative Radio (www.alternativeradio.org), the independent award-winning weekly series based in Boulder, Colorado. He has been working in radio since 1978. His interviews and articles appear regularly in *The Progressive* and *Z Magazine*. He is the author of several books, including *Propaganda and the Public Mind: Conversations with Noam Chomsky*; *Eqbal Ahmad: Confronting Empire*; *The Decline and Fall of Public Broadcasting*; *Culture and Resistance: Conversations with Edward W. Said*; and *The Checkbook and the Cruise Missile: Conversations with Arundhati Roy*.

Barsamian travels internationally lecturing on US foreign policy, the media, propaganda, and corporate power. The Institute for Alternative Journalism named him one of its "Top Ten Media Heroes" in 1994. He is the winner of the ACLU's 2003 Upton Sinclair Award for independent journalism.

About South End Press

South End Press is a nonprofit, collectively run book publisher with more than 250 titles in print. Since our founding in 1977, we have tried to meet the needs of readers who are exploring, or are already committed to, the politics of radical social change. Our goal is to publish books that encourage critical thinking and constructive action on the key political, cultural, social, economic, and ecological issues shaping life in the United States and in the world. In this way, we hope to provide a forum for a wide variety of democratic social movements, and provide an alternative to the products of corporate publishing.

From its inception, the Press has organized itself as an egalitarian collective with decision-making arranged to share as equally as possible the rewards and stresses of running the business. Each collective member is responsible for core editorial and administrative tasks. The Press also has made a practice of inverting the pervasive racial and gender hierarchies in traditional publishing houses; our staff has had a female majority since the mid-1980s, and has included at least 50 percent people of color since the mid-1990s. Our author list—which includes Arundhati Roy, Noam Chomsky, bell hooks, Winona LaDuke, Manning Marable, Ward Churchill, Cherríe Moraga, and Howard Zinn—reflects the Press's commitment to publish on diverse issues from diverse perspectives.

For current information on our books, please request a free catalog by mailing: 7 Brookline Street, Cambridge MA 02139, or emailing southend@southendpress.org. Our web site, www.southendpress.org, offers the most extensive information on our titles, as well as information on author events, important news, and other interesting links.